$u.$

PENGUIN BOOKS

THE NEW WRITER'S SURVIVAL GUIDE

Dianne Bates B.A. (Wollongong), Dip. Teach. (Wollongong Teachers Coll.) started her literary career as Assistant to the Editor of the NSW Department of Education *School Magazine*. Since then she has co-edited the children's magazine, *Puffinalia*, worked as writer-in-residence and tutor at numerous institutions, toured with the National Book Council and written a number of books for young people. She has worked as a teacher, newspaper journalist, radio DJ, advertising representative, editor/manager of a provincial newspaper, and youth worker in a home for delinquent teenagers. In 1987 and 1988 she was awarded Writing Fellowships from the Literary Arts Board of the Australia Council.

Her hobbies include collecting toucans, making ceramic dragons, painting, reading, swimming and canoeing. Her life ambition is to establish a national magazine for young people.

OTHER BOOKS BY THE AUTHOR

Terri (Puffin, 1981)
Piggy Moss (Puffin, 1982)
The Belligrumble Bigfoot (Roo Books, 1984)
Madcap Café and Other Humorous Plays, co-written with Bill
   Condon (Brooks Waterloo, 1986)
Thirteen Going on Forty (Hodder & Stoughton, 1986)
Grandma Cadbury's Trucking Tales (Angus & Robertson, 1987)
   (winner of WA Young Readers' Book Award, 1988)
The Worst Cook in the World (Methuen, 1987)
The Magician (Rigby, 1988)
The Slacky Flat Gang, co-written with Bill Condon (Brooks
   Waterloo, 1988)

Educational material

The Little Red Hen (Macmillan, 1987)
The Musicians of Bremen (Macmillan, 1987)
Operation Lily-Liver, co-written with Bill Condon (Macmillan, 1987)
When Melissa-Ann Came to Dinner (Harcourt Brace Jovanovich,
   1988)
A Night at Benny's (Harcourt Brace Jovanovich, 1989)

Anthologies

The Puffin Book of Fun (Puffin, 1980)
The Two Chefs (ABC Radio publication, 1985)
Plays for Pleasure (Macmillan, 1986)
A Swag of Stories (Oxford University Press, 1986)
Telling Tales (Oxford University Press, 1986)
All Australian English, Bk 3 (Macmillan, 1987)
Raising Spirits (Macmillan, 1987)
Stories to Share, Bk 6 (Macmillan, 1987)
State of the Heart (Omnibus Books, 1988)

THE NEW WRITER'S SURVIVAL GUIDE

An Introduction to the Craft of Writing

DIANNE BATES

PENGUIN BOOKS

For my dearest friend and partner, Bill Condon, with love

Penguin Books Australia Ltd
487 Maroondah Highway, PO Box 257
Ringwood, Victoria, 3134. Australia
Penguin Books Ltd
Harmondsworth, Middlesex, England
Viking Penguin, A Division of Penguin Books USA Inc.
375 Hudson Street, New York, New York 10014, USA
Penguin Books Canada Limited
10 Alcorn Avenue, Toronto, Ontario, Canada M4V 3B2
Penguin Books (N.Z.) Ltd
182-190 Wairau Road, Auckland 10, New Zealand

First published by Penguin Books Australia, 1989
10 9 8 7 6 5

Typeset in 11.5/12 Berkeley, by Midland Typesetters, Maryborough, Vic.
Made and printed in Australia by Australian Print Group, Maryborough, Vic.

Bates, Dianne, 1948-
The new writer's survival guide.
Includes bibliographies.
ISBN 0 14 011508 0.
1. Authorship - Handbooks, manuals, etc. 1. Title.
808'.02

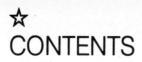

CONTENTS

CONTENTS ✱ CONTENTS ✱ CONTENTS ✱ CONTENTS ✱ CONTENTS ✱ CONTENTS ✱ CONTENTS ✱ CONTENTS ✱ CONTENTS

Introduction   1

1 ☆ WHAT IS A WRITER?   3
WHAT WRITERS SAY ABOUT WRITING   4
GET THE WRITING HABIT   6
ADVICE FROM ESTABLISHED WRITERS   7
HELPFUL BOOKS   7

2 ☆ WRITING FOR A PURPOSE   8
HAVING AN AUDIENCE   8
WRITING METHODS   9
IDEAS FOR WRITING PROJECTS   9
HELPFUL BOOKS   20

3 ☆ GETTING IDEAS   21
SOURCES OF IDEAS   21
KEEPING A JOURNAL OR DIARY   24
CONDUCTING INTERVIEWS   25
HELPFUL BOOK   26

4 ☆ TOOLS OF THE TRADE   27
DISCIPLINE   27
PERSISTENCE   30

READING	31
WORKSHOPS	31
USING A DICTIONARY AND THESAURUS	32
TYPEWRITERS AND WORD PROCESSORS	33
LEGAL MATTERS	33
HELPFUL BOOKS	34

5 ☆ WRITING PROSE 35

PROSE GENRES	35
NON-FICTION	35
FICTION: THE BASIC STORY ELEMENTS	39
METHODS OF PLOTTING	44
USING DIALOGUE	45
WRITING A NOVEL	45
A FICTION WRITER'S CHECKLIST	49
ADVICE FROM PROSE WRITERS	49
HELPFUL BOOKS	51

6 ☆ WRITING POETRY 52

WHAT IS POETRY?	52
GETTING STARTED	53
CREATING POETIC IMAGES	56
DRAFTING A POEM	57
RHYME AND RHYTHM	61
OTHER POETIC DEVICES	62
POETRY FORMS TO EXPERIMENT WITH	63
WHY NOT TRY FREE VERSE?	67
COMMON FAULTS IN BEGINNERS' POEMS	68
SUBMITTING A POETRY MANUSCRIPT	69
ADVICE FROM PUBLISHED POETS	69
HELPFUL BOOKS	72
USEFUL CONTACTS	72

7 ☆ WRITING DRAMA 73

WHAT IS DRAMA?	73
PLAYSCRIPT FORMAT	74

GETTING STARTED 79

CONFLICT AND CHARACTERS 82

A CHECKLIST FOR TESTING YOUR PLAYSCRIPT 84

ADVICE FROM PLAYWRIGHTS AND DIRECTORS 85

AUSTRALIAN NATIONAL ASSOCIATION OF YOUNG PLAYWRIGHTS 88

HELPFUL BOOKS 89

USEFUL CONTACTS 89

8 ☆ EDITING YOUR OWN WORK 90

WHAT EDITING IS 90

WHAT TO EDIT 92

MAKE EVERY WORD COUNT 93

WORDS, WORDS, WORDS 94

MAKING A RICHER BREW 97

USING THE ACTIVE VOICE 97

WRITE WITH NOUNS AND VERBS 98

GETTING IT RIGHT 99

SHOW, DON'T TELL! 99

IMPROVING DIALOGUE 100

THE SOUND OF SENTENCES 103

WHY WORRY ABOUT SPELLING, PUNCTUATION AND GRAMMAR? 106

A FIRST DRAFT EDITED 108

HELPFUL BOOKS 111

9 ☆ CO-OPERATIVE WRITING AND PUBLISHING PROJECTS 112

CO-OPERATIVE PUBLISHING 113

Five Islands Press 113

VOLUNTARY NON-PROFIT PUBLISHING 114

Women's Redress Press Inc. 114

PRODUCING A COMMUNITY OR SCHOOL NEWSPAPER 117

Connexions - A Multilingual Community Newspaper 117

Emu - A Literary Magazine for Young Australians 118

Live Wire - An Inter-school Newspaper 120

Lake High Link - A School Newspaper 122

COMMUNITY THEATRE - A CO-WRITING VENTURE 124

COMMUNITY RADIO 127

Radio 2CHY/FM - A Student Venture 127

10 ★
SO YOU WANT
A CAREER IN WRITING?   129

WORK EXPERIENCE   129
JOURNALISM   130
PUBLISHING   132
ADVERTISING COPYWRITER   133
PUBLIC RELATIONS   133
FREELANCE WRITER   134
COURSES   135
FURTHER INFORMATION   136

11 ★
PUBLISHED WRITERS SPEAK   137

INTRODUCTION   137
ADULT WRITERS   140
John Roarty – Novelist   140
Ruby Langford – Novelist   141
Serge Liberman – Short-story Writer   143
Mary Baarschers – Freelance Educational Writer   146
Nola Hayes – Scriptwriter   147
Sue Edmonds – Songwriter   149
Judith Worthy – Romance writer   151
David Foard – New writer   154
Richard Echin – Wordsmith   156
Merle Glasson – Poet   157
ADULT WRITERS WHO STARTED YOUNG   160
Michael Dugan – Freelance Writer and Editor   160
Sally Farrell Odgers – Freelance Writer   163
Anne Farrell (Heazlewood) – Fiction and Non-fiction Writer for
   Adults and Children   165
Doug MacLeod – Poet, Dramatist, Editor   167
Mavis Thorpe Clark – Children's Author and Non-fiction Writer   171
Simon French – Children's Author   172
Debra Oswald – Scriptwriter   174
Robin Gurr – Poet   177
PUBLISHED YOUNG WRITERS   179
Jodilee Eckford – Newspaper Reporter and Book Reviewer   181
Miriam Cullen – Playwright   183
Adam Boulter – Film-maker   185
Michael Winkler – Poet   187

Helen Sargeant – Fanzine Contributor   189
Sonya Harnett – Novelist   191
Sarah McLeish – Novelist   194
Claire Williams – Newspaper Columnist   195
Helen Cerni – Short-story Writer   198
POSTSCRIPT – A CAUTIONARY TALE   199

12 ☆
SUBMITTING YOUR WORK   201

KNOWING WHERE TO SEND YOUR WORK   201
HOW TO PRESENT A MANUSCRIPT   202
WHAT TO DO AFTER SUBMISSION   204
ADVICE FROM EDITORS AND PLAYSCRIPT ASSESSORS   207
GETTING WORK ACCEPTED   213
HOW TO COPE WITH REJECTION   214
VANITY PUBLISHING   215
SELF-PUBLISHING   216
CO-OPERATIVE PUBLISHING   217
HELPFUL BOOKS   218
USEFUL CONTACTS   219

13 ☆
MARKETS AND COMPETITIONS   220

ADVICE FOR THE AMBITIOUS   220
SHORT-STORY AND POETRY MARKETS   220
MAGAZINES AND NEWSPAPERS   221
BOOK PUBLISHERS   225
THEATRE COMPANIES   228
FILM COMPANIES   230
ANNUAL WRITING COMPETITIONS   231
FESTIVALS   240
WRITING WORKSHOPS   245
MANUSCRIPT ASSESSMENT SERVICES   248
WRITERS' ORGANISATIONS   250
OTHER USEFUL CONTACTS   251
A FEW DOs AND DON'Ts   251
HELPFUL BOOKS   252

Appendix: Useful Addresses   253
Sources   259
Acknowledgements   260

★
INTRODUCTION

The New Writer's Survival Guide is for you, a would-be writer with a dream. Perhaps your dream is of sharing your innermost thoughts and feelings on paper with the people in your immediate world. Or perhaps your ambitions are loftier: you would like to write the perfect poem, a block-buster novel or the film-script of the century. Maybe you suspect you have some writing talent, but it's not worth thinking about seriously because you're too old anyway (or too young), you wouldn't know where to start, you never had much schooling, you can't spell for peanuts, and who'd want to read what you wrote, anyway?

These, as you know, are all excuses for not pursuing your dream. If you *truly* want to write – whether for personal fulfilment, for your family and friends' amusement or for commercial publication – no barriers exist, except those which *you* put in the way.

The purpose of this book is to motivate you to explore a variety of possibilities in the writing world, and to show you how to hone your techniques if you are serious about submitting work for publication. I have tried to include as much practical information as you will need, as well as words of advice and encouragement from published writers. These are people who were once like you, wondering where and how to start writing.

Why not decide, right this minute, to do as they once did and harness your creative powers? Learn how to become a writer. You can do it! You are never too young or too old to start writing. Creativity flourishes at any age with the proper nourishment.

> *Consider bonsai –*
> *There, but for constricting bowl,*
> *Would be a giant.*

Note: For details of the addresses and telephone numbers of all names with asterisks throughout the book, see the Appendix.

1 ☆
WHAT IS
A WRITER?

A writer is a person who sits at a desk and keeps his eyes fixed, as intently as he can, upon a certain object: human life.

Virginia Woolf

A writer is born with talent and fights all out to use that talent to the utmost.

Irwin Shaw

Writing can be a real joy, a pleasure. Some writers might tell you, however, that being published is a greater pleasure. American Dorothy Parker put it succinctly when she said:

HATE WRITING, LOVE HAVING WRITTEN.

Can one be born a writer or is writing a talent one develops? This is hard to say really. Personally, I believe you need to have some degree of natural talent, but many people who are 'born writers' never develop their writing gift. Writing is a discipline; only those who are disciplined and persistent will be successful.

Effective writers appear to have common traits. Generally, in addition to being persistent, they are imaginative, sensitive, observant, analytical and reflective. They are conscious of words and enjoy learning about and experimenting with the pronunciation and meanings of them. They use their senses constantly and intelligently to record the world around them. Interested in people, they notice and remember unusual characters and stories. They

3 ☆

watch and listen carefully, developing a 'good eye' for descriptive detail and a 'good ear' for dialogue. The way things work intrigues them. In a sense they are 'nosy'. Writers are readers.

If you were to examine an effective writer's work habits, you would find a dedication to writing over and beyond the dedication given to a normal job. Not having a boss standing over them, or a clock ticking from 9 to 5 in their office, writers need to be self-motivated. Regular, hard work produces manuscripts. The ability to criticise one's work plus regular hard work and rewriting produces publishable manuscripts. Thus, organisation and the ability to structure their own working hours are essential qualities writers need to have if they are to produce work or to meet deadlines. Writers need to be meticulous about checking details (so they will not be sued or have readers sending them irate notes). Other skills, such as being able to type or conduct an interview or operate a tape recorder, are useful, but not all writers have, or need them.

Some people have a vision of 'the typical writer': eccentric appearance and behaviour, wealthy, middle-aged. Not true. Writers came from all walks of life, from all classes. They can be staid middle-class men or women, prisoners, ministers, accountants, teachers, dentists, actors, butchers, university students, solicitors, circus clowns, maniacs and geniuses. They pop up everywhere! Most writers are not wealthy; that is why they usually have a life outside their writing. Novelists, for instance, make only a small percentage - usually 7½ to 10 per cent - of the sale price of their books. Only if they are *extremely* lucky (for example, they write a best-seller or sell film rights to their book) can they make a living from writing. If making a mint from writing is your only motivation for writing, THINK AGAIN! Writing is not your passport to great fortune.

WHAT WRITERS SAY ABOUT WRITING

Writing is easy: all you do is sit staring at a blank sheet of paper until the drops of blood form on your forehead.

Gene Fowler

There is no art to writing but having something to say.

Robert Frost

I find the more I write the more I enjoy writing and the better I write.

> Michael Moorcock

Writing and rewriting are a constant search for what one is saying.

> John Updike

Have something to say, and say it as clearly as you can. That is the only secret of life.

> Matthew Arnold

To write simply is as difficult as to be good.

> W. Somerset Maugham

It is always hard work, sitting alone at a typewriter. It's lonely and it's difficult and you're scared. You can't ever be quite sure of where you're going.

> Diana Trilling

You should write . . . to please yourself. You shouldn't care a damn about anybody else at all. But writing can't be a way of life; the important part of writing is living.

> Doris Lessing

The quality I look for in any kind of writing . . . is that of complete sincerity and earnestness. The writer must have something he wants to communicate.

> Bruce Catton

The most important thing about writing is to have something to say. We don't write, we write about . . .

> Marjorie Barnard

. . . writing has to be a part-time occupation. More than any other serious profession, it feeds and grows on living and living is what a writer must do full-time. Living full-time takes more energy and discipline than any writing I know of. It demands that one not let oneself become uninvolved with life; or forget or fear to look at it.

> Virginia Hamilton

GET THE WRITING HABIT

> Write something every day, though it may be poor;
> write something even if it's only your diary. Just get into
> the habit of putting words down, and try not to miss a
> day . . . it's important just to write, consistently,
> persistently.
>
> Emily Hahn

This section briefly outlines some techniques you can employ *now* to put yourself on the road to authorship. Most of the points here will be expanded later in the book.

There is a lot of advice that could be given about writing, but the main thing to remember is that writing is something you *do* – talking about it doesn't fill pages. Here are some other helpful tips:

Get into the habit of writing. Write regularly, every day if you can. Don't wait for inspiration to strike. A journal is a good investment.

Write out of your own experience and observations; your writing will be better if you write about what you know than if you write about what you don't know.

Learn to be critical of your own work. Never be satisfied with a first draft. Be prepared, always, to rewrite.

Listen to other people's criticisms of your work. It is your *work* that is being criticised, not you. Learn from constructive criticism.

Be willing to experiment; try different styles of writing, different genres.

Learn how to use a thesaurus; use it often.

Learn new words – at least ten – every day. Expand your vocabulary.

Read widely. By reading widely you will be exposed to different styles and different ways of thinking. Subconsciously you will absorb structure. You will learn new words. You will learn how language can be used effectively.

Experience. Don't let life pass you by. Get involved: go to the theatre, meet new people, take up new sports, travel, learn.

ADVICE FROM ESTABLISHED WRITERS

I would say that the thing for a beginning writer to do is to write, and to rewrite; to read; to avoid asking people what they think of what he does; to follow what is intuitive within him. In other words, whatever it is that simply has to be said is the thing that the writer should write.

Eileen Bassing

New writers should do three things: look, listen, read. The material is all around. The sharp eye and the sharp ear will sharpen the mind and the heart. A detailed plan is often a great help for the first few novels. This allows the writer to begin anywhere, preferably at an incident that appeals to him and will enable him to catch the atmosphere. If, for those first attempts, the new writer chooses something he *knows* and something about which he has *felt*, then the rest will follow.

Thea Astley

Never miss an opportunity to live or an opportunity to write. *Nil desperandum.*

Ivan Southall

Watch. Experience. Inwardly digest. Read the right models. Plan – in your head which is where it has to come from – what you're going to write. Then, and only then, is it time to get the blank paper, the wet ink, the clean pen. Nothing else now but sit down – and write.

Hal Porter

HELPFUL BOOKS

Candida Baker, *Yacker*, Picador, Sydney, 1986. *Yacker 2*, Picador, Sydney, 1987.

Carmel Bird, *Dear Writer*, McPhee Gribble/Penguin, Melbourne, 1988.

Jennifer Ellison (interviewer), *Rooms of their Own*, Penguin, Ringwood, Vic., 1986.

Pamela Lloyd, *How Writers Write*, Methuen, Sydney, 1987.

John Quinn (ed.), *Portrait of the Artist as a Young Girl*, Methuen, London, 1987.

M. Jerry Weiss (ed.), *From Writers to Students: The Pleasures and Pains of Writing*, International Reading Centre, Delaware, 1979.

2 ☆ WRITING FOR A PURPOSE

HAVING AN AUDIENCE

The audience is the reward of the speaker.
> Babylonian Talmud

My purpose is to entertain myself first and other people secondly.
> John D. MacDonald

No man but a blockhead ever wrote, except for money.
> Dr Samuel Johnson

You have made the decision: you are going to be a writer. Where do you start? The first thing to learn is that the most important influence on any writer is the writer's audience. Without doubt, you will get the greatest thrill of your writing career when you have someone with whom to share your written thoughts. You do not have to send your manuscript to a publisher or producer to find an audience. You have one all around you right now: your immediate family, other relatives, friends, neighbours, people in your community. Having an appreciative audience is a good reason for writing.

The purpose of this chapter is to suggest different ways in which you can improve your own publishing prospects while you are still learning the craft of writing. This chapter also invites you to experiment with different forms of writing and to share them with people close to you. It also urges you to be ambitious and to aim for a wider audience if you have the confidence.

WRITING METHODS

The Bottom Drawer Method

Most beginner writers start by writing confessional poems or short, personal prose pieces in their diaries. Usually, because they feel too embarrassed, they don't share them with anyone. They put their pieces of writing away in a bottom drawer somewhere where they are soon forgotten. It's as though their efforts have died and are now buried. What a waste!

The 'Making it Live' Method

Writing should *live*. The best way to make it live is to share it. By exposing your writing to others, you not only entertain or communicate your thoughts, feelings or ideas, but you get 'feedback'; that is, you find out if your writing has been effective in achieving what you set out to do.

You don't need to stick to poems and prose or diary entries. Why not increase your range of writing? Take the challenge - have a go at writing the wide variety of forms listed in the next section.

IDEAS FOR WRITING PROJECTS

Become a Newspaper Columnist

There is no reason why you can't offer to write a weekly, fortnightly or monthly column for your local newspaper. First, though, you will need to have some idea of the sorts of issues you intend raising, or an idea of the proposed content of the column. You might want to start an 'agony', historical or gardening column, discuss youth issues, interview colourful local identities, comment on political issues, or write about the rock scene. It is probably a good idea to supply a sample column to the editor at the same time that you make your initial approach; this will give the editor an idea of your writing style and ability. If you do get excited about the idea of becoming a newspaper columnist, before setting out to see the editor, just remember that you are making a long-term commitment to supply material. Ask yourself if you have time to spare, and if you can come up with new material every issue. Newspapers have deadlines so you need to be well-organised as well as committed. Sometimes, because of space limitations, your column might be cut short or even left out. Be prepared for this! (By the way, editors are busy people; make an appointment before you rush off to the newspaper office. You could also write a polite letter of enquiry.)

Quite often opportunities exist for you as a columnist in non-profit publications (such as a social club, community or welfare group's newsletter), school or inter-school newspapers (see chapter 9, 'Co-operative Writing and Publishing Projects').

Become a Book Reviewer, Theatre, Concert or Art Critic

As with the columnist suggestion (above) you may like to approach your local newspaper editor with the idea of writing occasional reviews. The idea of a young person reviewing a rock concert, for instance, might appeal to an astute editor. If you fancy yourself as a gourmet, think of writing restaurant reviews. If you are a film buff, offer your services as a film critic. Your municipal or school librarian would probably be delighted if you wrote book reviews for display on their noticeboards or for their regular library newsletter. Local authors would no doubt be co-operative if you offered to interview them for community publications. If you *can* get space in a newspaper for a book review column, write to major book publishers, detailing the sorts of books you wish to review; you will be amazed at the response (you also get to keep the books)! Another possibility is that you could set up a joint book review arrangement with local bookstores. The nicest thing about reviewing (as well as seeing your name in print) is that you get freebies (for example, free theatre, concert tickets).

Write a Revue

A revue is a series of sketches – satirical, dramatic, comic and musical – presented live on stage. Usually the sketches make political or social commentary; for example, they might make fun of politicians or rock stars, television commercials or government policy. The idea is not only to entertain your audience, but to make them think.

You might like to try your hand at writing a revue sketch. A popular method of presenting a satirical song is to write a parody of a well-known song. If you are 'sending up' a personality who regularly appears on television, study his or her use of language, noting any peculiar speech mannerisms. You might decide to use puppets to get your message across. Whatever you do, make sure your material is lively, witty and up to date.

The fun of writing a revue is doubled if you are able to collaborate with zany, enthusiastic co-writers.

Stage a Play

Writing a play with a friend or a group of friends is fun, but you may prefer to work alone. There is an infinite variety of plays which you could write: comedy, melodrama, tragedy, community theatre, music drama, documentary drama, shadow play, pageant, etc. You can also write your play in any number of styles from farcical to satirical, absurdist to naturalist. You can choose to write in verse; you might like to incorporate a song and/or dance chorus or to use puppets, masks, film clips, music and sound effects.

You might have as your starting point (especially if you find plots difficult to devise), the adaptation of a folk tale or novel. You might decide to parody a well-known play or take a nursery rhyme as your starting point. On the other hand, you may prefer to explore what is familiar to you and base your drama on a real-life situation. The possibilities for writing drama are endless. As a playwright, you will learn a great deal about the technicalities of theatre if you also involve yourself in the production of your play. An important lesson you will learn is that your script is only *part* of the play.

Present a Cartoon Show

If you have access to an overhead projector, this is an excellent way of incorporating your skills as an artist with your writing skills. Map out your storyline, then make a sequence of rough drawings to match each section of the story. Next, draw your cartoons on sheets of acetate with felt-tip markers. When you present your cartoon show to an audience, have someone present the cartoons as you read the 'voice-over' parts. Alternatively, you can prerecord the dialogue and/or commentary and show the cartoons yourself. You might also consider using the overhead projector to present a shadow play. Cut out cartoon characters from fairly stiff paper, and attach each of them to a cane stick. When the projector is turned on and your characters placed on its screen, silhouettes will be projected. You will need to write a story (with dialogue) to give life to your characters. You can use sound effects and music if you wish; you might also like to experiment with the possibilities of using coloured cellophane to achieve interesting visual effects.

Present a Slide Show

If you have access to a slide projector why not write commentaries to accompany slides, and present a show? At home you could devise a sequence showing your family holidays, the baby's first birthday party, your daughter's graduation, your son's engagement or Christmas Day in your household. A slide show can enliven your social club's get-together or annual general meeting. Alternatively, it could be the highlight of a colleague's retirement party, or a fun way of saying 'bon voyage' or 'welcome home' to holidaying friends and relatives. At school you could show slides of your class's excursions, people in the playground or school visitors. Libraries often have slide collections suitable for natural and social science classes; you could write documentaries to accompany each set.

Write an Operetta, Musical or Pantomime

To do this you will most likely need the assistance of someone with musical abilities who can write the score. However, it may be possible to use existing music to which you can set your own lyrics. Writing an operetta, musical or pantomime is very much like writing a play; you need characters and conflict, setting and plot. The only extras are singing and dancing. If possible, see an opera, musical and/or pantomime and try to use them as models. The musical you write may be the highlight of your social club or school's end-of-the-year concert!

Start a Radio Club

Many schools have broadcasting equipment operated from a central location which reaches classrooms and/

or the playground. You and a group of friends can get together to start a radio club, broadcasting during recess or wet weather periods. The programming could include radio plays, true life stories, short stories, serials, poems, school news, historical features, rock music items and so on, which you have researched and/or written. You can intersperse announcements with music, humorous 'advertisements' and interviews with visiting celebrities.

Numerous opportunities exist for adults to become involved with community radio stations. The Public Broadcasting Association* will put you in touch with your local station. (See also chapter 9, 'Co-operative Writing and Publishing Projects'.)

Make a Film

The only limitation here is access to equipment. If you don't own your own home video equipment, then council community workers or staff at neighbourhood centres may know where you can obtain a Porta-Pak camera and recorder at little or no hiring cost. (They often know, too, where video skills classes are conducted.) Some community organisations – such as sporting or leisure groups, or women's co-operatives – may have equipment you can borrow. Alternatively, for advice and practical assistance, seek out amateur film/movie makers' clubs (listed in your local library's community groups register). For young film-makers most schools have film equipment stored away somewhere.

Your film might be as simple as a home movie or as complicated as a full-length feature film. Whatever sort of film you decide to make, you will need to write a script or a rudimentary story-board before you commence shooting (for directions on this refer to chapter 7, 'Writing Drama'). You might like to make a documentary, a video rock clip, or an animated cartoon, or write a TV play; these could be shown to audiences at home, school, in the local hall, wherever you can find room to set up a projector and screen.

Write Fiction

The sky's the limit here: anything from a short story to a full-length novel. You can write a romance, a choose-your-own-adventure, an illustrated book for younger readers, a narrative written in the first-person or third-person, or in diary form, a mystery, a detective story, a fairy tale, a fable, a fantasy, a sci-fi novel, a school story, a family story, a tale about an animal. Your literary style can range from irony and satire to comedy, tragedy or social-realism.

The subject matter available to you as a writer is limited only by your knowledge of the world and by your imagination.

Write a Non-fiction Book

Non-fiction covers an incredible range, including autobiography, biography, history, true-life stories, how-to manuals, encyclopedias, textbooks, recipe books, general interest subjects, nature studies, sports manuals, and so on. Writing one of these can be a real learning experience as well as enormous fun.

Create a Picture Book

What a good idea for a birthday or Christmas present for your favourite little person! If you don't know any children but you still want to make a picture book, you could present your finished effort to an infants' class, to your local children's library or to a children's hospital.

Commercially published picture books generally have thirty-two pages, so you might like to use this as your starting point. Small children enjoy reading stories about their own lives; if you are writing and illustrating a picture book for a child you know, why not use the child's name in the story? Study picture books by well-known authors and learn what you can about sentence length, vocabulary, storyline and placement of text on the page.

If you have a picture-book story you think is suitable for publication, you can submit the text only; you do not have to have illustrating skills to write a picture book. Often the author and illustrator of a picture book never meet one another; the editor commissions an illustrator if the text is good enough.

Write a Song

If you don't have the faintest idea of how to write a tune, then practise by using the tune of an existing song and setting new lyrics to it (of course, you would not be able to perform this song in public because you would be infringing copyright). You can write a song to sing to a patient in hospital, a friend embarking on an overseas trip or going to a new school, for a birthday or for any celebration you think of. (For further help, see chapter 11, 'Published Writers Speak' under heading, Sue Edmonds, songwriter.)

Self-publish

Self-publishing need not to be an expensive business. It can be as simple as typing a poem or short story on a piece of A4 paper and photostating copies for distribution to friends or relatives, etc. You can pin your literary masterpiece on the canteen noticeboard, even send a copy to your local member of parliament. Whatever you wish!

If you wish to self-publish on a much grander scale, for example, a 50 000 word novel, you will need to be wealthy. However, with much hard work (and a lot of running around) it can be done.

Once you've published your book, you will have the problem of distribution, so be aware of *that* problem. Many people self-publish, and there are some excellent books available that explain how to go about self-publishing (see below). My advice, though, is *don't do it*. If you believe your novel is publishable, send it to a reputable publisher. If it is good enough, it will find a market. After you've sent it to a dozen publishers and no one wants it, perhaps you ought to think about putting it in your bottom drawer. Sometimes a first novel is just laying the groundwork for a bigger and better (publishable) book.

By the way, some people don't know that *reputable publishers pay authors* to publish their work. Vanity publishers ask authors (generally young and/or inexperienced) to pay for publication – say 'no'!

DON'T EVER PAY A PUBLISHER TO PUBLISH YOUR WORK.

(For further information, see chapter 12, 'Submitting Your Work'.)

Start a Newspaper or Magazine

Organisations to which you belong – such as a parents' and citizens' association, a sporting body, unemployed workers or neighbourhood centre – may decide to publish a newspaper, newsletter or magazine on a regular or irregular basis in order to communicate your group's news, views and forthcoming events. Your writers' group may vote to publish its own anthology. Or, as an individual with a hobby, you may wish to start a specialist magazine (for example, on gem fossicking or dog breeding).

The problem with starting a newspaper or magazine is money. And distribution. The problem is solved if you have the backing and resources of a large organisation such as a business company or educational institution. However, don't be daunted by the task.

It can be done. Catherine Jaggs and Evelyn Tsitas started a national youth literary magazine without any monetary help (see the discussion of *Emu* in chapter 9, 'Co-operative Writing and Publishing Projects').

Before you do anything, you need to decide the function of your publication (that is, what it aims to do, its intended readership, its editorial philosophy and proposed content), its format (size and layout) and how often it will be published. You might, for example, have a single broadsheet, folded in the middle, containing neighbourhood news and views. On the other hand, you might aim for a sixteen-page A2-size literary magazine, stapled in the middle, or a thirty-two page rock magazine, A3-size, with colour photographs. Distribution is another sizeable problem for small publications. You must take *costs* into account before you make any commitments to people like contributors or printers, otherwise you can have *big* headaches. Avoid being over-ambitious.

If you start up a community, school or classroom newspaper, and you are seeking contributions from people outside your immediate circle of staff, colleagues or classmates, make strict deadlines. Getting articles in on time will probably be your biggest problem. Make sure you do not print anything libellous. If in doubt, leave it out. It's a good idea to model your publication on an actual example and have all its main features.

Be sure to put copies of your finished product in your local libraries. (For more information on producing a newspaper, read chapter 9, 'Co-operative Writing and Publishing Projects'.)

Compile a Local or Family History

If an older member of your family has a birthday coming up, why not prepare a family history, complete with family tree, photographs, mementoes, and comments from other members of the family? You could collect anecdotes from interviews with relatives and transcribe them onto neat handwritten or typed pages. Lay out the book as attractively as you can. It will most likely become a family heirloom, to be passed down from generation to generation.

If you have a special interest in history as well as writing, then compiling a history of your town or local area would most likely appeal to you. Newspaper records are a valuable resource, while your local library will also be able to direct you to suitable references. Elderly people have a valuable storehouse of memories (and sometimes memorabilia). You could also approach your local historical society or museum for information. Your completed local history could be donated to the regional library, school, council, museum or historical society. The National Library in Canberra also collects documents of historical significance, including taped interviews.

Write Letters

One of the best ways of practising your writing is to write letters. You can write to anyone: to your local newspaper, overseas penfriends, your best friend, boyfriend, girlfriend, Amnesty International, your mum or dad, interstate relatives, your local member of parliament, authors, hospital patients, rock stars, companies, the Prime Minister of Australia, etc. You can think up slogans for competitions, seek autographs, present your point of view, swap news, request information, tell someone you love them, and so on.

Most professional writers write interesting, amusing letters. Write frequently and it will improve your fluency.

Write Verse for Greeting Cards

You can design the greeting card, or you can buy a blank one. By making up your own verse, you use your talent as a poet in a practical but personal way. The recipient will value the card even more than if you had given a commercial one.

Why not go further and write verses for all occasions: to be read at your cousin's wedding; for your brother when he's feeling down; for Dad when he's baked an especially nice dinner; for Mum when she's just got that job she wanted; for your best friend when you've just had a fight; for your teacher who gave you a lot of help. Some overseas publishers purchase greeting card verse (refer to the *Writers' and Artists' Yearbook*, chapter 12, 'Submitting Your Work' under Helpful Books).

Don't let your poems die in the bottom drawer.

Conduct a Prose or Poetry Reading

Another way of making your writing 'live' is to share it with an audience at a prose or poetry reading. Find some other brave writers who would like to take part in the reading and arrange a program with them. Arrange material so you have an interesting balance: try to include humorous material if you can; you could also consider including a musical item or two. Have at least one rehearsal before the actual performance.

You could conduct the reading in someone's home, in a hotel lounge, library, town hall, school auditorium, park or beach. Make sure you publicise the event in advance. Whether or not you charge admittance is up to you and your co-performers.

Become a Hired Scribe

Some people are lousy writers. They'd do anything to be freed of the chore of writing that letter to their aunty or to their creditor. That's where multi-talented *you* comes to the rescue. You can advertise by word of mouth, by posters or by paid advertisements in the local or metropolitan press. You will need to decide in advance what (if anything) you are going to charge for your services. If you prefer to write for love (not money) your local retirement home or general hospital may know of patients who need the services of a competent letter writer.

Other writing you might seek to do is writing comedy scripts for comedians, audition monologues for would-be actors, thank-you speeches for a wedding party, poems for a tongue-tied lover, references, *curriculum vitaes*. The possibilities are endless.

Form a Writers' Club

Writing can be a very lonely business. There may come a time when you have writer's block or you wish to share your work with others or you think your writing can do with workshopping. If you don't know any other serious writers, you could (as I once did) place an advertisement in the local newspaper, inviting other writers to contact you with the view of setting up a writers' club. If hiring a room or a hall is too costly, arrange a meeting in your own home.

Invite participants to bring work to be read and you'll be well on your way to establishing a lively writers' group. Future activities might include workshops, spontaneous writing on set subjects, talks by invited speakers, readings, competitions, seminars and club visits to arts festivals.

Form a Writers' Circle

For this you will need a group of people who have unpublished writing they wish to share. Form a circle. Only contributors are invited to sit in. Each writer reads from his or her own work, then every person in the circle is invited in turn to offer a constructive comment, criticism or question. The contributing writer should be able to gauge the effectiveness of the piece from the overall response of the audience. If you are commenting on another writer's work in the circle, you will be as careful with your response as you can be, as that person will eventually be analysing and commenting on your own work. Remember you are criticising the literary worth of the writing, not the writer personally.

Display Your Writing in a Public Place

If you can't get your writing published, and you don't want to relegate it to the bottom drawer because you still think it's good, then display it! Put it up on your workplace or school noticeboard. Ask your local bank or shop if they will display it and/or the work of members of your writers' club. Send it to the local newspaper – chances are the editor may not be interested, but what have you got to lose?

Conduct a Writing Competition

Hard work, this one, but loads of fun. You'll learn a lot about writing from comparing the relative merits of entries. Before you announce the competition, decide the conditions of entry (for example, types of writing, poem or story lengths, age groups, closing date, number of copies to be submitted, whether or not names should be on the entries). You will also need to decide where entries are to be sent, whether or not they will be returned (if they are, then you will need to insist on a stamped, self-addressed envelope (s.s.a.e.)), if there is to be an entry fee, who will judge the competition and the date of announcement of winners.

You will have to be firm about disqualifying anyone who doesn't abide by the contest rules; for example, if conditions of entry state no name must be on the piece submitted and someone disobeys this, then their work is ineligible, no matter how good it is. You will be surprised at how many people forget to include their name, address and/or s.s.a.e. One positive outcome of this venture is that you will get a very good idea of the standard of writing of other people; you will also learn how competitive the writing game is.

Make a Riddle and Joke Book

Instead of compiling riddles and jokes you already know, why not write down your own original humorous ideas? They could be made up, or they could be taken from real life:

a record of funny things you say, hear or see. Sometimes commercial magazines such as *The Reader's Digest* publish humorous real-life stories and jokes; you might even find a market for pieces which first appear in *your* riddle and joke book.

If you want to share your side-splitter with other people, a good place to leave it is in your loo!

HELPFUL BOOKS

Joanna Beaumont, *How to Write and Publish Your Family History*, Orlando Press, Rozelle, NSW, 1985.

Hazel Edwards, *Writing: A Piece of My Mind*, Edward Arnold, Caulfield East, Vic., 1986.

Pat Edwards, *Hey, That's a Good Idea!*, Primary English Teaching Association, Rozelle, NSW, 1985.

Leonard Knott, *Writing for the Joy of It*, Writer's Digest Books, Cincinnati, Ohio, 1982.

Peggy Teeters, *How to Get Started in Writing*, Writer's Digest Books, Cincinnati, Ohio, 1981.

Gordon Woolf, *How to Start and Produce a Magazine*, Cromarty Press, Narrabeen, NSW, 1986.

3 ☆
GETTING IDEAS

SOURCES OF IDEAS

I don't get ideas: they get me. I am assailed on all sides by ideas. In fact, my definition of a writer could nearly be 'a person who suffers from ideas for books, poems, articles, stories . . .' The frustration lies in the number of ideas that go to waste because they crop up constantly while you're working on something else.

Anne Farrell

Once you have begun collecting ideas, you see them everywhere.

Joan Aiken

Often a problem for a beginner writer is that of finding ideas for stories and poems. Your whole surroundings are actually made up of basic material for plots. What you have to do is to acquire the habit of recognising it. Many writers keep a special book for recording observed or spontaneous ideas. This acts as a valuable resource, especially when they are suffering 'writer's block' or need imaginative stimulation. A glance through my own ideas book shows snatches of overheard conversations, unusual names of people, places I've visited, pieces of graffiti, newspaper clippings of stories that have intrigued me, childhood memories, story titles I might use in future, comments from other authors, and many other titbits of information. Once you start becoming an ideas collector, you will be surprised at the snowballing effect your new hobby will have.

BE CONSTANTLY ON THE ALERT FOR IDEAS.

Here are a few clues about ways in which you can collect ideas:

Listen in on conversations. As well as getting valuable ideas for plots, you learn to develop 'an ear for dialogue'.

Be observant. Look out for the unusual even if you are just taking a walk. Watch how people interact with one another. Watch the way the seasons change. Notice colours and smells, shapes and noises. Be ever-ready to use your senses to record the world around you. Be sensitive to people's relationships.

Take note of newspaper items. Often a small story or an unusual advertisement may prompt an idea for a storyline.

Listen to the stories of relatives, friends and acquaintances. Other people's lives are a storehouse of potential stories.

Record your dreams when you wake. Writers often use dreams as an inspirational source.

Read widely. Sometimes another person's story may trigger a response in you which paves the way to a quite different story. There is nothing to stop you from using someone else's idea as a starting point; however, if you copy their story or even a part of it, this is known as 'plagiarism'.

IT IS ILLEGAL TO PLAGIARISE ANOTHER WRITER'S STORY.

(See chapter 4 'Tools of the Trade' under Legal Matters.)

Experience life as much as you can. Try new experiences. Be daring. Do the unusual. Travel. Love. Experiment. Get out of a rut. Absorb – and record – as much as you can of life's wonderful possibilities. The more you experience, the wider store of knowledge and emotions you have to draw upon.

Think. Challenge conventional notions. Don't be complacent about accepted values or practices. Record your developing philosophies about social, moral and religious matters.

Retrieve memories. Early childhood memories can often be used as springboards for writing. Interview other people about their lives; use their memories as the basis of stories.

Make a record of your day-to-day life. Working writers often keep and/or refer to journals or diaries for source material.

There are as many potential story topics as there are people in the world. If you are still scratching about for something to write about, surely you could find something in this (very limited) range of topics:

ANIMALS: living, extinct or mythological.
BEHAVIOUR: bullying, crying, dating, depression, friendship, kind-ness, gossiping, lying, prejudice.
CONSERVATION: buildings, earth, forests, nuclear testing, recycling, seals, whales.
DISABILITIES: anorexia nervosa, cancer, cerebal palsy, dwarfism, leprosy, rubella.
EMOTIONS: anger, fear, jealousy, hatred, suspicion.
FASHION: clothes, plastic surgery, pop stars.
GENERATION GAP: bringing up troublesome teenagers, caring for the elderly.
HEROIN: drug addiction, other narcotics.
INVENTIONS: the safety pin, motor car, roller skates, record players, television, false teeth.
JAZZ: rock and roll, country and western, new wave, pop music, rastafari.
KISSING: mating rituals, keeping your marriage alive.
LANGUAGE: advertising, body language, graffiti, malapropisms, slang, sign language, spelling.
MASS MEDIA: newspapers, film, television, radio.
NOSTRADAMUS: the future, tarot cards, crystal balls, astrology, psychics, palmistry.
OLYMPIANS: training of, rewards of.
PEOPLE: artists, ballerinas, cannibals, designers, electricians, fortune tellers, geneticists, hang glider pilots, inventors, jillaroos, kite-makers, lepers, marine biologists, navigators, Olympians, park rangers, quarantine officers, retarded children, safe-crackers,

teenagers, undertakers, violinists, waiters, X-ray technicians, Youth Line counsellors, xenophobes.

QUADS AND QUINS: multiple births, how parents cope.

RECREATIONAL ACTIVITIES: aerobics, badminton, camping, dancing, equestrian sports, fishing, golf, hiking, ice skating, javelin throwing, knitting, lifesaving, marathon running, nude bathing, occult studies, partying, quilting, raging, stamp-collecting, tie-dyeing, underwater hockey, volleyball, writing, X-rated activities, yachting, xylophone playing.

SOCIAL ISSUES AND PROBLEMS: drugs, death, shyness, war, voting, smoking, swearing, colour, race, illegitimacy, disease.

TELEVISION: actors, backstage crew, comedies, detective shows, employment opportunities, producers, ratings, reception.

UNEXPLAINED: supernatural, mysteries of the world, disappearances, the Bermuda triangle, Hanging Rock.

VIRTUES AND VICES: heroism, courage, physical endurance, cowardice, wickedness.

WISH-FULFILMENT: success, fame, wealth, power.

XXXXXXX: love, marriage, St Valentine's Day.

YOWIES: The big foot, yeti, abominable snowman.

ZZZZZZZ: sleep, dreams, nightmares.

Note: Why not make up your own A-to-Z of topics for your ideas book?

KEEPING A JOURNAL OR A DIARY

A journal and a diary are personal records of a person's life and thoughts. For me, a diary is a day-to-day record, while a journal is used on a less frequent basis and may include material (such as poems and prose passages) recorded from other people. Both diaries and journals can be effective in developing self-awareness as well as written skills.

There is no 'best' or 'correct' way to write a diary or journal. Because they are personal you can record whatever you wish in them. You can tell the story of your life. You can explore all your pent-up emotions, your anger, love or jealousy. In a journal and diary you can 'think in words'; sorting out your emerging or changing values and beliefs. As a writer you can practise your craft without fear of others' judgement, or you can write freely and intuitively without worrying about redrafting. A diary can also be an invaluable means of overcoming a 'writing block' (see below).

In a diary and journal you can experiment, play, loaf, relax or confess. You don't have to impress an audience so you will not write in a self-conscious style. Use your diary to examine your inner self and your outer self closely. What 'makes you tick'? What motivates you to behave the way you do? What are your positive and negative traits? How do other people perceive you? To 'know yourself' is perhaps the first step towards understanding others. A good writer always strives to understand what makes people 'work'.

Your life may seem very mundane at the moment, but in a few years' time you will be surprised (and probably amused) at how your younger self viewed the world. Writing daily in a diary or journal helps to improve your writing fluency.

CONDUCTING INTERVIEWS

Writing, whether it be fiction or non-fiction, often involves research. You may need to check facts in an encyclopedia or atlas or year book. Most research, though, involves some element of talking to other people who have personal experience, or knowledge and skills, in a subject area you are not familiar with. In order to gather information for my novels, I have interviewed a zoologist, a women's refuge worker, battered women, juvenile delinquents, a solicitor, officers from various government departments and youth workers, to name but a few. You might not be writing a novel, but you may wish to write a newspaper or magazine article, a non-fiction story, a biography or even a play where specialist information is needed.

It is important for a writer to learn the essential skill of interviewing people. You can conduct an interview over the phone or face-to-face. The most important thing to know is that the more thoroughly you prepare for your interview, the better the quality and greater the number of facts you will gather. The more frequently you interview people, the better you will become at doing it.

Once you have decided who you need to speak to, your object should be to obtain as much information in the least possible time and with the least possible inconvenience to yourself and your subject. Before your interview, work out *all* the things you want to ask. It is a very good idea to write down a list of possible questions, listing them in order of priority. List more questions than you possibly need in case you or your subject 'dry up'.

If you are interviewing someone face to face, arrange an appointment by phone. Make sure the date, time and place of the interview suit your interviewee. It is a good idea to specify how much time you wish to take for the interview; this prevents time wasting. On the day nominated, be punctual. Throughout the interview be polite and show interest in what the person is telling you. Allow the interviewee to talk; don't interrupt and don't offer your own opinions. If he or she gets off the subject, be tactful in guiding the conversation back to it. If you don't understand an answer, ask for clarification.

You may wish to use a tape-recorder to record the interview; ask for permission to do this in advance. Before you leave home, check that the machine is operating and that your batteries are fresh. Always carry a writing pad and several pens or pencils with you. If you are writing an article for publication in the media, your interviewee may ask to see it before publication to check for accuracy and bias. I believe the journalist has an ethical obligation to honour such a request.

Don't let the interview go over time. When it has finished, thank your subject enthusiastically for his or her time. A gracious gesture is to send a follow-up thank-you note.

HELPFUL BOOK

Tristine Rainer, *The New Diary*, Angus & Robertson, Sydney, 1985.

4 ☆
TOOLS
OF THE TRADE

DISCIPLINE

Discipline in writing, to me, means honing your style, your rhythm, and most of all, your own thinking, till everything has a true sharp edge, as precise and delicate as a craftsman's tool.

Lilith Norman

The discipline of writing can refer to crafting one's writing until it is the best effort that can be achieved. This is certainly an excellent discipline to acquire if you want to be a good writer. For many beginner writers, the first discipline in writing that needs to be acquired is that of actually sitting down and producing something. Some people say they can only write when 'inspiration' strikes – a poor excuse for not writing! Often a person will sit down with the intention of writing, but will find his or her mind wandering. If you are serious about writing, then you will need to be serious about being productive. What you need to learn is how to organise your writing time.

Organisation

Declare yourself a writer; set up a writing corner. It may only be a desk with a bookshelf nearby, but an 'official' writing area will help to give you a sense of purpose as a writer. On hand have stationery and pens – perhaps a typewriter – a dictionary, thesaurus and reference books (such as a world almanac, a style manual (see chapter 8, 'Editing Your Own Work' under Helpful Books), encyclopedias, books on writing and trivia, books of quotations, and so on). A handy book in my reference collection is an onomasticon, a little book of amazing names of real people. Other valuable resources are my books of publishers' addresses and writers' newsletters.

You will also need some sort of filing system for your newspaper clippings, journal, ideas and despatches books, letters, copies of completed manuscripts and writing projects still in progress. I need a four-drawer filing cabinet to contain all this; a cardboard box (indexed) might be enough for you to start with.

Work Schedule

If you want to ensure the maximum chance of getting writing done, organise a work schedule. This schedule can be as flexible or as rigid as you like. It depends on your other work, school or social commitments. If you find you 'don't have time to write' (a common cry), then you probably aren't giving writing your top priority. Nobody *forces* writers to sit alone for hours to produce the goods; writing is their profession and/or first love. It needs a great deal of self-motivation. It needs discipline.

Since starting a 'writer's diary' to record time spent at my desk, I've discovered that I produce my most (and best) work if I can get off to an early morning start and work through undisturbed until lunch time. On average I spend 30–40 hours a week in writing; this does not include time spent reading or doing research. You might find that keeping a record of actual time spent writing motivates you to work at least a minimum number of hours a week.

A writer needs to set aside regular working times, during which writing should be done. The best course is to plan time for writing every day. Even if this is no more than an hour a day, a great deal can be done. By keeping a continuity of work you preserve interest and excitement in your writing project/s. Also, if you write regularly, you will get into the habit of mentally planning your work in advance. When you see what regular writing can produce you will have a great sense of achievement.

Deadlines

One way of disciplining yourself as a writer is to impose deadlines on what you produce. This can be self-induced (for example, 'I will finish the first draft of this short story by next Friday') or you can decide to enter writing competitions.

It is a very good idea to start a 'despatches' book. In this you record work you have sent off to competitions and markets. You could rule pages up into columns marked Date of Submission, Name of Story/Poem etc., Place of Submission, Date of Return or Acceptance, and Payment (if any). You could also have another column to note any special features such as whether you have sent a stamped self-addressed envelope, the closing date of the competition, cost of the entry fee and the date of announcement of competition winners. A despatches book enables you to see at a glance what work you have out, how long it has been out, and how successful overall you have been in achieving publication. The book also acts as an incentive to submit work.

Writer's Block

Sometimes, even with the best of intentions, you find your mind is blank. You sit and think, and the more you think the less your brain responds. White paper glares at you from your desk. How do you overcome this block?

One way to prevent it in the first place is to get into the habit of finishing by the clock. Next time you sit down to write, tell yourself you will finish at a particular time. At the stroke of the clock, stop writing, even if you are in mid-sentence. When you return to your writing next day, you will have half-finished work to resume. It is easier to finish old work than to start new.

Some people with writer's block use a 'stream of consciousness' approach. They decide not to write on a set topic, but to write aimlessly, scribbling down all that is in their mind. They may be preoccupied with a personal problem, or with a fly crawling up the wall. Everything which flashes or wanders into their mind is recorded. If you write like this for even a short while, you will be surprised at how soon an idea for a story will come to you.

You might even try the technique of 'writing out your writing block'. Write a letter to yourself. Tell yourself why you think you are having this problem of not being able to write. Again, you will be surprised at the results.

A perusal of your ideas book or a look through writing you have done previously might motivate you to begin writing afresh.

Alternatively, try your hand at a different form of writing; if you normally write prose, try writing a dialogue between two people. Compose verse to be sung. Finally, what you can do is to sit for your allocated time, then if nothing has happened, go and immerse yourself in a totally different activity. Consciously get your mind off your writing. Your mind will still be working subconsciously and when you next return to your desk, ideas will probably tumble out.

PERSISTENCE

Persistence is the first, second and third requirement for an author in my opinion. When I first started I was writing pretty horrible stuff. The very first literary encouragement I had was when I entered an eisteddfod. I was about thirteen, and I had a little poem which won my section for the under-fourteen-year-olds. I'm afraid it won because it was the only entry. But a girl that I knew had a poem in the under-sixteen section, and I came across it many years later – it had been published in the local newspaper. Her poem was still a very fine poem – it could be published without any hesitation today in a major anthology – whereas my poem was one that you screwed up and hoped no one would ever uncover. However, I am now a professional poet and she isn't. What I am suggesting is that you can start off with a very, very clumsy apparatus, but you'll get there if you have the persistence to keep going and the belief in yourself that you've got something worth saying. I think that is the most essential thing about being a writer.

Tom Shapcott

You don't know what it is to stay a whole day with your head in your hands trying to squeeze your unfortunate brain so as to find a word. Ideas come very easily with you, incessantly, like a stream. With me it is a tiny thread of water. Hard labour at art is necessary for me before obtaining a waterfall.

Gustave Flaubert (to George Sand)

Throughout this book writers offer advice to people like yourself who want to become writers. If I had only one piece of advice to offer an aspiring writer, young or old, it would be to persist. <u>Nothing succeeds like persistence.</u> Believe in yourself. Believe in your talent. Learn from rejection. Keep trying. Keep learning. Keep writing. So many give up so easily. It doesn't matter what sphere of work you are involved in, if you have some talent, if you work hard, if you persist, then you will succeed.

READING

One sure-fire way to become a better writer is to read widely and critically. Every writer I know is an avid reader. I suppose you could say that by reading one learns to write, just as by listening, one learns to speak. Reading not only offers a writer an imaginative experience, but constant exposure to a vast range of literature provides opportunities to think about and reflect on language. By reading good and varied literature, you will be able to study different literary styles. Subconsciously, you will absorb the mechanics of writing: how authors use sentence structure, diction, syntax, symbolism, metaphor and rhythm to create illusion. Subconsciously, you will learn about plotting, characterisation, point of view, setting and theme.

The more you read, the better equipped you will be to develop your critical faculties. This, in turn, will enable you to judge what is good writing. Make use of professionally trained librarians; seek their advice if you want to devise a rich reading program to complement your writing attempts.

WORKSHOPS

At some time or another you may be fortunate enough to participate in a writing workshop. Workshops are simply classes where the emphasis is on the practical rather than the theoretical. Students' writing is made public so that others can comment on it.

If you attend a writing workshop, you may be asked to submit written work in advance but usually your tutor will suggest a topic/s or writing style to practise in class. Then you will be given a certain time in which to write. After that, there is usually a sharing session in which participants in turn read their efforts aloud. The tutor may comment on each writer's work or may invite general criticism or discussion of it from the other students.

Do not be sensitive about someone criticising your writing in a workshop. That is the main purpose of the session: for others to look at your early draft/s and offer advice on how to improve it. If you hate 'going public' like this, it's probably best not to attend workshops. Remember, too, that if you wish to criticise someone else's work, not to attack it viciously. Give advice graciously. Try to *help* the other writer. Comment on flaws in the plot, undeveloped characters, poor grammar, the use of clichés, repetitious sentence beginnings. Alternatively, praise original ideas or images, unusual presentation, vivid phrases, the natural use of dialogue. If you *are* critical, back up your statements with facts and/or helpful suggestions.

Writing workshops where participants respect one another's work can be highly beneficial learning experiences.

Note: For more information about workshops, see chapter 13, 'Markets and Competitions'.

USING A DICTIONARY AND THESAURUS

Whatever you write – fiction or non-fiction – two tools of the trade are essential. Heading the list is a thesaurus and running a very close second is a dictionary.

When the exact word to describe something eludes you, a thesaurus will help. It can provide you with a very wide range of possible alternatives for any single word. (Refer to chapter 8, 'Editing Your Own Work', under the heading Words, Words, Words.) Using a thesaurus regularly will improve your vocabulary more than you can realise.

As well as using your dictionary to check word meanings, use it to check when you are proofreading your finished piece of writing. Never submit work to a publisher or competition if you even *suspect* a word may be misspelt. When in doubt, check.

TYPEWRITERS AND WORD PROCESSORS

If you are serious about being a writer, you will need to learn how to type or have someone type up your work for you. Publishing companies *refuse* to look at manuscripts unless they are typed.

If you don't have a typewriter, but you want to send work to markets and/or competitions, see if you can borrow a typewriter or persuade a friend to type your work for you. (For instructions on how to present a manuscript, see chapter 12, 'Submitting Your Work'.)

There are various kinds of typewriters, ranging from manual to electric to electronic (with visual displays). They may be cheaper than word processors, but if you can afford to buy (or persuade your fairy godmother to buy) the appropriate software and printer, you can convert your home computer to a word processor. A word processor allows you the freedom to experiment with your writing and makes revising and editing easier. From personal experience, I believe that using a word processor also increases my output. Without the benefit of my computer, I am quite sure I would never have attempted to write this book.

LEGAL MATTERS

All writers should avoid libel: that is, writing statements which damage other people's reputations. Libel can land you in the law courts. To avoid this, do not use a real person's name or other criteria which can identify any real person when you are writing fiction. Do not invade other people's privacy (for example, do not tape-record what they say and use it without their permission). Always be careful not to write anything which can be challenged, or which may be offensive (see chapter 11, 'Published Writers Speak', under Postscript: A Cautionary Tale).

Another matter which will cause you legal problems is if you plagiarise another writer's work, that is, if you deliberately and with intent publish another writer's original work under your name. You can, with impunity, be *influenced* by another writer's ideas or storyline – just don't pass off their actual words or ideas as your own.

To indicate that this is your own work, and to discourage plagiarism, make sure you attach a copyright © sign and your name to all pieces of completed work.

Dealing with publishers' contracts – if you are ever in that fortunate position – can also be a tricky business, fraught with all manner of legal complications. Always use the services of a solicitor or other professionals before signing your name to a contract. Published writers are wise about contracts and particular publishers' quirks; consult them for advice.

The Arts Law Society,* the Australian Society of Authors* and the Australian Copyright Council* will be able to advise you on legal matters.

HELPFUL BOOKS

Colin Golvan & Michael McDonald, *Writers and the Law*, Law Book Company, Sydney, 1986.

5 ☆
WRITING PROSE

> Good prose is like a window pane.
> George Orwell

PROSE GENRES

Prose can be fiction (invented) or non-fiction (true). Prose is different from poetry in that prose is usually written in sentences. There are an enormous number of prose genres. They can take the form of: novels, short stories, plays, dialogues, essays, articles, reviews, prayers, proverbs, parables, scripts for stage, film or television, diaries, journals, logbooks, surveys, questionnaires, anecdotes, reports, memoirs, business minutes, narratives, instructions, reminiscences, tall tales, myths, legends, science fiction, fantasies, character sketches, biography, historical fiction, jokes, puns, letters, description, announcements, telegrams, petitions, signs, notices; the list seems endless.

This chapter will concentrate on three popular forms of prose: non-fiction, the short story, and the novel.

NON-FICTION

Non-fiction is enormously varied and includes: autobiography, biography, true-life stories, how-to manuals, encyclopedias, recipe books, textbooks, history, nature studies and sports manuals, general interest subjects, etc. Often a non-fiction project starts from the writer's own interest in, and a need for, a book on the subject. This book illustrates these points. My starting point was an interest (and involvement) in writing, a background in teaching, editorial experience on youth magazines, and the knowledge that there were few comprehensive resource books on the market aimed at helping new writers. It's been a lot of hard work, but I've honestly enjoyed every minute of writing and compiling it.

Writing a Non-fiction Book

The first thing you need to do, after deciding on the subject area of your non-fiction book, is to break the subject down into smaller components, that is, chapters. Next, break the chapters down into even smaller sections. This break-down will prove to be an important guide when you are writing the book. You will next need to research your subject more closely. Read extensively, gather notes. You need to be a good organiser to write a non-fiction book. If you intend writing a non-fiction book to coincide with a specific event, you should plan it at least eighteen months to two years in advance.

The degree of work involved in researching and writing non-fiction will, of course, depend on your intended readership. You may not aspire to writing a book for commercial publication; your need may be personal. If you decide, for instance, to write a biography, you could chose someone very close to you, say your mother. Collect as much information about her life from as many different sources as you can (for example, informal talks with your mother; interviews with her parents, your aunts and uncles; photograph albums; your mother's friends and acquaintances; your own childhood recollections). When you have transcribed all the information and written your mother's story, illustrate it with drawings or photographs. Surprise Mum with her 'This is Your Life' book on Mother's Day. Guaranteed to bring a tear to her eye.

Perhaps you have a special interest in a subject – such as computers, trucks, doll collecting, stamps, flags of the world, toucans, the psychology of brother and sister relationships, the life and times of Adolf Hitler. Why not attempt to write a non-fiction book on the subject? You can always present it to a school library, your infant child, niece, nephew, or young cousin.

Commercial publication

Many 'one off' non-fiction books have been written and published by people who had specialist knowledge of particular subjects. Brothers Ken and Steven Laitin, for example, decided the world could use a better soccer book, so they wrote *The World's #1 Best Selling Soccer Book* which was published in America. Fourteen-year-old New Zealand girl, Lisa Vassal, wrote about her life as a cerebal palsy victim in a book titled *Just an Ordinary Kid*. Australian housewife Julie Stafford compiled recipes of foods she cooked for her invalid husband; they were later published in the immensely successful *Taste of Life* series. Bookshelves all over the world are heavy with books by people who have written about aspects of their own or others' lives.

If you are ambitious enough to attempt to write a non-fiction book for commercial publication, you would be wise to take time first to assess the market for the kind of book you intend writing. Supposing you have wide experience in grape growing and you wish to write a book for the amateur grape-grower. First, look around bookshops, in libraries and in publishers' catalogues and see what books already exist on this topic. If, after doing this, you still believe there is room on the market for your book, do not rush off to write your tome. You will save yourself considerable time and energy if you first prepare a proposal to submit to a publisher. Chapter 12, 'Submitting Your Work', discusses in detail the process of researching the market, submission of your manuscript and what you might expect should it be accepted.

Writing Articles for Magazines

Your world is filled with opportunities for you to write articles: social, sporting and community organisations are constantly crying out for publicity officers to write press releases. If you decide to turn your writing hobby into a profitable freelance business, you need only look around any newsagency at the vast array of local and international newspapers and magazines to get some idea of the opportunities awaiting you. Depending on the publication, you might find yourself wanting to write: an inspirational article; an article based on a personal experience; a humorous anecdotal piece; a personality profile; a travel article; a historical piece; a how-to article; an informational article.

Market research

Before you rush into print, you would be advised to study your market. The first rule in writing for magazines is

'Give them what they want'. To do this, you must examine carefully the publications you wish to write for. You can obtain information about specific magazines and their editorial requirements such as word-length, the kinds of material the editors say they need, whether a query is necessary or if finished articles are preferred, from the *Writers' and Artists' Yearbook* (see chapter 12, 'Submitting Your Work', under the heading Helpful Books). Find further clues to an editor's needs by studying all aspects of the magazine you intend submitting to, from the types of articles run to the illustrations used. A careful analysis of the magazine's advertisements will also help you form an accurate idea of what the 'typical' reader of the magazine is like.

Finally, make sure your subject matter is appropriate for that publication. Even if your idea is sound, it could be that your style of writing or approach is wrong.

Getting an idea

Fresh, new ideas for articles are always welcomed by magazine or newspaper editors. Annual events – Christmas, Easter, school holidays, national holidays – are excellent opportunities for you to show your versatility as a writer. The trick is to think of a novel variation on an old theme (easier said than done).

Ideas for articles can come from a million-and-one places: from newspaper headlines, overheard conversations, meeting people, photographs, witnessed incidents, reviews, personal experiences, holidays, other people's anecdotes. You may be an expert at growing petunias, raising children, pickling vegetables, balancing a budget; make use of your valuable background. Later, when you have more confidence in your ability to place articles, you can attempt to write researched articles.

The query letter

Query letters save writers time and energy. Once you have decided on an idea for an article which you believe will suit a particular publication, write a brief letter to the editor, outlining your proposed article. Your query letter should include main points you would cover, the length and tone of the piece, your suggested delivery date, and the rights you are selling (for example, first Australian rights, non-exclusive rights, serial rights only). You might also like to include a brief résumé of your previous publication experience.

If the editor likes your idea, you will be given the go-ahead to write the article. However, don't submit your query letter a week before the publication is due to go to the printer; it will be relegated to the waste paper bin. Editors and publishers schedule ahead (sometimes as much as two or three issues ahead) and so must you. As a guide, your deadline for a weekly magazine should be at least six weeks ahead of publication, for a monthly magazine three months ahead, for a quarterly magazine six months ahead; for a weekly newspaper you would be looking at approximately four weeks ahead.

Photographs

Editors prefer to get text and photos in the one package, so you would be advised to learn how to take saleable photos or to get hold of someone who is willing to snap away for you. It is probably a good idea to make a query first about the magazine's basic photo requirements (that is, does it print only colour, black and whites, transparencies or glossies?) Most editors will want your shots to be captioned. Never submit photos without attaching details of photographer, title of article it accompanies, and so on. If someone other than yourself took the photo, obtain their permission (in writing) before submitting it for publication.

FICTION: THE BASIC STORY ELEMENTS

The first thing you have to consider when writing a novel is your story, and then your story – and then your story!

Ford Maddox Ford

All fiction has certain elements in common which makes it work as a story. If you want to write good stories, you will need to carefully examine your use of theme, plot, characterisation, point of view, setting and style. Other story components such as conflict, dramatic action, tension, climax, atmosphere, motivation and tone should arise from your use of these main elements.

Theme

The theme is the main concept or message that you, the writer, are trying to express. Typical themes are concerned with the meaning of life, the search for freedom, conflict between the classes, the struggle to find love, the rewards of goodness and faith. You may strongly believe in peace in our time, that children have rights too, that politicians should not play with people's lives, that apartheid is wrong, that the world will be destroyed by nuclear war if we do not take action soon; these motivating ideas form the theme of your story. The way in which you express your idea or theme is through your plot.

Plot

> The most important and difficult thing about writing fiction is to find a plot. Good original plots are very hard to come by.
>
> Roald Dahl

Some people confuse story with plot. A story is what happens, the sequence of events. A plot, on the other hand, is the plan and design of the story. It is to do with *why* things happen. The plot involves the interaction of the elements of character, motivation and action.

Basic to plot is *conflict*. A story must have conflict of some sort, arising out of the situations in which the characters find themselves. The working out of this conflict is the crux of the story. First you have a problem for the main character to overcome. Then comes an adversary or an obstacle (conflict) to the easy solution to the story. With the solution of the problem, you have the resolution – or satisfactory ending – of your story.

Conflict can involve:

a person against another person (for example, a bully and his victim, a sportsperson and the umpire, a child against a parent, a teacher and student);

a person against his or her conscience (for example, guilt at having stolen something, or jealousy towards someone);

a person against nature (for example, a board rider drifting out to sea, a woman caught in a raging flooded river, a man facing an escaped circus lion).

By putting your characters under stress (conflict), you will reveal a great deal about them. (You will find more about conflict in chapter 7, 'Writing Drama', under the heading Conflict and Characters.)

Characterisation

When I begin a book, I start out with a character. I have
no plot in mind. The character begets other characters
and soon they begin to take over the novel and chart
their own destinies.

Sidney Sheldon

People are too elusive, too shadowy, to be copied; and
they are also too incoherent and contradictory. The
writer does not copy his originals; he takes what he
wants from them, a few traits that have caught his
attention, a turn of mind that has fired his imagination,
and therefrom constructs his character.

W. Somerset Maugham

Characterisation is the way you present and
develop a story character so that he or she is known to, and understood by, the reader. You can reveal a character through actions
and idiosyncracies, through dialogue, by what others say about
the character, and by his or her relationships with others. You
can also develop a character through attributes such as gesture,
physical expression, dress, speech mannerisms, vocation, even
through Christian names and surnames.

As the story progresses, your story character can be shown to
change (for better or worse); this is what is known as character
development. A character who is sufficiently well developed to
involve the reader's identification is said to be 'well-rounded' or
'three-dimensional'. 'Flat' or 'one-dimensional' characters (sometimes referred to as 'types') are not fully developed. The main
character (or protagonist) in your short story or novel should be
three-dimensional.

When creating story characters, do not base them totally on
anyone you know. This can cause legal problems for one thing,
and for another it limits your opportunity for shaping a character
creatively. How do you project a fictitious character with some
force in order to make that character come 'alive' on the page?
A good way is to ask questions about the character, just as you
would ask questions about some new acquaintance. What does
my character look like? What does she want out of life? Who are
her friends, her family? What distinguishes her in a crowd? Is
she a good listener? What habits of speech and manner does she
have? What are her personality traits?

These are just a few questions you could ask of your invented
character. By asking questions you make the character come clear.

I never start a new novel until I have asked so many questions of my characters that I feel I know them intimately. If you do not know your characters, how can you hope to get others to know them?

Make up names to suit your characters. Endow sympathetic characters with pleasant names, give your villains evil-sounding handles. Collect names (from real life, books, newspapers). Some I have used from my ideas book are Willie Macbeth, Lola Rose, Sheila Fangboner, Dora Agnes Kelly, Stephen ('Cadbury') Perrin, Angela Devine and Michelle Towers.

Point of View

If there is a story, then there must be a story-teller. A short story is usually told from the point of view of one of its characters, though in the novel the point of view can switch from one character to another. Before you begin to write your short story, you need to know whose story it is for the story will belong to your central character, who should command more interest and sympathy from the reader than any other. The story can be told from the point of view of:

First person. (Told by the main character, using 'I'.)

Third-person narrator. (This narrator tells the story from another person's viewpoint of the main character, using the pronoun 'he' or 'she' to refer to that character. This narrator may be known to the protagonist.)

The omniscient narrator. (This narrator knows everything about all the characters in the story and may – or may not – reveal everything. The omniscient narrator is not known to anyone in the story.)

Multiple narrators. (Several narrators can tell the story by the use of devices such as letters, notes, reports, documents and so on. This method is rarely used in short stories but is sometimes used in novels.)

The point of view you decide to use can be of any kind but you must use it consistently. Do not change viewpoint in mid-story as it can weaken the narrative.

Setting

Without setting, some books (such as a mystery novel, for example) would be totally devoid of atmosphere. Using setting you show your characters against an environment which may have shaped or may be about to shape the way they are. The environment may be a French castle in the nineteenth century, a reform school for juvenile delinquents, the Amazon jungle, slum tenements in the Philippines, a Hollywood film studio, a clothing factory, an ordinary middle-class Australian home. Setting is thus the background against which the action unfolds and the characters move. It can refer to location (actual place), period (historical time) or the characters' social backgrounds. In contributing to the design of the whole, setting supports the plot and often reveals character.

When you are writing prose, you will need to think about how important setting is to your story. Before you describe a scene, imagine every detail as vividly as you can. Not only are the visual details relevant, but also those of sound, smell, taste and touch. Record setting using all of your five senses. The art of descriptive writing lies not in crowding a passage with details but in knowing how to leave most of the detail out. You must know how to select and feature the *essentials* of a scene. Suggest just enough to kindle the imagination, relying on the reader's mind to supply the rest of the scene.

Style

 To write well, express yourself like the common people, but think like a wise person.

Aristotle

Style is the way in which your writing shows your personality and character. It involves the way in which you choose to use words; this is reflected in tone (serious, humorous, sarcastic, sophisticated, straightforward), in diction (your choice of words) and in the precise (or other) way you express yourself. You may use plain, everyday language or you may use very vivid words. You may write literally, or, on the other hand, you may use figurative language (frequent use of metaphors and similes. For a discussion of figurative language, see chapter 6, 'Writing Poetry', under the heading Creating Poetic Images).

The essentials of good style are: clarity, simplicity, and originality. You can develop your own style by studying the styles of other writers, and by experimentation. Verbs (action words) are very effective in communicating an idea or mood, or event. Use strong verbs and this will help improve your writing style. Writing can never be too clear or too simple. If you work hard at your craft, attempting to eliminate errors such as faulty grammar, repetition, clichés and clumsy sentences, and if you strive for original images and fresh ways of looking at the normal, your style will improve.

Carefully study chapter 8, 'Editing Your Own Work'. If you can learn the lessons of this chapter, then you will be well on your way to developing your own individual, distinctive voice. With continued practice, you will eventually write with style.

METHODS OF PLOTTING

My plots derive from everyday life, from asking 'what if?' and 'what would happen then?'

Monica Hughes

'Plot is action. Action of language, language of action. Plot is story . . . plot must not cease to move forward.

Elizabeth Bowen

I strongly advise beginning writers not to write without an outline. Writing without some kind of blueprint can lead to too many blind alleys.

Sidney Sheldon

Keeping in mind that plot involves the interaction of character, motivation and action, a good idea to help plot your story is to ask – and find answers for – the following questions:
1 Who is the story about? (protagonist)
2 What is his or her need? (motivation)
3 What stops or thwarts the protagonist from achieving this need? (antagonist)
4 Does he or she achieve this need?
5 How does he or she succeed or fail? (resolution)
Using the answers to these questions, plan an outline of your story before you attempt to write it. Jot down all the events in the plot in the order in which they will occur in the finished story. List the crises which are designed to sustain interest in the middle of the story. Make notes on the characters – their problems and situations, and their relationships with others.

Plots basically grow out of characterisation and conflict. It is really a matter of one thing leading to another. As well as using character, you can devise plots based on:
emotions (for example, fear, jealousy, hatred, cowardice, anger);
situations (physical dangers such as a capsizing boat, a runaway truck, an enraged bull, a raging river);

themes (A stitch in time save nine; too many cooks spoil the broth);
titles (My Wife's a Werewolf, Every Day Is Sunday)

USING DIALOGUE

Dialogue is particularly important in revealing character and in showing relationships between people. A person's speech will reveal more than his or her appearance. For example, you can make your story characters glare at each other, avoid each other or even hit each other, but the conflict becomes more real when they erupt into words. Points to remember when using dialogue:

Communicate the essence!

1 Don't write down *everything* people might say in conversation; when you are writing dialogue, find the *essence* of what is being communicated and write that. If you tried to be absolutely true to everyday speech, what you would write would be boring. Nevertheless, you must try to make speech sound natural.

2 Keep speeches short. Only people delivering a sermon or a political speech are long-winded. Lengthy soliloquies are boring and you must never, *never* bore your reader.

3 Remember that people speak in character. If in doubt about dialogue, read it aloud. Ask yourself, is that how my character would speak? Be careful in using slang; it can date quickly. Remember that most people use contractions (e.g. I've, don't, haven't); often too, they speak in phrases.

4 To capture the basic rhythm of speech, vary sentence lengths.
   For further pointers on using dialogue in writing, refer to chapter 8, 'Editing Your Own Work', under the heading Improving Dialogue.

WRITING A NOVEL

You have to have determination, discipline, dedication and drive. You have to be obsessed with a book. Without it it won't work. You've got to want to write more than anything else, and you've got to be prepared to make sacrifices for it. Also there is a D for distraction. Nothing or no one must intrude.

Barbara Taylor Bradford

I find the first draft pure torture.
> Judy Blume

It takes me about a year to write a book, but I spend
another year thinking about it and polishing it.
> Betsy Byars

Writing a book is a horrible, exhausting struggle, like a
long bout of some painful illness.
> George Orwell

People write novels in different ways. Some start
without a plan and let the writing find its own course; others
meticulously plan the structure of their novel before they commence
writing. After experimenting with both these methods, I find it
best to have a very good idea of what the novel is going to be
about before I start writing, even if I don't know its eventual
destination. What I *do* need to know very well before I begin are
my characters, especially my protagonist (lead character). I need
to know everything about her – her personality, what she looks
like, her family relationships, her social contacts, her schooling,
what motivates her, her ambitions, her problems. Armed with this
information, I can create a world for her in which she will live
and learn and grow. I make many written and mental notes before
I tackle a novel.

Another major decision which I have to make is the matter of
viewpoint. How will I narrate the story? Should I use first person,
third person, an omniscient narrator, multiple narrators? What tense
is my story going to be in, present or past? Often I have to experiment,
using different narrators before I can decide which best suits a
particular story.

Planning a Novel

Writing a novel is a long and often difficult
business. You need a great deal of concentration in order to keep
in contact with all the threads of the story, and with characters.
It is, of course, easier to write a novel without the distraction of
outside employment, and to have a longish period – up to two
years or more – in which to do this. (This is probably why so
many new writers concentrate their energies on writing poems and
short stories.) If the idea of writing a full-length novel daunts you,
remember this: you start with a sentence, then you write another

and another. Soon you have a chapter. After twenty (or less) chapters, you have a book. The whole prospect becomes less frightening if you break it down into smaller components. Meet one challenge at a time and before long you will have written that 40 000-word novel.

I write books one chapter at a time, always trying to start at a crucial moment in my protagonist's life, a time when that person is about to experience challenge and/or change. At the end of each chapter, I spend a lot of time reading, thinking about, and rewriting the chapter before I go on to the next. Other writers work their way right through the novel before they read it and make changes. Different methods suit different people; no one method is *the* best.

The First Chapter

In your first chapter avoid using flashbacks and long detailed explanations and descriptions. Concentrate on *action*. Confrontation is a good idea. Spend a long time working on your first paragraph; it may be what decides your reader to keep on reading. At the end of the first chapter, don't give away too much; again, you want your reader to continue reading. A good place to start a novel is in the *middle* of the story; make the assumption that the reader knows all that has come before.

Titles

A good title is a title that 'sells' a book. It should be catchy and to the point. It should make itself be remembered. Find a title that matches the mood of the book. Here are some titles which grab your attention:

The Moon's A Balloon/Plumbum/The Most Beautiful Lies/Foxybaby
The Undertaker's Gone Bananas
Pardon Me, You're Stepping on my Eyeball
Love's Tender Fury/As I Lay Dying/Woolworth Madonna/
My Uncle Bertie (Alias Fangs)
The Cat Ate My Gymsuit
Boss of the World
Psycho

When you are using titles, be original. Don't use titles others have used before you. Titles (for both short stories, novels, even articles) can be of the following type:

Questions (*Who Says the World Is Flat?*)
Striking statements (*Cats Are Smarter than People!*)
Puns (*Little Red Riding, the Hood*)
Negative (*God Does Not Exist*)
Positive (*Kids Win, Hands Down*)
How, What, Why (*How to Win Friends. What If You Died Tomorrow?
    Why My Dad Went Crazy*)
Frightening (*Two Hours to Death*)
Topical (*Nuclear Nightmare*)
Paradoxical (*Bad Angels*)
Quizzical (*So You Don't Believe in the Money Tree?*)

Openings

In your story opening, you must
• immediately catch the interest of your reader
• introduce the characters
• set the stage
• introduce the problem or the situation
• set the mood.

A good idea is to show your main character in action in an interesting setting as soon as you can. Read a wide variety of books to compare and contrast how other writers 'hook' the reader's attention at the start of a novel. Some writers use the following kinds of openings:

Character. The protagonist is introduced immediately. Preferably he or she will be involved in some sort of action which captures the reader's attention.

Dialogue. The narrative will be revealed through speech. This type of opening suggests a story of human communication.

Emotion. The mood of the story is quickly established. This would suit a story about relationships.

Atmosphere. A description of setting is ideal for a mystery story.

Situation. This type of opening sets the scene, introduces the characters and poses the problem of the story.

Action. No beating about the bush; this is a good way to open an adventure story.

Philosophical. The story's narrator presents his or her view of life (but action must start soon or you will bore your reader). This could suit a science fiction story.

Dialogue and action are the most effective means of generating interest in your story's opening. Start where the story's action begins.

A FICTION WRITER'S CHECKLIST

Once you have finished writing your short story or novel, you could re-read it to consider the following points:

1 Is the title intriguing? What kind of a story does it suggest?
2 Does the first paragraph grab your attention? Is there any way at all that it can be improved?
3 Does the story maintain interest? What story-telling devices have you used to create suspense (for example, dialogue, 'cliff-hangers' at chapter ends, flashbacks, description, the supernatural)?
4 Are there any parts of the story which are confusing?
5 Are the sentences concise or longwinded? Have you a good variety of sentence structures and sentence openings?
6 Did you make good use of dialogue and action or have you written too many slabs of description? Have you told the reader too much?
7 Is the writing economical?
8 Are the characters three-dimensional and true to life? Or are they flat and/or stereotyped?
9 How would you describe your story? Is it lively, humorous, dull, moralistic, patronising, superficial, original?
10 Have you used conflict in your story to create tensions?
11 Is the ending satisfactory? Are all the conflicts in the story resolved?
12 What theme/s emerge from your story?

ADVICE FROM PROSE WRITERS

The Australian literary scene at the moment is more pervasively dominated by conservative interests than before. There is less Australian-owned and small publishing than in the period 1968–80, and more publishing of Australian authors by multinational companies.

The prevailing style in prose is bland, non-controversial, non-experimental and inauthentic. To get published in establishment areas you must not only have this type of style but also have the right connections. There is a huge need in Australia for new and young writers to join with the people who have been promoting small press and writer-owned productions to set up, continue and retain productions and networks which serve our own interests as writers.

Information about small presses and alternative writers' groups is hard to find and rarely seen in any major newspaper. Sources of this information are the Poets' Union*, the Collected Works Bookshop* (and catalogue) and the Experimental Art Foundation Bookshop.*

Anna Couani

I urge you, the writer-to-be, to set out with high levels of hope, application and self-criticism, a grim level of determination, and a commitment to your own uniqueness. If you're a writer at heart, you've got to believe in the validity of your contribution to what at times may seem to be an already too-large mass of existing literature. If you're committed at heart, what exists already doesn't matter to your objectives as a writer. You may respect what exists, but you are never to be daunted by it.

The writer you're going to be may not show for years, but if you don't go through those years, if you don't serve the sentence, you'll never savour the excitement of the ultimate self-discovery. Finally, if the critics have anything useful to say, be honest enough and modest enough to accept it. But if they're trying to build empires and don't give a damn whether you're a writer or a cockroach, refuse to allow them to dishearten you.

Ivan Southall

The biggest sin you can commit in writing is to be boring. Start the action on the first line and put in hints of future exciting or terrible events to come. Don't use one unnecessary word. Create a real world so that the reader feels he or she could jump right into that story and be a part of it. Use simple grammar. Writing that draws attention to itself detracts from the plot. Don't waste time describing the fine points of your character's personalities – let their actions do it for you. If someone kicks the cat the reader won't like them. You don't have to bother writing that this person is cruel. Don't preach either. If you have a moral don't state it – let the readers draw their own conclusions. If you are writing a short story you must finish off with something interesting, insightful or surprising. The last line of a short story must draw an 'ah ha' from the reader or the story is no good.

Paul Jennings

HELPFUL BOOKS

Australian Book Scene (magazine), published annually, available from D. W. Thorpe, Port Melbourne, Vic.*

Joanna Beaumont, *You Can Make $25,000 a Year From Writing in Australia and New Zealand*, Orlando Press, Rozelle, NSW, 1986.

Louise Boggess, *How to Write Short Stories That Sell*, Writer's Digest Books, Cincinnati, Ohio, 1984.

Connie Emerson, *Write on Target*, Writer's Digest Books, Cincinnati, Ohio, 1981.

Cassidy Maddens et al., *The Writer's Manual*, E.T.C. Publications, Palm Springs, California, 1979.

Jill Morris & Mary Lancaster, *Writing Freelance Articles for Newspapers and Magazines*, Interface Publications, London, 1985.

6 ☆
WRITING POETRY

WHAT IS POETRY?

When a poet writes a poem, he (she) is saying something more important than the things said in everyday life.

James Reeves

It is not easy to define poetry. Prose writing is continuous, whereas poetry usually consists of a sequence of short lines. Poetry is different from verse in that most verse sets out to create a deliberate pattern of rhythm and rhyme. In an intense and concentrated form poetry uses language to create images that convey the poet's perceptions of the world. Thus rigid rhyme and rhythm are not the main concerns of poetry; what is of the utmost importance is the way the poet sees and writes about the world. Rhyme and rhythm are merely the technical means by which a poem's form is achieved. The Australian poet, Judith Wright, says that poetry deals with experience, physical, emotional or mental; nothing learnt from books or other poets can teach the poet to make a poem, unless the things written about are experienced and known so deeply that they become a personal truth.

Thus, if you wish to become a poet, you would do so because you are a sensitive, perceptive being who wants to share your feelings and experiences. Poets learn to use their perceptions more directly and consciously than most other people.

GETTING STARTED

A poem may be worked over once it is in being, but may not be worried into being.

Robert Frost

A real poem is sort of an idea caught in dawning; you catch it just before it comes. Think it out beforehand and you won't write it.

(source unknown)

Inspiration, the sudden, strong urge to create, is usually considered the starting point for poetry. What inspires the writer is an overflow of powerful feelings. If you write poetry, you might have noticed that your best writing was motivated by something that moved you deeply. It may have been something you saw, a physical, emotional or spiritual experience you underwent, or a strong response to someone else's experience.

Getting started on writing a poem is often a difficult business. You could sit around waiting for inspiration to strike (which may take some time!). On the other hand, it is possible to draw on your inner store of feelings, thoughts and memories, or to stimulate your senses in order to create a draft of a poem at virtually any time.

Here then, are some strategies you can use to evoke poetic responses at those times when inspiration isn't tapping on your shoulder:

Read poetry. Surround yourself with poetry. Read it aloud often. Sometimes another writer's expression of an experience can act as a springboard for your own (different) response to the same subject.

Explore your senses. Listen to stirring music, stand alone in a cathedral, hike through the bush, walk barefoot through muddy puddles, explore a rubbish tip, visit your favourite painting in an art gallery, smell aromatic flowers or leaves, pretend blindness to 'feel' the world. Experience! Inspiration often arises when one is totally absorbed in an experience.

A good way of evoking images is to concentrate on a single sensory perception. Let's use the example of taste. Close your eyes and concentrate on a particular food you like or dislike. Imagine you are eating that food. What is its texture? What does it smell like? Is it hot or cold? How does it feel in your mouth? Is it sweet or salty? How do you eat it – with chopsticks, knife and fork, spoon, your fingers? Try to remember every single detail of your eating experience. If you prefer a real experience to an imagined one, take a food, such as an apple; cut it up, explore its colour, smell and texture, listen to the sound it makes as you bite into it, concentrate on its flavour as you eat it. Explore all of your senses.

Use your memory. Use your vast store of memories to draw upon for writing material. You can train your mind to dig back into your earliest years. Write down events as you recall them. Be specific, try to remember as many concrete facts as you can about any particular happening. Try to capture the emotions you experienced at the time. Dig deep for details. Often it is the inclusion of details which makes a piece of writing vivid, which makes it stick in the reader's mind. Some experiences which you may concentrate on could be listening to your parents quarrelling, being afraid of the dark, being left alone, having a birthday party, feeling very small and helpless, your first day at school or at work, making a new friend, your first date, being scared of thunder and lightning, moving away from home, building a cubbyhouse, playing with your brother or sister.

Use brainstorming or freewriting (below) to build on the memories of your earlier childhood that you have reactivated.

Brainstorming. Explore your head; gain access to that host of experiences stored in your memory. One way to do this is by brainstorming. First, decide on a topic. Then, jot down at random all the thoughts you have associated with that topic: words, phrases, ideas, snatches of dialogue, lines, doodles. Don't push yourself, don't be selective, just take what comes. Do this for about ten to fifteen minutes. At the end of this time your mind should be alert, focusing on that topic (or something else which may have occurred to you during the brainstorming).

Freewriting. Another way of exploring your head is by freewriting; that is, writing without stopping. You could do this for five to ten minutes, writing either prose or poetry. This is a very quick and simple way of starting writing. Don't worry about spelling, punctuation, sequencing, grammar, neatness. Nobody needs to see what you've written. The main idea is to let your pen follow the ideas that flow into your mind. Your mind might wander all over the place – let it! At the end of the freewriting time, look through what you've written; you might find ideas, phrases and so on which you can use to shape a poem.

Associating. This exercise is similar to brainstorming. Start with a topic. Anything will do. Let's say you chose 'sleep'. Write it down. Now write under it another word or phrase that you associate with sleep. It could be 'darkness'. Write that underneath 'sleep'. Now find a word/s to associate with 'darkness' . . . get the idea? After a while your list of idea associations might read like this:

sleep
darkness
creeping shapes
fear
I want my daddy
nobody is coming
alone
pounding heart
footsteps
the blanket is over my head
murder
dripping blood
last thoughts
vampires, bats, dracula
teeth in my neck

The list could go on forever! What is happening is that you are beginning to focus your attention on the topic. After a while you will want to stop your associations in order to work on the drafting of your potential poem.

Describing. This exercise works in the same way as associating except that you use a specific object to work with. You may choose your hands as an example. Look at them, explore their contours, lines, skin texture, colour, smell. Close your eyes and think of your hands in action; they could be shaping something in sand, tugging, gesturing, caressing, slapping, waving. Imagine them performing specific actions such as washing up, tying shoe-laces, playing the piano, typing, making a cake. Think of hands that belong to other people: the hands of a dancer, a surgeon during an operation, an old lady, a baby. Make up images for hands. Focus as closely and as intensely as you can on your subject. Explore it from as many angles as you can.

CREATING POETIC IMAGES

Imagery is the picture or pictures that a poem makes. The best images are those that are fresh and original, giving the reader a new way of viewing the world. Often images come from the poet's immediate experience of taste, smell, touch, sight and sound.

As a writer you can sharpen your senses and become more responsive to them by being constantly aware of the physical world around you, by opening your attention to everything that comes to your mind, and by recording your responses. As well as having a literal meaning, a word may arouse a variety of associated meanings. You need to be as accurate as possible in your choice of words to recreate in your readers' minds the ideas and feelings which you wish to convey. The success of an image also depends on its suitability for its context.

There are many ways to pinpoint your sensuous perceptions and to evoke an image that you can use in a poem, either as a stimulus to write it, or as a line within it. Here are just a few:

Direct description. One way is simply to describe the image as it appears to your senses, for example, 'the apple is red, round, sweet-smelling and juicy'.

Similes. Another way is to ask what the image is like. As soon as you make literary comparisons, you are dealing with similes and metaphors, that is, you are comparing one perception with another. A simile says something is like something else, for example, 'your smile is like the sun lighting up the day' or 'the lake was like a mirror'. A simile leaves less to the imagination than does a metaphor.

Metaphors. A metaphor is much more subtle than a direct description or a simile. It is a non-literal use of language which is often heard in everyday speech. For example, we might say someone pulled the wool over our eyes. We don't literally mean what we've said, rather we wish to give the impression that we have been tricked by someone, blinded by their deceit. Metaphors thus make comparisons but in such a way that they give us a fresh view of something that may be commonplace. Poets try to invent new metaphors to give a deeper layer of meaning to their work. Some other examples of metaphors are: 'the dancer wafted across the stage' (the dancer's movement is compared to a breeze); 'beauty is a rose'; 'cut these words and you will find blood'; 'the poet is spawning ideas'.

Symbolism. Sometimes a particular object or image is made to stand for some idea. Eve, for example, is the symbol for womankind and Adam the symbol for all men. In a poem climbing a hill and tottering down the other side could have a double meaning: that of the living of life. The use of colours often has symbolic significance, as do certain animals. If you wish to use symbols to create images in your poetry, you would be advised to consult a dictionary of symbols. However, be careful not to be too vague or too complicated in your use of symbols – your first obligation is to your reader; make sure your symbolism is accessible.

You can practise ways of creating images by making word pictures of various sensory subjects. Try to think of original ways, either through direct description, simile, metaphor or symbolism, to create images for sights, sounds, smells, tastes and tactile sensations of the world around you. Go to places rich in sensation such as the zoo, a kindergarten, park, hospital, factory; reflect on controversial issues such as war, survival, the future; observe the people around you; read, look at paintings and photographs. Get out, get involved, get motivated, write.

DRAFTING A POEM

I write a poem in about an hour, but it takes me about six weeks to edit it down to what is virtually a telegram from me to myself.

Marty Feldman

Poetry is not principles, but processes. The poet is a doer, not a thinker.

Percy Bysshe Shelley

It has been said that in writing one begins hot and ends cold; that the first draft is motivated by some strong, 'hot' emotion and is thus written with passion, but that in redrafting it, in trying to improve it, one needs to be dispassionate, to be 'cold'. A poem is really never finished; the vision you had when you first conceived it is never really captured when you finally decide that the poem is as good as you can make it.

The most difficult part of writing for most writers, is rewriting. After being totally involved in the heat of creating, you then need to be cool and detached in order to examine your poem for ways of improving it. One of the best and most useful ways of revising a poem you've written is to read it aloud. If you stumble over a word or hesitate, it could be that the rhythm of your poem is not right. Make sure that your line breaks are in the right place. This is something which is often difficult – knowing where to end a line before you go onto the next – but reading the poem aloud will help you 'see' where to place the lines of text. Your natural breath phrases as well as the clusters of meaning will be what helps you discover this.

In redrafting your poem, you need to keep asking yourself, 'What's wrong with this poem?' You must go over it time after time, 'chewing' on it, spitting out words, phrases, sometimes whole lines or verses which don't taste right. Here are some questions which you could ask yourself about the poem you've written:

1 Is the title right for the poem? Does it sum up its subject matter and the spirit of the poem? Could I use something more appropriate?

2 Does the poem really start after the first few lines? (Often the first line or two can be cut out without altering the meaning of the poem.)

3 Is my message clear to my readers? Can I make any part of my poem clearer or simpler? Have I repeated myself anywhere?

4 Are all my images fresh or are they clichés? Is every word just right? How else can I say what I have said? Is there a better way?

5 Have I used concrete or abstract words and images? (Be specific, don't generalise.)

6 Have I used too many adjectives or adverbs? (Adjectives and adverbs tend to weaken nouns and verbs. See if you are able to strengthen your nouns and verbs first; if not, make sure the adjectives and adverbs you use are extraordinary and concise.)

7 Have I explained too much? Have I finished at the right place, or have I overstated my message?

8 Does my poem have unity? Do all parts of it link together to convey my message?

9 Does my poem have a strong rhythm? Does it flow?

10 Are the line breaks in the right places?

There are some poets who believe that their first draft, just as it comes, is perfect, or at least the best they are capable of. This is rarely, if ever, the case. Even famous poets redraft their poems, not just once or twice, but many, many times before they are satisfied with them.

A Poem in Process

Although I don't consider myself a good poet (my vision is always much clearer than my communication of it), I would like to share the drafting of one of my poems with you.

This poem was inspired by my experience of living in a block of flats. Here is the original draft which I wrote in the early hours of one morning when my upstairs neighbours were partying. It's not very tidy at all, but I'm sure you can get some idea of my drafting process.

Here is the poem as it is at the moment:

NEIGHBOURS

They are above,
noisy as rats
mapping the story of their lives
with a cacophony of rock.

A baby, tied to the world
by its wail
frets the hours
its fathers move like tyrants,
wood thunders,
godless creatures creep in walls.

Above where I lie they
stamp words
on my face
detonate mortar and brick
until every night
is dream-fractured,
my world filled with theirs.

I conspire to eradicate vermin,
devise devious plots,
dream myself rising
through layers of paint and plaster
to hover darkly above,
smother them with my terrible outrage.

I still don't feel right about this poem; even as I was typing it just now, I changed a word ('rats' from 'mice' in the second line). Perhaps I should change the word 'smother' to 'poison'; after all, my earlier references to my neighbours are as 'rats' and 'vermin' – 'poison' would more appropriately extend the metaphor. Why do I want to retain the word 'smother'? Is it because it's a more direct method of extermination, one which I feel more inclined to do?

Every time I look at this poem, I make some adjustment to it. Perhaps I have not yet become detached enough from that situation to write 'coolly'. You really have to create a distance between the initial inspiration and the redrafting period. If I put this poem back into my filing cabinet and take it out at a much later date, I will most likely find the flaws in it which I know are there, but which I can't fix just now.

What to Do with a Failed Poem

Never throw it away. Put it in your bottom drawer and let time pass. If you continue reading and writing and developing as a poet, you may eventually be able to return to it and find what is wrong with it. Perhaps it really is a mess, but you may discover a phrase, an image, a word that you can use in another poem. If something moved you enough to write the poem, there must be something in it worth salvaging.

RHYME AND RHYTHM

The unity and power of a poem can be as easily shattered by an inappropriate rhythm or rhyme as by a wrong connotation or image.

Ron Pretty

Poetry depends for its unity, balance and emphasis upon a certain amount of repetition. Such repetition in poetry is achieved principally through use of rhythm and rhyme.

Rhythm

Rhythm is what people sometimes call the *music* of poetry. It is achieved by the rise and fall of spoken speech according to how words are stressed. Stress is the emphasis that is placed on words or parts of words. Poets make use of these stresses in spoken language to give rhythm to their poetry. They arrange the stresses into patterns. It is very easy to see stress patterns in nursery rhymes such as:

> There was an old woman
> Who lived in a shoe,
> She had so many children
> She didn't know what to do.

In this verse, the lines have two stressed and two unstressed syllables each, until the last line where unexpectedly there are four unaccented syllables. If you say this nursery rhyme aloud, you will find the first three lines have a sing-song lilt, but the last line needs to be said in a hurry to keep the pace going.

Rhythm is arranged in meters according to different sorts of stresses (for example, long, short or long, short, short) in various words. The different meters include iamb (the most common), trochee, spondee, dactyl, anapaest and amphibrach. If you want to experiment with these rhythm patterns, there are many books available which provide comprehensive examples for you to follow.

Rhyme

Rhyme, as well as rhythm, is what gives music to poetry. Rhyme is the echo of similar sound (such as train/plain, please/tease, go/no). Usually it is the last word in a line which carries the rhyme. The most common arrangements are rhyming the lines in pairs (a,a,b,b), rhyming alternate lines (a,b,a,b) or rhyming even lines only (a,b,c,b). In writing poetry you can, of course, devise your own rhyming scheme.

You might like to use *internal* rhymes. These sorts of rhymes occur within the lines themselves (eg. My foe outstretched *beneath* a *tree*) or *near* (or *half*) rhymes (friends/fronds, leaves/loves, killed/cold). Rhymes can be placed anywhere in the poem, though most people are more aware of *end* rhymes (i.e. rhymes at the ends of lines).

If you decide to write a poem with rhyming lines, don't *force* rhymes. Don't make words rhyme merely because you want a rhyme; the sense of the poem is more important than its mechanics. Too many inexperienced poets write poems with rhyming lines that don't make sense simply because they are less concerned with meaning than they are with matching sounds. Try not to make your rhymes obvious; don't put down the first thing that comes into your head – search about for alternatives. Rhyming dictionaries are a good investment for a poet.

OTHER POETIC DEVICES

Sometimes tricks of sound add to the 'music' of a poem and help to create and intensify its mood and to sustain imagery. Here are some sound devices you might like to experiment with in your poems:

Alliteration. Alliteration commonly refers to the repetition of the beginning consonant sounds in a series of words. The repeated sound attracts the reader's/listener's attention; it creates effects, feelings, moods and movements. Often it is used in tongue-twisters for humorous effect. The main aim of alliteration is to make a parallel of sound and meaning, or to give the poem a 'musical' quality.

Some examples of alliteration are:
- Full fathom five thy father lies.
- Over the cobbles he clattered and clashed in the dark inn-yard.
- Around the rugged rocks, the ragged rascal ran.

Assonance. Assonance is the repetition of identical or similar vowel sounds. The atmosphere developed from use of assonance comes as much from the sound of the words as from the picture they convey.

Some examples of assonance are:
- In the walls of the Halls where falls
- And the cheers and the jeers of the young muleteers
- A slosh a galosh slosh a galosh

Onomatopoeia. In the sound they make, onomatopoeic words attempt to echo meaning. Some examples are: ooze, swish, slurp, slap, rustle, hiss, buzz, bang, crackle, squawk, blubber. If you were trying to capture the atmosphere of the sea, the sound of drums banging, the whine of a mosquito, the squeaking of a door, the use of onomatopoeic words would help.

Repetition of words or phrases. This is a device for emphasising ideas, feelings or sounds.

Some examples are:
- And moveless fish in the water gleam,
  By **silver** reeds in a **silver** stream.

- **Do you remember an Inn,**
  Miranda?
  Do you remember an Inn?

POETRY FORMS TO EXPERIMENT WITH

Every poem has its own distinctive form or shape. The sort of poem you write will dictate how you shape it. For example, you are more likely to use a limerick form than a sonnet to write humorous doggerel. A sonnet form would better suit a love poem. If content is your main aim in writing a poem, you cannot force a shape. Alternatively, you change, rewrite and experiment until you find the right shape and pattern for your subject. There is a tremendous range of forms which your poem can take, including: epic, tanka, ode, rondolet, rondeau, villanelle, clerihew, haiku, triadic stanza, free verse, blank verse, concrete poem, elegy, diamentine, epigram, epitaph, sonnet, ballad, cinquain.

This is not to mention types of stanzas contained within various poetry forms: one-line stanza, couplet, triplet, quatrain, cinquain, sextet, septet, octave, etc.

If you are serious about poetry writing, you will read poetry extensively to discover how other poets have solved the problem of matching form to subject. Then you will train yourself in traditional forms, even if you don't intend to write strictly in every case. Here are some simple poetic shapes and forms which you might like to experiment with:

Form poems. Write a poem, rhymed or unrhymed, so it has a pattern of so many words per line, for example 4/3/4/3:

> MOVIES
>
> *Popcorn, icecream, tickets, seats,*
> *   Music, cheers, hush,*
> *Actors, actions, glamour, violence,*
> *   Stirring, time-stopping, starry-eyed.*

Acrostics. In these poems the first, last or other letters in the lines form a word or phrase, for example:

> Boldly
> And
> Lightly –
> Agility
> Needed –
> Carefully
> Examine your every step.

Repetition forms. Choose a word or phrase, and use it to begin every line. For example, 'Green is . . .', 'I wish . . .', 'Hard as . . .' Here is a more sophisticated variation of this idea:

> Greed in the world,
> In those who exploit,
> In the making of money without conscience
> In deliberately neglecting the needs of the poor
>   In   taking,   not   giving,
> In profiting from other's woes
> In thinking you are the only person on this planet.

Quatrain. A four-line stanza, generally with the second and fourth line end-words rhyming:

> I eat my peas with honey,
> I've done it all my life:
> It makes the peas taste funny,
> But it keeps them on the knife.
> **Anonymous**

Haiku. A Japanese nature poem of three-line verses with a total of seventeen syllables in the pattern of:
   1st line - five syllables
   2nd line - seven syllables
   3rd line - five syllables:

> Sliding through long grass,
> Sly-eyed lord of Summer earth –
> Red-bellied black snake.

Diamentine. A pattern for writing that has seven lines and shows a comparison between things:
   1st line - a noun that names an object or thought
   2nd line - two adjectives that describe the noun
   3rd line - three participles ('ing' or 'ed' words) that relate to the noun
   4th line - four nouns, two referring to the noun in line 1, two referring to the noun in line 7
   5th line - three participles that relate to the noun in line 7
   6th line - two adjectives that describe the noun in line 7
   7th line - a noun that names an object or thought that is the opposite of the noun in line 1.

CRY

loud, frantic
squawling, ear-splitting, caterwauling
baby, wakefulness, sleep, peace
enveloping, resting, welcoming
rapturous, total
SILENCE

Cinquain. A five-line poem with this pattern:

- 1st line – one word (or two syllables) gives title
- 2nd line – two words (or four syllables) describes title
- 3rd line – three words (or six syllables) expresses action
- 4th line – four words (or eight syllables) expresses a feeling
- 5th line – one word (or two syllables) gives another word for the title.

FOOTBALLER
agile ball-handler
surging, kicking, scoring
heart-stopping, exhilaration, joy, pride
HERO

Association poem. One thought leads to another:

Married sister
telephone call
long distance
phone rings
'hullo sis!'
you are so far away
how are the children?
your husband?
they want to say 'hullo'?
hullo Julie, hullo Amy, hullo Linda
they all sound well . . .
measles?
oh no!
raining?
roof being replaced?
everything so expensive
and new shoes?
she left it on the beach?

nothing but worries, eh?
pips
have to go, costing a fortune
bye! Love to you all.

Wonder how she really is?

WHY NOT TRY FREE VERSE?

Traditional poetry has definite forms and shapes that rely on devices such as rhyme and rhythm. Most people expect poetry to look and sound 'like poetry'. Sometimes, though, poets can (and do) change the shape of a poem so that it is different from what readers expect. Free verse does not rhyme and has irregular rhythm. Some people are uncomfortable with it and say it isn't poetry. It is.

Free verse frees the poet. It enables the poet to vary line lengths and rhythms in a poem, and to experiment with using occasional rhymes. If you were creating a free verse poem, you would probably divide the lines according to cadences, or natural speech patterns. Free verse is generally more concerned with conveying emotions and showing the world than with narrative. The theme of a free verse poem and the way it is developed is limitless. 'Neighbours', my poem in process (above) is an example of a free verse poem. Here is another, written by a ten-year-old girl. You will notice it contains some internal and end rhymes, but because it does not use a regular rhyming scheme it is free verse.

WHAT A DIFFERENCE IT WOULD BE

The whistle of the wind
through the leaves of the trees –
the greenness –
it pleases me.
I listen to the twittering
of the working birds
who hold their heads high
and call to the sky,
'the trees are my home'.

But what if there were
no trees at all,
if the log trucks came
and all you could hear
was the sound of the dreaded
chain saw declaring war
against those beautiful trees?

Then stumps would be a forest –
hardly a forest I guarantee!
On the earth's floor
there would be no mating call,
no birds at all!
There's a reason I guess
why trees aren't a pest –
they give happiness and homes
to birds.

Claire Williams

COMMON FAULTS IN BEGINNERS' POEMS

Certainly we shall never write a good poem unless we
are not afraid to write a bad one.

Michael Baldwin

The section 'Drafting a Poem' earlier in this
chapter included a list of questions to ask of your poem when
you are in the process of working on drafts. Here are some further
points you might like to consider in evaluating your 'completed'
poem; they show the kinds of faults that feature in a poor poem:
1 Is the poem sentimental? Does it use well-worn ideas?
2 Are the words and phrases hackneyed (e.g. black as velvet, blood
   red, tears falling like rain)?
3 Have mixed metaphors been used (e.g. His face, a ripe tomato
   burnt by the sun, shone like a beacon.)?
4 Does the poem abound in archaisms (e.g. 'amongst', 'whilst')?
   Does it use overly poetic language ('doth', 'morn', 'betwixt')?
5 Have poetic devices such as alliteration, metaphor or simile been
   over-used?
6 Does the poem use abstract nouns (e.g. 'the weary corridors of
   doom') instead of concrete ones?

7 Does the poem contain wordy descriptions? Is it as concise as it can be?

8 Is the rhythm monotonous?

9 Have obvious rhymes and forced rhymes been employed?

SUBMITTING A POETRY MANUSCRIPT

There are a number of factors to consider when submitting any manuscript for publication (see chapter 12, 'Submitting Your Work'). However, when you send off a poem or poems, there are further points to consider:

• Put each poem on a separate page with your name and address at the bottom. Do this even if you are submitting a batch of poems (it is easy for the poems to become detached). If the poem is longer than a single page, type the title of the poem and page number on the second and subsequent pages, then put your name and address at the end of the last page of the poem.

• Position the poem centrally on a sheet of A4 paper. It is imperative that you type your poem on unlined white paper.

• Title every poem. If you don't, the poem will be called by the first line.

• Send around six poems at a time – don't send your life's work.

Note: If you are hoping eventually to have a book of poems published, first establish a reputation by getting your poems published in as many different magazines as you can. The average volume of verse by a new poet is about 50 pages and contains 25 to 30 poems.

ADVICE FROM PUBLISHED POETS

Poetry is the rhythm of your life and your imagination. It has a beat and an insistence just like music. But you have to learn to listen.

Your use of language creates this poetry's voice. Every word, from the pedestrian to the exotic, is potentially poetic. But there are some useful tricks. Some words have more energy than others. Verbs usually give a poem its guts and pace. Don't decorate your poem with superfluous adjectives. They can make a poem look like a supermarket Christmas tree. When you're writing a poem, imagine you're dancing. Keep moving. Be light-footed.

For many people poetry means high-minded or sentimental verse in rhyme. No wonder hardly anyone wants to read it! If you want to be a poet, regard rock music, films and television as legitimate competition. Aim to be more exciting. And less crass.

Remember poetry's roots are in magic. A good poet writes powerful spells.

Dorothy Porter

The hardest thing to learn, yet the most necessary, is to be yourself – to see for yourself, to hear for yourself, to think for yourself. Always the young poet is bombarded with pressures to imitate—pressures from other poets, from teachers, from friends, from TV, from what you read: 'See it my way! Do it my way!' is the constant call, sometimes strident, often seductive, always to be resisted.

But that does not mean that you shouldn't learn from others. You must read widely – poetry as well as all kinds of modern prose, biography, science . . . everything. Read to discover the possibilities open to human beings as well as the possibilities of language and the forms available to poets. But don't read looking for models to imitate or information to pass on. That's for poetasters and critics.

The poet is a person prepared to be alone, game to go searching into his or her own mind for new connections and new meanings in things others take for granted.'

Ron Pretty

Find your own voice. Write even when inspiration is scarce. Read, listen and practise different styles of poetry from ballads and free verse to haiku. Only by practice will you find your own poetic voice. When I first started writing poetry, people wanted me to be less personal and to use end rhymes. I persevered, but it wasn't me. Now I use rhythm and sometimes internal rhymes, assonance and imagery but I rarely use end rhymes. However, I still write personal poetry.

Always carry a notebook with you and try to write down initial ideas and 'inspiration'. Editing is the hard work of writing. I enjoy the challenge of changing and rearranging words and images. Sometimes I can spend hours looking for the right word and may have twenty drafts for a five-line poem. The only time I have patience is when I am writing. Remember, each poem has its own tempo and it won't be rushed into being.

Colleen Burke

Between the ages of fifteen and twenty I wrote a number of very bad poems; poems overloaded with reflection, sentiment and statement; heavily descriptive poems, full of clichés; poems that were overdressed, gross imitations of works studied at school and university. In the poem *Untitled*, I wrote:

Parched lips reaching to taste the
purple-staining, grape-drawn wine
Are bittered, with gall-soaked spikes.

I knew something was wrong with my writing. I knew it was drowning in a sea of words and feelings. Still, I had an urge to keep writing. What I didn't realise at the time is that I was being weighed down by a false belief that poetry must be intense and deeply reflective – 'poetic'. By thrashing around, trying to imitate the poetry of the past I was in fact writing in a foreign language, a foreign voice.

In 1970 I went to London. There I slowly found my 'feet'. I went to lots of poetry readings where I was inspired by listening to the poets of my time, more down-to-earth poets; poets who were using contemporary language, images, speech rhythms; poets writing of contemporary issues, concerns. I visited the bookshops and libraries looking for poetry in recently published books and in the many little magazines that were around then. I began to feel part of something that was alive.

This gave me new confidence and energy. I commenced pruning my words, simplifying my language. I started using colloquial, contemporary idioms. I sharpened what I wanted to say by using images and metaphors that implied plenty and yet were succinct. That is, I was trying to say more by writing less. I started to get poems published in small magazines, poems like this:

she had more friends
than you could fit
into the back of a truck

that's why she didn't mind
leaving them parked
on a cliff edge

while she went
for a stroll
with the brake in her pocket.
                              Joanne Burns

HELPFUL BOOKS

Peter Finch, *How to Publish Your Poetry*, Allison & Busby, London, 1985.
Rory Harris & Peter McFarlane, *A Book to Write Poems By*, Publishing Design Studio, Adelaide, 1983.
Margaret J. O'Donnell, *Feet on the Ground: An Approach to Modern Verse*, Blackie & Son, London, 1962.
James Peek, *Exploring Poetry*, Reed Education, Sydney, 1976.
Ron Pretty, *Creating Poetry*, Edward Arnold, Melbourne, 1987.
Frances Stillman, *The Poet's Manual and Rhyming Dictionary*, Thames & Hudson, London, 1966.
Ruth Whitman, *Becoming a Poet*, The Writer Inc., Boston, 1982.

USEFUL CONTACTS

The Poets Union* conducts poetry and prose readings as well as occasional seminars. You can contact the NSW branch for details of that state's activities, or for addresses of other state branches.

Addresses for the Tasmanian Writers Union* and Friendly Street Poets* (SA) are listed in the Appendix.

7 ☆
WRITING DRAMA

WHAT IS DRAMA?

What is crucial [in drama] is the emphasis on action.

Martin Esslin

The dramatist is always commenting on people, and the problem is to comment effectively and make art out of it.

Edward Albee

There can be no drama without actors, whether they are flesh-and-blood people or puppets or projected shadows on a screen. This is about the best definition of drama because drama can take many forms: it can be portrayed by means of dialogue or action (mime); it can rely heavily on costumes and scenery or use none at all; lines can be delivered in prose or verse; they can be sung or spoken.

Drama can happen anywhere, anytime. Drama is action. It can take the form of real-life drama; unscripted plays (impromptu; shadow plays; mime); readers' theatre (adaptations of stories or poems); scripted stage plays (comedy or tragedy; pageant; pantomime); ballet; opera; radio plays; television plays; puppetry (marionettes; shadow, glove, stick or papier mâché puppets); film.

This section will concentrate on scripted plays for stage, radio and film.

The First Thing a Playwright Has to Learn

If you think as a writer that every word you write is
sacred and that only your vision can work then it
probably isn't a good idea to write for the theatre and
it would be an even worse idea to write films.

Dorothy Hewett

Because scripted drama is meant to be acted,
your script may be handled by dozens of other people before it
reaches production: producers, directors, actors, lighting and sound
technicians, property and stage managers. Scripts have to be worked
on, rewritten, improved, cut down. You might have to add or build
up scenes, chop out others, develop characters – be prepared!
Writing drama is not the personal activity that poetry or short-
story writing is. You have to share – to listen to and to act on
criticism – if your script is to be produced successfully.

PLAYSCRIPT FORMAT

Like taking up a new game, the rules have to
be learnt first. The setting out of a play is not very difficult; it's
merely a matter of observing the conventions so that the script
is easy for the director, actors and technicians to follow. However,
you should constantly be aware of technical problems you may
be creating for the other people who are responsible for producing
your play; keep your play as *simple* as possible. Epic scenes set
in exotic locations with casts of thousands are for film-makers
with million-dollar budgets.

Stage

Writing a stage play is probably the most gratifying
form of drama writing for a new writer. It can use as little or as
much spectacle (lighting, sound, costume) as the writer (or director)
wants. Your stage-play script can also be adapted to suit other
drama forms such as puppetry.

Setting out a script
Set the script out using double spacing with wide
side and top and bottom margins. The speakers' names are always
in *capitals* and are placed well to the left of the margin of the

speech. Everything not spoken must be *underlined*. This includes stage directions and directions for sound and lighting. Sometimes instructions appear before a speech (for example, to show the actor how to deliver a line); put *brackets* around these so the actor doesn't read them, and underline them as well.

Rules for writing a stage play

1 *Conflict is essential.* If there is no conflict in your play, the dramatic qualities are lost; the play will be *boring.* (This is discussed further under Conflict and Characters later in this chapter.)

2 *Start with a one-act play.* A full-length play is twice to three times as long as a one-act play; it also has more stage problems. If you start with a shorter play you will have fewer characters and fewer incidents. Because a one-act play is not as complicated as a full-length play, you'll be able to concentrate more on the actual writing. Aim for your play to run for thirty minutes or less.

3 *Use realism.* Realism deals with the world you know. Because it is a familiar scene, your early plays will be easier to write if you stay in realism. Later you might like to experiment with symbolism, absurdism, expressionism and other dramatic modes.

4 *Limit the number of characters.* Three is a good number for your first play. Too many more and you get more and more complications which will most likely cause you to lose the thread of the story. Three characters allow development of action, conflict and variety.

5 *Keep your characters on stage for as long as you can.* Learn to keep all your characters actively contributing to the play's action. You need action that involves all the characters. If you have a character who keeps leaving the stage, perhaps this character ought not to be in the play.

6 *Beware of shifting scenes and time lapses.* Try to have all the action of your play in one location and in a single time-span. Your play needs your concentrated attention on *action.* If you have numerous scenes your play will be difficult to stage, and if you jump around from one time to another, you'll lose the audience's attention and interest.

7 *Keep speeches short.* Long speeches are boring. As well, the other actors on stage are left standing around like dummies. Short speeches – particularly if they involve quick exchanges between characters – keep the dialogue flowing. The play will have more pace and thus more interest for the audience.

8 *Be selective with your dialogue.* You don't have to write down *everything* your characters might say in real life. Pick out only what is relevant to the action. If you write a speech, its sole purpose must be to advance the plot or to show characterisation.

9 *Get into the action quickly.* Drama is action. Don't waste time trying to establish mood, character, foreshadowing, etc. Start the plot as soon as you can.

10 *Limit your props.* Here is another example of where you will have to take into account the people producing your play. Keep it simple: the fewer scenes, costume changes and props the better. One prop which you should especially avoid is food: if your play is shown over a number of sessions, food will need to be recooked or repurchased, an expensive business.

Radio

Producing a radio play is much easier than producing a stage or television play. You can put it on tape and replay it whenever you wish. The main thing to remember when writing a radio script is that only sound comes over on radio. (For suggestions on starting a radio club, see chapter 2, 'Writing for a Purpose'.)

Setting out a script

Set out the script as you would a stage-play script (above). As well, remember that everything that is heard apart from speech is called *effects*; these are usually shown by the letters FX. Effects include music and other sounds.

Rules for writing a radio script

1 *Write only what is heard.* Sometimes it is easy to forget the medium you are writing for, and to include directions for movement. Radio is words, sound effects and music; this is what you must concentrate on.

2 *Make sure your characters are easily identified.* Because you are relying on sound alone to get your message across, you have to make sure your listeners understand who your speakers are. It is important to use their names as soon as you can after starting the script, and later to use them every now and again. It is also important to make it clear what the relationship is between the characters (are they friends, relatives, strangers, business acquaintances?).

Another bonus with writing a radio play is that you can use as large a cast as you wish – actors can read two or even three parts.

3 *Make sure the places are clear.* Let the listener know *where* the action is taking place by using sound FX (for example, a knock on the door, followed by the door opening, a voice welcoming whoever it was who knocked, footsteps; this indicates to the listener that the action is taking place in a house or flat). You can use as many scenes as you wish in a radio play.

4 *Begin and end scenes with fading.* This means that the volume is turned up slowly at the beginning of the scene, and down slowly at the end of the scene. This is an aural clue for the listener who then knows the scene is starting or ending.

5 *Use music frequently.* If you use music to introduce your radio play, it can set the atmosphere. Fade it up and play it for about twenty seconds, then fade it down slowly when dialogue commences. Use music to link scenes.

6 *Narrator.* It's all right to use a narrator to introduce the play or to link scenes.

Film

Writing for film means writing for a visual medium. This means that, wherever possible, you must *show* your viewers rather than *tell* them.

Setting out a script

Type your script on the right-hand half of the page only; this gives the producer/director/actors and technicians space to write in directions, etc. on the left-hand side of the page. All instructions and descriptions are in *capitals*. Only the actual words spoken by the actors are in lower case letters.

Rules for writing film-scripts

1 *Silence is as important as dialogue.* Because film captures both sight and sound, you don't need as much dialogue as you do in either a radio or stage play. Speeches should be short and as few as possible. Let the camera do the 'talking'.

2 *Try to restrict your play to one set only.* It is expensive for the film-maker to set up numerous indoor scenes and to light them.

3 *Use a variety of outdoor scenes.* These scenes give the viewer a change from indoor scenes, they often act as links to indoor scenes and they can add atmosphere to the story. In these scenes, you don't need to have people talking to one another. Some examples of outdoor scenes might be a person walking along a deserted street, trees blowing about in the wind, a plane taking off, an outdoor shot of the house in which action is taking place.

4 *Restrict the number of people being filmed at any one time.* If your script is going to be shot in Super 8 (and chances are it will be), the screen which shows your work will be small. Therefore, when writing you must consider the intimacy of your medium and use no more than three to four people in a scene; use close-ups as much as possible.

5 *Make your characters' relationships clear.* The viewer must be shown who the people are in your film and what their relationships are to one another (as in radio).

Visual and sound terms and abbreviations

Here are some visual and sound terms and abbreviations you need to understand depending on whether you are writing a film or a radio script:

Close-up, medium shot, long shot, medium long shot: these are all directions to show where the camera should be viewing the scene from; for example, a close-up can be used to enlarge some detail such as a person's face.

Cut: a quick change from one scene to another, or from one angle to another.

Dissolve: the camera slowly fades out of a scene. Another term used (for both film and radio) is 'fade in', 'fade out'.

FX (effects): sound effects or visual effects.

OFF: sound coming from a distance or outside the scene actually being portrayed.

O.O.V. (out of vision): the speaker is heard but not seen.

O.S.V. (off-screen voice): as for V.O.; you can hear what is being said, but cannot see the speaker.

Pan: the camera moves around the whole scene, perhaps showing the faces of all the characters at a particular moment.

P.O.V. (point of view): used when the writer wants to show the scene as though the viewer is looking through the film character's eyes.

V.O. (voice over): used when a viewer is looking at a scene but hearing something being said without the speaker being in the actual scene.

Zoom: the camera moves in quickly from a long shot to a close shot.

GETTING STARTED

It begins with a character, and once he stands up on his own feet and begins to move, all I can do is trot along behind him with a paper and pencil trying to keep up long enough to put down what he says and does.

William Faulkner

You make many false starts and you're always playing with ideas and concepts and then suddenly something happens, something clicks inside and you know you have a hold of something.

William Inge

All plays come out of some inner tension in the playwright.

Tennessee Williams

You can start a play with a theme, a story, a character, a setting. What motivates you to write depends very much on your own feelings, responses, thoughts, attitudes. Something may have been bugging you: the way adults treat young people; a feeling of alienation; the worry of unemployment or nuclear war. On the other hand, you could have a flair for comedy and decide that what you want to do more than anything is to make people laugh. You may be intrigued by a particularly forceful character and want to model your play character on this person. You may want to explore your own personality and how you would react in given circumstances. Relationships within a family or other social group may intrigue you. Any number of things motivate the writing of playscripts. The more strongly you feel about a topic, the more motivated you will be not only to start writing your play, but to continue.

Characters are the essential ingredient of drama, so you need to decide *who* is going to be in your play. You need to keep practical considerations always in mind (for example, the size of the cast) when planning your play. You could then sketch a diagram of your stage, showing where the action will take place. You could have two (or even three) stage areas. After you've more or less decided on characters and setting (remembering that things are likely to change in the course of writing), you will need to have some general idea of the outline of you play. Where is it going? What is going to be the end result? Map out a plan of the play, then try to organise the action into scenes.

When you have this organised, then start writing. Start at the point of *action*. Let the audience know who your characters are, and what the conflict is, as soon as possible.

A Play in Process

In collaboration with playwright Bill Condon, I have written a book of plays, *Madcap Café and Other Humorous Plays* (Brooks Waterloo, 1986). Bill and I were writing for secondary school students so we knew we needed to have large casts and simple sets. As well, we aimed to make our plays humorous and lively, full of zany characters and situations. The titles of our plays probably reflect this: 'Madcap Café', 'Numbers at the Gate', 'The Great Quiz Biz', 'Super Snoops', 'The Brute Family', 'The Godmother Gang', 'Operation Lily-Liver', 'Warts and All', 'Rockwinkel's Rise to Stardom', 'Just Another Day on the Inside', 'The Revved-up Rest Home'. Let's look at the evolution of one of the plays, 'The Godmother Gang', my favourite.

When planning this, we started off with a vague idea of writing a play about goodies versus baddies, say a play about gangsters. First we needed a goodie. He could be a detective. Name? Sam Diamond sounded good. He would be our hero.

Next we needed an antagonist, someone to oppose Diamond (conflict!). Who would that be? Suppose that instead of one person, we had a whole gang poised to eliminate him? OK. What would we call this gang? Who was its leader? What if it were ruled by a tyrannical old lady, somebody like a Mafia godfather? The Godmother, we decided. Then we listed her evil colleagues, creating interesting backgrounds for each:

Louie Q. Weasel, hit man
Elsie Scarlett, woman of ill-repute
Fingers Bent, safe-cracker
Ivan Didit, the Godmother's butler
Professor Pickel, a mad scientist turned to crime
Sir Jonathon Tetley, a millionaire crook who is also
    the Godmother's husband.

Now, how to show conflict between the intrepid Diamond and the dastardly Godmother gang? What if Diamond was tracking down the gang but the gang tricks him instead? Maybe they could lure Diamond into danger when he least expects it? What method would they use? Where would the action take place?

This then, is how the play evolved, and here is the first part of scene 1:

SCENE 1   *[The curtains are closed. Theme music (such as Harry Lime's theme from 'The Third Man'), is being played as the Narrator enters to address the audience.]*

NARRATOR   Sam Diamond, Private Eye, was on another case. He was bright-eyed and bushy-tailed, his trigger finger was itchy. Otherwise, he was perfectly healthy. Nothing could stop him . . . except an extremely poor sense of direction . . . *[Curtains onstage remain closed. Sounds of knocking on wood.]*

SAM   *[Voice over.]* Open up or I'll break the door down!

WOMAN'S
VOICE   No!
    [There is the sound of wood splintering. The woman screams.]

SAM   Don't nobody move. I gotcha covered . . . now slowly step out of that bath and reach for the sky. *[Pause]* By the way, this is number thirteen?

WOMAN   It's fifteen!

SAM   Sorry, madam. You can go back to sailing your boats. *[Theme music continues.]*

NARRATOR   Moments later at number thirteen . . .
    [Curtains open to reveal Ivan opening the door to Sam.]

SAM   Open up! I'm conducting a house-to-house search for a house . . . Is this number thirteen?

IVAN   Yes, it is, sir.

SAM   The name's Sam Diamond, Private Eye. I've been called here to investigate a murder.

IVAN   May I take your coat, sir?

SAM   This coat was a Christmas present. But here's fifty
        cents for coffee.

IVAN   I expect you'll want to see . . .

SAM   The body. Lead the way, Jeeves.

The gang, in fact, had reported a fictitious crime so that Diamond, when sent to investigate, would be brought face to face with his most bitter enemy, the Godmother. What follows is the criminals' attempts to dispose of the detective, but their eventual discovery that Diamond simply cannot be eliminated, that he is actually – well, I won't tell the rest; you'll have to read it for yourself to find out how we resolved the conflict.

CONFLICT AND CHARACTERS

Conflict

Be very clear in your own mind what the central conflict of your play is. Then be very clear as to what the basic desires and driving forces of each of your characters are. Unless it's in the nature of the play to do otherwise, make your characters as fully developed as possible and avoid using them solely to fulfil a plot point or present a particular point of view.

Ron Haddrick

Almost all conflict can be traced to the environment, the social conditions of the individual.

Lajos Egri

Conflict is the essence of drama. Without it, there is no drama. Conflict is forces opposed against each other. It can be one person against another person or group; it can be a person pitted against nature; conflict can be entirely within a person's mind or can be the thwarting of a person's ambition to fulfil a goal. Most conflicts are between people. The vast majority of stories and plays are based on the resolution of conflict.

You can find conflict all around you. People's traits – cowardice, cruelty, dignity, morbidity – can be the soil from which a conflict springs. Conflict is based on attack and counter-attack. Good versus bad, strong versus weak; or, to use the above examples, bravery versus cowardice, kindness versus cruelty, slovenliness versus dignity, cheerfulness versus morbidity. Conflict grows out of character.

Characters

A play that lasts is one in which the human dilemmas faced by the characters are enduring dilemmas, which have been caught and illuminated by perceptive dramatic writing.

David Williamson

Plays are about people; thus you need to feel that you know your characters thoroughly, their backgrounds, strengths, weaknesses, habits and so on when you are writing a script. People have three main dimensions: what they look like (physical), how they live (sociological) and how they behave (psychological). Thus, when you are developing a character, you need to consider these aspects. Before you begin writing your play, think deeply about your characters, chart their particulars. You could do it like this:

Physical. Male or female? Age? Name? Physical appearance? Manner of dress? Any distinguishing features (for example, tattoos, moustache, wrinkles)? Manner of walking/talking?

Sociological. Where does this character live? Family? Home life? Friends? Race? Occupation? Education? Sports/hobbies?

Psychological. What sort of a person is your character? Likes? Dislikes? Fears? Secrets? Problems? Ambitions?

As with prose writing, the main play characters are known as the protagonist (person to whom the action happens) and antagonist (person who is against the protagonist). Characters can be 'rounded' (fully-developed) or 'flat' (only one aspect of the character is shown).

When you are planning your characters, try to make them strong and different, bigger than life. Dull characters make for dull plays. If you try to create marked differences between the various characters' temperaments or personalities, you will add greater interest. During the course of your play (and this is true in prose writing), characters should change; the protagonist in particular should grow in understanding of self and of others.

. . . and a note about dialogue

In chapter 5, 'Writing Prose', under the heading Using Dialogue, we saw how character is revealed through speech. In writing plays, you need constantly to be aware that characterisation is conveyed by dialogue, and, to a lesser extent, by action. Thus dialogue is vitally important in drama; you must get it right.

The main things to remember are:
* to make what each character says consistent with his or her personality;
* to keep speeches short and natural;
* to keep moving the action forward; don't write in a speech unless it reveals character or advances the action of the play.

A CHECKLIST FOR TESTING YOUR PLAYSCRIPT

When you have completed writing your playscript and written the words 'Final Curtain' at the end, then is the time for double-checking. Before you hand over your script to a reader/ potential producer, here are some questions you might like to ask yourself:

1 Does the play have an easily identifiable protagonist (main character)? Will the audience care about this character? What does your protagonist want? (If your central character doesn't want something, then he or she will be boring.)
2 Does the play have conflict? What is the central character's conflict? Is it against another person? Self? The environment? A play without conflict is not a play.
3 Does your protagonist change as a result of conflict? Conflict causes people to change.
4 Are your characters interesting? Average people are boring; your characters should be lovable, hateful, full of strength or extremely weak: in other words, they should be memorable.
5 Is your play full of emotions? Will it totally involve the audience's attention?
6 Is there plenty of on-stage action through the script?
7 Does the plot build and keep on building?
8 Does every line move the play forward? (If not, cut out static lines. *Now.*)
9 Does the play preach to the audience or explain too much? Is information repeated?

10 Is the dialogue natural?
11 Is this a play or a manuscript? Have you written action, action,
    action? Or have you written a page of words more suited to
    reading? Plays are for acting.

ADVICE FROM PLAYWRIGHTS
AND DIRECTORS

What I learned about playwriting I learned by reading
other plays and going to the theatre.

Peter Weiss, director

See as much of film, drama or whatever it is you want
to write as you can. Be persistent. Join the Australian
Writers' Guild as an associate and study how to lay
scripts out and format them professionally. Keep
submitting scripts to theatre companies and
production houses despite inevitable knockbacks.
Attend any drama or film conferences you can and
try to contact working professionals in theatre or film
(not writers but producers, directors, actors) to get a
feel of how the industry works. Enter scripts in competitions and events such as the Annual Playwrights'
Conference.

David Williamson, playwright, screenwriter

One of the difficulties we have found in choosing
plays, is that some authors are quite oblivious to the
difficulties they present to the technical side of the
operation, that is props, lights and sound . . . an early
awareness of this to the budding playwright would be
a great advantage to directors and producers. Also
from an economic point of view, a small cast is more
practical.

Hayes Gordon, director

Before you begin you should know what you want to
say and the approximate destination of your story. The
play is a journey, hopefully one of discovery. Map out a
rough outline of scenes before you begin. Characters
who don't change through the course of a play are

unlikely to excite or enthuse their audience. You have
to know how they will act and react. Draw up charts
of each one showing their personality, physical
description, age, job, marital status, etc. If the dialogue
you've written doesn't sound the sort of thing your
characters would say, cross it out and try again. Be
ruthless in editing. Others will be. Look for ways of
varying the pace of your writing so it has highs and
lows. Swing the action around to surprise and breathe
new life into a dull scene. People go to the theatre
hoping to be astonished. Stretch their minds (and
yours). Go to the theatre frequently, read as many
playscripts as you can, learn from those who have
been successful. If you have what it takes, it's yours for
the taking.

Bill Condon, playwright

Keep your own voice clear. Listen, listen to everything – ideas, language, conversations, criticisms,
suggestions – but do not distort your work to make it fit
someone else's idea of perfect. It's hard to keep your
voice clear. Some people will try to distort it because
they want you to believe what they want to believe,
others because they are frightened of what you want to
say, or outraged by it, and want to keep you quiet,
though they might not be honest with themselves, or
with you, about their motives.

Beware, too, of censoring yourself. Guilt and fear
and the desire to be approved by other people can sit
on a writer's shoulder and stifle courage before it
comes out of the pen. Keep your courage. Keep your
voice. But listen, listen to everything. Look for people
who will help you learn the craft of writing, so that
when you put your voice on paper it is clear to other
people as well as yourself. I send you courage.

Alison Lyssa, playwright

The first thing to remember if you are writing a script is
that it is only *part* of the play. A play is much more than
dialogue: it also includes physical movement, posture,
gesture, facial expression and position on stage in
relation to other people. Sometimes all this is
conducted in silences and stillnesses. Thus, in
presenting only dialogue and limited stage directions

(and don't overdo these), a script can go only part of the way to the completed play.

Try to imagine the rest of the action as you write. Begin by constructing your stage. A sketch of it by your side is essential. Walk around an actual stage and imagine your play on it. Ask yourself: where are my entrances and exits? Where is the furniture? Where is the audience in relation to the stage? As you write, ask yourself: what is my character doing as he [or she] says this? What are the other characters doing? How are they reacting? You cannot, of course, include all the answers in your script, but they will help you in framing your words. Try to have your dialogue indicate a lot of the rest of the action.

Be sparing in dialogue. Don't feel you have to explain everything. The director will supply a great deal through movement, facial expression, gesture, etc. Try to make dialogue as close to actual speech patterns as possible. A good ear is required for this, so listen to how people speak around you. Remember that how a person speaks is often influenced by his [or her] personality, education, the time in which the person lives and relationship to the person being addressed. People talk mainly in ensemble situations. That is, they speak *to* others and much of what they say is in reaction to what is said to them.

Try to workshop your finished script. Make sure each scene, or situation says what you want it to say and has appeal for the audience. Be prepared to make alterations. A good script is usually the result of much polishing and often bears little resemblance to the first draft.

Allan Mackay, playwright

Because I value workshopping, I recommend sending a new script to the Australian National Playwrights' Conference. All scripts are read by at least two people and an assessment is sent to the writer. If chosen, the script is workshopped or given a rehearsed reading by top actors and is seen by theatre representatives from all over Australia, giving it a better chance of being snapped up for professional production than if it had simply landed on someone's desk. A similar scheme, if you don't feel ready to compete with older writers, is

the National Young Playwrights' Weekend run annually
by the Shopfront Theatre* for young people in Sydney.
I'd also send my play to companies such as Sydney's
Griffin Theatre which specialises in Australian work. See
lots of theatre, learn how it's done, and discover for
yourself which companies are likely to respond to your
style of playwrighting.

Alma De Groen, playwright

AUSTRALIAN NATIONAL ASSOCIATION OF YOUNG PLAYWRIGHTS (ANAYP)

If you are twenty-five years or under and write
playscripts, you would be well-advised to join this relatively new
but vitally important association which offers a wide range of services
to its members.

The Association was formed as a result of work done at the
National Young Playwrights' Weekends° held at the Shopfront
Theatre over a number of years and from Interplay, an international
festival of young playwrights, held in Sydney several years ago.
ANAYP's headquarters are the Shopfront Theatre in Carlton, Sydney,
which provides an office and reading room and a large library
of young writers' scripts. The Shopfront Theatre's facilities are also
available to run rehearsed readings, discussions and workshops
from time to time.

Services available and being developed through ANAYP include:
a script reading service; a regular newsletter; a regular magazine,
Roles (see chapter 13, 'Markets and Competitions', under the heading
Magazine Markets for Young People); rehearsed readings; a Theatre-
in-Education scheme; practical assistance from theatre professionals; a library; a writer exchange scheme; and an international
exchange scheme.

In addition to these services, the Association will help full
members in contacting and dealing with theatre companies which
may be interested in producing their work.

° For information on the Australian National Playwrights' Conference and the
National Young Playwrights' Weekends, see chapter 13, 'Markets and Competitions', under the headings Writers Workshops and Young Writers' Workshops,
respectively.

HELPFUL BOOKS

Oscar G. Brockett, *The Essential Theatre*, Holt, Rinehart & Winston, New York, 1980.

Brian Cooke, *Writing Comedy for Television*, Methuen, London, 1985.

Alan Cram, *How to Write and Sell TV Scripts in Australia and New Zealand*, William Heinemann, Richmond, Vic., 1985.

Lajos Egri, *The Art of Dramatic Writing*, Simon & Shuster, New York, 1960.

T. E. Hardin, *Let's Write a Script*, Georgian House, Melbourne, 1972.

Lyndy McNair, *Play Write 1*, McGraw-Hill, East Roseville, NSW, 1983.

Walter Wager (ed.), *The Playwrights Speak*, Longman, London, 1969.

USEFUL CONTACTS

The Australian Writers' Guild Ltd* is an organisation for amateur and professional writers, directors, actors and others connected with the dramatic arts. It is very helpful and will provide information on a wide range of drama-related topics such as scriptwriting courses in Australia, theatre companies, festivals, etc. It also has a library which includes original scripts for theatre, radio, film and television.

8 ☆
EDITING
YOUR OWN WORK

Don't write merely to be understood. Write so that you cannot possibly be misunderstood.

Robert Louis Stevenson

Writing and rewriting are a constant search for what one is saying.

John Updike

WHAT EDITING IS

No passion on Earth
No Love or Hate
Is equal to the Passion to Change
Someone Else's Draft.

H. G. Wells

In an interview once, the great American novelist and short-story-writer Ernest Hemingway commented that he had rewritten the last page of *A Farewell to Arms* thirty-nine times before he was satisfied. 'Was there some technical problem there? What was it that had you stumped?' the interviewer asked, to which Hemingway simply replied, 'Getting the words right'.

GETTING THE WORDS RIGHT IS WHAT EDITING IS ALL ABOUT.

Anyone can write – but it is the good writer who rewrites, who constantly searches for the right words, the right way of expressing his or her thoughts so that the reader understands what it is the writer wishes to communicate.

It doesn't matter how wonderful you think your first draft is; invariably it can be improved. Accepting this, and being prepared to do something about it, is probably the hardest fact a new writer has to come to terms with.

YOUR WORK WILL NEVER IMPROVE
UNLESS YOU *ARE* PREPARED TO REWRITE.

Have you ever asked someone for an opinion on your writing and had them criticise some aspect of it? Rigorous, honest evaluation of that poem or short story you wrote, exposing your intimate feelings or perceptive observations, can be hurtful.

The fact is you are not personally under attack when someone offers critical assessment of your work. If you ask for an opinion, do you really want that, or are you just after praise?

PRAISE NEVER IMPROVED ANY PIECE OF WRITING.

You can strengthen your writing by learning from and acting on honest assessment from an experienced reader. Relying on other people – your parents, teachers, friends – for opinions about your writing is all very well, but the ideal method of evaluation is for *you* to become so detached from your work that you can see the faults in any piece of your own writing.

How do you become detached? There are several ways. The best one is the 'bottom drawer' method; put your precious manuscript away, out of sight, for as long as you possibly can. When you look at it a few days, a week, a month later, you *will* notice mistakes. Time is a great detacher.

Another way is to imagine that someone else wrote the piece of work, a simply dreadful writer who needs your sound, critical advice. Look for everything wrong, mark it in pencil, make notes in the margin. Being able to distance yourself from your writing is the way to find objectivity when editing it.

Let other people see your writing, listen to their comments, accept that they are far more objective than you are, and pay attention to what they say. Follow their advice. Rewrite. Keep rewriting. Don't take anything as a personal slight. Believe that following well-meant criticism will improve your writing. It will.

WHAT TO EDIT

Good writers are those who keep the language
efficient. That is to say, keep it accurate, keep it clear.
                                        Ezra Pound

The approach to style is by way of plainness,
simplicity, orderliness, sincerity.
                                        E. B. White

 The first thing you ought to remember about writing *anything* for publication is that *writing is an act of communication*. You are trying to get across an idea, a story, an emotion, a description to another person.

IF YOU CANNOT MAKE YOURSELF UNDERSTOOD,
THEN YOU HAVE FAILED AS A WRITER.

You cannot fail to communicate if you do as both Pound and White (above) say:

KEEP YOUR WRITING CLEAR: KEEP IT SIMPLE.

This doesn't mean you can't use complex ideas and formal language; of course you can. But when you are trying to communicate, your top priority should be to *do it clearly and simply*.

There is, of course, more to editing. When you are assessing your draft manuscript, you need to look at such areas as:

How you have organised and arranged your ideas and information. The organisation of a story is called plot. Methods of plotting a short story were dealt with in some depth in chapter 5, 'Writing Prose'.

How you have presented your material. Have you used concrete images or vague generalisations? What is the tone of your writing (is it suited to the content?) Have you always used the best, most appropriate words? Is your writing free of *all* unnecessary words, of tautology, euphemisms, clichés? Does your writing have the overall clarity that helps the reader to understand what you have intended? Have you checked your work for spelling errors?

The appeal of your writing. What effect(s) has your writing created? Have you achieved what you set out to do? What do you feel about the choice of words, form and style used? Is your piece of writing vague or definite? Is what is communicated relevant and meaningful? How does the overall presentation feel (pleasing, boring, exciting, interesting)?

Your use of grammar. Are the sentences written so their parts (words, phrases, clauses) are clearly placed and understood? Have you used correct punctuation?

MAKE EVERY WORD COUNT

If it is possible to cut a word out, always cut it out.
George Orwell

Life is the elimination of all that is dead.
Wallace Stevens

Clear writing is concise; that is, every word counts. You must take out every unnecessary word. You must check phrases to see if they can be simplified. The following section deals with common errors of wordiness.

Verbosity

This merely means the use of too many words. Below are sentences before and after editing. The first sentence in each pair is too wordy; the second sentence is concisely written.

1 The old man walked with a limp along the narrow city road.
  The old man limped along the alley.
2 Colleen, who is my aunty, has two daughters who were born on the same day and who look exactly like each other.
  My Aunty Colleen has identical twin daughters.
3 The idea was thought of by John at four o'clock early in the morning.
  John thought of the idea at 4 a.m.

What you will have noticed is that the edited sentences are not only shorter than the original sentences, but they contain the same information. You must constantly search for unnecessary words in your sentences and remove them.

Tautology

Tautology is repeating something that has already been said. Here are some examples of sentences containing tautology.

1 That is past history.
  (History is the past.)
2 She was riding a two-wheeled bicycle.
  (A bicycle has two wheels.)
3 The final conclusion of the weekend camp is tomorrow.
  (The words 'final' and 'conclusion' mean the same thing.)

WORDS, WORDS, WORDS

Whatever you wish to say, there is but one word to express it, but one word to give it movement, but one adjective to qualify it; you must seek until you find this noun, this verb, this adjective.

Gustave Flaubert

Style in writing is a special quality that commands interest or gives pleasure; it makes the reader 'sit up and take notice'. One way in which writers develop style is through their choice of words. Look at the aptness (and originality) of the italicised words used in the following sentences:

1 Like I say, Devola is *cloudy-headed* and this is one thing I cannot understand because none of the rest of us Luthers is that way but Devola is for sure, so each day I have to explain the whole of our existence to her. (From *Where the Lilies Bloom* by Vera and Bill Cleaver)
2 Away out in the Mungalongaloo Mountains in the middle of Australia, where the *jaggedy* peaks are all purple and primrose and pink and *prune-coloured*, there is a wonderful waterhole called Willawallawalla. (From *The Super-Roo of Mungalongaloo* by Osmar White)
3 The social worker slowed and stopped beside a dirty white fence. The house it *penned* was old and brown with a porch that gave it a sort of *potbelly*. (From *The Great Gilly Hopkins* by Katherine Paterson)
4 Matty Stubeck was a little *nut* of a man, aggressive, quick-witted, scheming, begging and obsequious or cheeky depending on what he was after. (From *The True Story of Lilli Stubeck* by James Aldridge)

WORDS ARE A WRITER'S PRINCIPAL TOOL.

If you want to write well, it is imperative that you learn to use the right word. How do you choose the right word? Obviously if you have a good vocabulary you will have a much better chance than does someone else who has fewer words to choose from. In chapter 4, 'Tools of the Trade', I discussed the ways to improve your vocabulary using a dictionary and thesaurus. You are well advised to make constant use of these two valuable sources of vocabulary. Meanwhile, here are some principles you might like to apply if you want to use the right word:

Prefer the simple word to the complex. If you have to make a choice between a short, familiar word and one that is polysyllabic and 'more dignified', choose the shorter word if it means exactly the same thing. Often, in an attempt to sound sophisticated, beginner writers try to impress their readers with long, formal words and phrases. The more formal, complex word may be used occasionally, but consistent formality will make your writing sound pompous and artificial. Don't try to impress with 'big' words.

Here are three sentences containing complex words:
1 I *informed* the *individual* I would *accompany* him to the city.
2 Robert *desired* to possess a *vehicle similar* to his father's.
3 The Bulldogs *emerged victorious.*
Put more simply, these sentences could read:
1 I told the man I would go with him to the city.
2 Robert wanted to own a car like his father's.
3 The Bulldogs won.

Prefer the right word to the almost right. With the huge English vocabulary available to you, there is no excuse for not choosing the word which means precisely what you wish to say. Just to give you an idea of the immense choice available, look at *some* of the possible variations that *Roget's Thesaurus* provides for the word 'little':
> *Petite, dainty, pigmy, Lilliputian, elfin, diminutive, wee, teeny-weeny, pocket-sized, runty, puny, dwarfish, squat, dumpy, microscopic, minute, minimal, imperceptible . . .*

Poverty of vocabulary is no excuse given the immense range available to you, not only in thesauruses but also in general dictionaries and dictionaries of antonyms and synonyms. Use the exact word; don't compromise with anything less.

Avoid abstract words and phrases. Writing has more appeal to the reader if you prefer the concrete to the abstract. Say exactly what you mean; don't be vague:

1 A period of unfavourable weather set in. (abstract)
   It rained every day for a week. (concrete)
2 The candidate in the examination graduated recently from a large secondary school institution. (abstract)
   Rick Dwyer received his Higher School Certificate last month from Sydney High School. (concrete)
3 The sailboat won the fourth race by a short distance. (abstract)
   Speedy Gonzales won the fourth race of the America's Cup by fifty-two seconds. (concrete)

Avoid the use of qualifiers. Some words in the English language are better left alone or avoided as much as possible. They are generally so vague they serve no worthwhile purpose. Such words are: rather, very, nice, pretty, a lot of, little, just.

Another word which is often overused is 'that' (for example, 'I was told *that* he would be soon leaving'; the sentence loses nothing if 'that' is omitted).

Be careful of the word 'there'; it can sap energy from your writing. Look at this sentence:

   There was something wrong.

Remove 'there' and you have a much stronger sentence:

   Something was wrong.

Here are further examples of how the above words weaken a sentence:

1 There was a fight.
   A fight erupted.
2 I was careful that I did not leave any clues.
   I was careful not to leave any clues.
3 He thought he was just so clever.
   He thought he was clever.
4 Martin was a nice sort of man.
   Martin was generous (kind, humble, gentle).
5 Somewhere there was a pretty strange creaking sound of a door.
   Somewhere a door creaked.

Avoid the use of 'exhausted' adjectives. Certain adjectives such as 'fantastic, fabulous, horrible, terrible, awful, incredible, amazing' have been so exhausted by overuse in daily speech and in advertising that they have become almost meaningless. If you want to use them, make sure you know their *real* meanings before you commit them to paper. (Did you know, for example, that 'fantastic' means 'extravagantly fanciful'? or that the meaning of 'terrible' is 'fit to excite terror'?)

MAKING A RICHER BREW

       In the section above, you examined how to use concrete images to make your writing more vivid. Sometimes you may use phrases or words which are too general. Look closely at each word you've written to see if it conveys precise information. If you give your reader more detail, the picture you convey will be clearer.

Here are sentences which provide scant information. Closer examination and attention to specifics will enrich each of them:

1 There were a lot of chickens in the enclosure.
  (What sort of chickens were they? Rhode Island reds, Orpingtons, bantams? Were they hens or chickens, roosters or pullets? How many were there? Twenty-five, six hundred, over a thousand? What sort of an enclosure was it? A yard? A cage? A box?)

2 She was an ugly woman with a mean streak.
  (What features mark her ugliness? How old is she? Does she have a name? How is her mean streak manifested?)

3 That house is worth a lot of money.
  (What are the features of the house? What size is it? What is it built of? Where is it located? Who owns it? What is meant by 'a lot of money'? Twenty thousand dollars? One hundred thousand? One million?)

USING THE ACTIVE VOICE

       In writing you should prefer the active voice to the passive. Active voice is direct, vigorous, strong; passive voice is indirect, limp and weak.

Writing in the passive voice uses the word order of object–verb–subject. Here is an example:

    Jack was hit by Jill.

The same sentence, written in the active voice, would read:

    Jill hit Jack. (subject–verb–object)

Thus you can see the active voice is more direct and economical than the roundabout passive. Here are some more sentences showing differences in active and passive voice:

1 The broth can be spoiled by too many cooks. (passive)
    Too many cooks spoil the broth. (active)
2 The class was interrupted by the appearance of a lion. (passive)
    The appearance of a lion interrupted the class. (active)
3 It was decided by the teacher that we could have a holiday.
    (passive)
    The teacher decided we could have a holiday. (active)

Sentences in passive voice lack suspense. Examine the verbs in the above sentences ('was spoiled, was interrupted, was decided'); the use of the auxiliary verb 'was' weakens them. If you wish to avoid the lifelessness that passive verbs lends to sentences, check the verb you have used as well as the sentence order. Remember, the order of a sentence using active voice is subject–verb–object.

When to Use the Passive Voice

Sometimes the passive voice is preferable to the active. An example of this is when the performer of an action is unknown or irrelevant. Here is an example:

The Prime Minister was struck by a bullet from a revolver.

The emphasis here is on the Prime Minister, rather than on the bullet. If the sentence was written in the active voice, 'A bullet from a revolver struck the Prime Minister', it would lose its full import.

Usually we put disaster in passive voice. (She was knocked over by a car. Hundreds were killed in an earthquake. The child was kidnapped.) The passive voice reduces the shock effect that the active voice creates.

Occasionally you will need to use the passive voice for the sake of clarity or to create a change of tone. However, it is generally weak and undesirable. You should avoid its use where possible.

WRITE WITH NOUNS AND VERBS

Classroom teachers are constantly telling their pupils to 'use plenty of adjectives and adverbs' to improve their writing. Adjectives and adverbs are indispensable parts of speech; however, it is nouns and verbs which give writing its power.

The following sentences show how appropriate use of nouns and verbs gives colour and toughness as well as brevity:

1 The haggard old woman walked slowly along the very wide road.
    The crone tottered along the highway.

EG.

2 A large number of destructive young people in their teens pushed hurriedly out of the stadium.
A thousand teenage vandals spilled from the stadium.

3 The quavering sound of the blue, satin-feathered bird caused Jim to move hurriedly towards the window.
The bower-bird's trill caused Jim to rush toward the window.

IF YOU WANT TO IMPROVE YOUR VOCABULARY,
USE A DICTIONARY AND THESAURUS CONSTANTLY. ✶

GETTING IT RIGHT

When you are editing your own or other's writing, you should be on the lookout for factual errors. If a writer does not research material carefully and is guilty of including incorrect information, credibility comes into question.

Here are some sentences which contain factual errors. Can you spot them and write the sentence correctly?

1 Billy went fishing for bream and dugong in the NSW inland town of Mallacoota.

2 A play I enjoyed reading during the school vacation was Charles Dickens' *Great Expectation*.

3 In 1986 – a Leap Year – my brother proposed to his fourteen-year-old girlfriend; two years later they married.

4 American tourists visiting Australia from the State of Cheshire were impressed by the ostriches, finches and budgerigars they saw in the Sahara Desert.

A number of mistakes were made in the sentences above; how many did you spot? To avoid factual errors, look as carefully at your own work as you did at these sentences.

SHOW, DON'T TELL!

One of the easiest mistakes to make when writing is to *tell* your reader what the characters in your story feel. Your writing will improve considerably if you can learn to *show* characters in action; this allows the character to reveal him/herself more clearly. Let's suppose, for example, that you have written this simple sentence:

Mary was angry

The reader will get a far more vivid impression of Mary's anger
if you show it:

'Don't you know anything about privacy?' Mary snapped.

or

Mary threw her arms around her diary and glared at the
intruder.

or

Mary spat every obscenity she'd ever heard as she charged
through the house, crashing doors behind her.

In each case, Mary's dialogue and action reveal her anger more
vividly than the statement, 'Mary was angry'. Notice the effectiveness
of the verbs used in the latter sentences.

Here are some more examples for you to examine:

1 The woman was upset.

The woman's body began to shake with giant sobs.

The crushing sensation in her chest continued until she felt
she was close to her last breath on this earth.

2 Rosanna disliked Mary-Beth.

'I can't stand your ugly face', Rosanna screeched at Mary-Beth.

Rosanna brushed past Mary-Beth, her eyes directly ahead, her
mouth pursed.

You can use the 'show' method in descriptive writing too:

1 Joe was an old man.

Joe was about eighty, his face brown and shrivelled like a walnut.

Joe creaked when he moved, his arthritic limbs bowed beneath
the weight of his eighty years.

2 The house was falling down.

The shack in the clearing leaned at an angle that made it seem
as though the first breath of wind would raze it.

A demolition order was posted directly beneath the 1831 foundation plate: THIS BUILDING CONDEMNED.

If you adopt the motto 'show, don't tell' in your writing, you
will avoid boring your reader.

IMPROVING DIALOGUE

While dialogue makes a story easier to read by
breaking up the look of the page, its most important function is
to show character. Words used by a person reveal more about

that person than do appearance or actions. They portray emotions and are the ideal means of showing interaction between characters. Dialogue crystallises relationships.

Because of the vital importance of dialogue in portraying characterisation, it is imperative that you carefully examine your use of it. Here are some points you should consider when you are editing speech:

Is the dialogue natural? To sound natural, the dialogue must bear out whatever traits you have given your story's characters. If a character is pompous, then the words the character uses must show this; they would not include slang, for instance, and the structure of the sentences used would be formal. A working-class character would probably use some slang, clichés and/or contractions when speaking. If you constantly consider characterisation when writing, you will avoid making all the characters sound exactly alike.

Does your dialogue flow? Dialogue must appear realistic without being so. If you were to capture speech exactly as it is spoken, you would find it vague, terse or trivial; words and thoughts are often repeated. Written dialogue must be condensed to keep the reader's interest at a high pitch. You do not need to include *everything*, right down to the last goodbye.

IF IN DOUBT ABOUT DIALOGUE, READ IT ALOUD.

Do the words sound natural as you say them? If they appear stilted or untrue in any way, rewrite them. To capture the basic rhythm of speech you need to work on variation of sentence length. Balance long sentences against short.

Do your characters talk too much? No character should be allowed to talk too long without a break. Long passages of dialogue become boring. Break up long speeches with interjections from others or with actions (for example, the speaker might pause, sigh, have a drink of water).

Never have a long tract of dialogue between two characters without occasionally identifying the person speaking.

Is the dialogue absolutely necessary? If dialogue does not advance the plot, it should be cut out, no matter how interesting or witty it may be. As well as characterising the speakers, dialogue is also used to build suspense, characterise other people in the story, inform the reader of impending action, reveal conflict – all of which further the plot. Dialogue can also be used to tie up the loose ends of a story (as in detective stories when the main character explains how he or she arrived at a conclusion); however, this function of dialogue should be used sparingly.

Other DOs and DONTs

1 Don't have invisible people speaking. 'Cue' the speeches to the speakers. Mention their facial expressions, mannerisms, physical appearance.
2 Weave in background details of where conversations are taking place. Don't let them happen in a vacuum.
3 It is not necessary to use 'he said', or 'she said', *every* time a character speaks, especially when there are only two characters having a conversation. Do remember, however, to identify speakers if the conversation is a long one.
4 Some words should not be used in place of 'said'. These include words such as 'sighed', 'beamed', 'shrugged'; these are descriptions of actions, not synonyms for 'said'.
5 'Said' is a perfectly good word; sometimes over-zealous new writers use their thesauruses to replace it with words like this: rejoined, expostulated, propounded, interrogated, grumbled, asserted, hissed, ululated. These are perfectly good words as well but should not be overused at the expense of 'said'.
6 Avoid using adverbs to qualify 'said' (for example, 'he said angrily' could be written 'he snapped').
7 Be very careful when using dialect. Unless you are perfectly sure you know how to present it accurately, it is best to avoid it. Readers find it difficult to interpret dialect on the page. You could use the occasional sprinkling of foreign words, for example 'Non!', 'Si', or 'Ach', to lend flavour to a character. Show the foreign character using stilted English phrases, rather than write his actual speech in broken English.

Setting Out Dialogue

1 Start new conversations (that is, by a different speaker) on the next line.
2 Dialogue is indicated by quotation marks around the actual words spoken, and usually by starting with a paragraph indention. Sometimes writers indicate speech in italics or by using a dash; these are unconventional methods of setting out dialogue, and you would be advised to remain with the traditional form until you have conquered it thoroughly.

3 Spoken words are separated from the remaining words of a sentence by commas, question marks or exclamation marks. Study these examples:

    'Sorry I'm late', said Fred.
    'Is it really eight o'clock?' asked Fred.
    'Golly!' exclaimed Fred.
    Fred said, 'I hope you'll forgive me'.
    Fred asked, 'Will you invite me again?'
    Fred exclaimed, 'I don't believe you said that!'

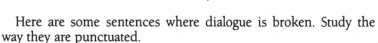

Here are some sentences where dialogue is broken. Study the way they are punctuated.

    'I like your drawing', Trudi said. 'It shows real talent.'
    'You can come if you wish,' Mum said, 'but you're not to misbehave.'

THE SOUND OF SENTENCES

In analysing the structure of your sentences as they 'sound' to the reader, you would be advised to concentrate on two main aspects: sentence lengths and sentence variation.

Sentence Lengths

A sentence can be as short as one word ('Help!') or as long as forty or fifty words. Longer sentences – obviously – are harder to understand than short ones. The ideal style of writing is one where short sentences are balanced against longer ones. You would be advised to

KEEP AVERAGE SENTENCES UNDER TWENTY WORDS.

Fewer words are even better, most of the time, and for readers of all ages. Break some of your really long thoughts or descriptions into shorter segments. You can make new, shorter sentences, or you can break longer sentences with punctuation (colons, dashes, semi-colons, etc.) to indicate a long pause.

Avoid writing a succession of long sentences or a succession of short sentences. Extremely long sentences tend to bog the reader down. A succession of very short sentences tends to be monotonous. Try to have a balance of long and short. The only exception to this is if you want to create a deliberate effect; you might, for example, want to capture a dramatic incident. Here, a series of short sentences would work well:

His knee lifts. He snorts. I see the underside of his shoe. Scuffed and coming at me. His boot lands on my cheek. My head bounces on the floor.

You can use a series of longer sentences for description, to evoke a lazy atmosphere, for example, as in these sentences:

Later that day, following a path worn by wallabies and other bush creatures, I came to a creek. Exploring further, swatted by shrubs that smelt of herbs, startled occasionally by scuttling lizards, I paddled through shallow pools, ankles confettied with sand, and came across a rock pool at the foot of a thirty-metre-high sandstone wall. It was shady, a relief from the harsh sun and, to my creative eye, full of possibilities for my sketch book.

Sentence Variation

Another way to get variety in sentences, is to vary the structure of sentences. Sentences that repeat a pattern become monotonous:

She was fourteen that summer. She became restless. She fought her parents and teachers; anyone who tried to stamp authority on her. Her friends were the only people she trusted. Even then she was wary of confiding her innermost thoughts. She determined not to reveal herself to anyone.

To vary sentence structure you can rearrange or invert the pattern; you can join sentences to make compound or complex sentences. Using the paragraph above, you might, after editing, arrive at the following:

That summer, aged fourteen, she became restless. Those who tried to stamp authority on her (including her parents and teachers) she fought, and only trusted her friends. Wary of confiding her innermost thoughts to anyone, she determined not to reveal herself.

Variety adds interest to a story, but a sentence should take its shape according to its particular job. A series of simple sentences constructed in like manner (for example, subject–verb–object) may suit your subject matter; go for it! However, be aware that monotonous sentence structure can be irritating.

Sentence Workshop

In addition to correcting faults of sentence length and variation, you should check if your writing contains the following:

Ambiguity. Sometimes, because of poor grammatical structure, vague expression or misplaced words, a sentence can have more than one interpretation:

Fran told her sister she had won the competition.
(Ambiguous; it is not clear whether it was Fran or her sister who had won.)

Fran congratulated her sister on winning the competition.
(Unambiguous; now we know.)

Sentences without a Subject. Ambiguities and confusions can arise if a sentence lacks a subject (that is, the person or thing which is being referred to):

Rounding the corner, a supermarket came into sight.
(Who is rounding the corner – the supermarket?)

As I rounded the corner, I saw a supermarket.
('I' is the subject.)

Incomplete sentences. Don't confuse a phrase with a sentence. Sometimes, especially if you start a sentence with a participial phrase (for example, 'Running into the yard'), you may finish up with an incomplete sentence:

Running into the yard with a rabbit in his mouth. (phrase)

My dog came running into the yard with a rabbit in his mouth. (sentence)

Sentences should always contain finite verbs (for example, 'came' in the sentence above). However, it should be pointed out that recently it has become an accepted practice, particularly with experimental writing, to use sentence fragments (for example, 'I used to wear dresses that were long and straight. Wash and wear.'). Nowadays, too, it is acceptable for sentences to start with 'and' and 'but'.

Be particularly careful to check sentences which start with verbs ending in 'ing', as in the first supermarket example above, or 'ed'. Often such sentences are ambiguous, lack subjects or are incomplete.

WHY WORRY ABOUT SPELLING, PUNCTUATION AND GRAMMAR?

This morning I took the hyphen out of Hell-hound and this afternoon I put it back.

Edwin Arlington Robinson

How may an author best acquire a mode of writing which shall be agreeable and easily intelligible to the reader? He must be correct, because without correctness he can be neither agreeable nor intelligible.

Anthony Trollope

Spelling is the passport to understanding language; grammar is the structure of language; punctuation communicates pauses, emphases and tone to make reading easier. Written English insists on rules for structure, punctuation and spelling to ensure clear communication between writer and reader.

IF YOU WANT TO BE A GOOD WRITER,
YOU MUST LEARN HOW TO USE CORRECT SPELLING,
PUNCTUATION AND GRAMMAR.

Spelling

After you finish editing your writing, proofread it carefully. If you are unsure about the spelling of *any* word, look it up in the dictionary. It is not sufficient to say, 'It's good enough'. Meticulous attention to detail marks the amateur from the professional.

Punctuation

Check your writing to see if you have used the following correctly:

capital letters
full stops

commas
semi-colons
colons
apostrophes
question marks
exclamation marks
hyphens
parentheses
dashes
quotation marks
paragraphing

If you do not know how to use some of these punctuating devices, obtain a handbook of written English and study their uses. The tool you use as a writer is the English language: you should have as much control as possible over it. Ignorance is no excuse.

Grammar

Here are some questions about the grammatical structure of sentences which you should ask about your writing:

Do the subject and the verb of each sentence agree?
1 Nancy and her sister were going to the concert. (The subject – Nancy and her sister – is plural; therefore the verb is plural.)
2 Our class has high standing in the school. ('Class' is a singular noun; therefore the singular verb 'has' is used.)
   However, in this sentence: 'Our class members have high standing in the school' the subject is 'class members' (plural); therefore the plural 'have' is used.

Have you used tenses consistently? When writing prose, you need to decide from the outset what tense you are going to use (for example, present, past, conditional, future, etc.) Use that tense throughout the story: do not switch from one to another unless you are doing so deliberately (perhaps for dramatic effect). Check your writing to see if unwittingly you have mixed tenses.

Have you used the correct form of the verb? Tenses cause new writers a great deal of trouble. Be careful to use the correct tense of verbs (for example, 'She saw you' *not* 'She seen you'; 'I rang you' *not* 'I rung you').

Do you know when to use 'shall' and 'will'? When to use 'may' and 'must', 'will' and 'would'? If not, you would be advised to make a study of verbs and how to use them.

Have you used the correct pronouns? Sometimes you might be confused as to whether to use the pronoun 'she' or 'her', for example:

Julie and her went to the cinema yesterday.

This is incorrect. The sentence should read:

She and Julie went to the cinema yesterday.

'She and Julie' are the subject of the sentence, and thus would usually be placed before the verb.

The way in which to spot the subject of the verb is to ask who or what did the verb? (Who *went* to the cinema? She went and Julie went, *not* Her went and Julie went.)

Subject pronouns are: I, she, he, we, they, who; object pronouns are: me, her, him, us, them, whom. Subject pronouns are placed with subject nouns, object pronouns with object nouns.

Have you used prepositions correctly? Special prepositions follow particular adjectives, nouns and verbs. There are no rules for saying which prepositions to use in specific cases; you just have to learn them by hearing and using them. Here are some phrases using prepositions:

dispense *with*	accompanied *by*
refrain *from*	rely *on*
care *about*/care *for*	unfitted *for*
worthy *of*	indifferent *to*
accustomed *to*	different *from*
confide *in*	prejudiced *against*
thankful *for*	

A FIRST DRAFT EDITED

The great artist is the simplifier.
Henri Frederic Amiel

To write simply is as difficult as to be good.
W. Somerset Maugham

Sometimes the best way to learn how to edit a piece of writing is to examine a student's first draft. These first paragraphs of a children's story were written by Jean:

LINDSAY'S TURN

Lindsay was a very happy boy. He was happy because he had a very important job. He knew that today he was going to be the boss of the assembly.

For the whole month of April Lindsay was the leader of the assembly. For this job Lindsay had to do two things. First, when it came time for the children to pick which songs the assembly was going to sing Lindsay had to decide which child would choose the song.

The second thing Lindsay had to do was to choose five children to tell news about something that had happened to them or just something they knew and wanted to share with the rest of the children.

The head teacher of the infants' school, Mrs Albert, told Lindsay and the rest of the assembly that this job was a big RESPONSIBILITY and every week she wrote the word on the board. Mrs Albert said that RESPONSIBILITY is when you have a special job to do and you must make sure that it is done well.

Lindsay's class teacher Miss Newbold had the responsibility of choosing a child from second class to be the leader of the assembly. Every month, Miss newbold [*sic*] chose someone who was doing very good work. She said that it doesn't have to be the best in the class, just someone who tries very hard. This was the month of April and for April Miss Newbold had chosen Lindsay Green, even though he wasn't very good at arithmetic.

(249 words)

With editing, the writing becomes more economical:

Lindsay was happy. Today, and for all April he was going to be boss of the school assembly. He had to decide which child could choose a song for everyone to sing. And he had to choose five children to tell news.

It was an important responsibility being in charge of the assembly. Mrs Albert, the principal, wrote RESPONSIBILITY in big letters on the board. 'It means having a special job and doing it well,' she said.

Lindsay's teacher, Miss Newbold, had the responsibility of choosing someone in second class to be assembly leader. She said, 'The child I choose doesn't have to be the best in the class, just someone who tries hard'. That is why she had chosen Lindsay, even though he wasn't very good at numbers.

(129 words)

You will notice that although there are fewer words in the edited version, the *content* of the paragraphs has not altered. The writing is said to be 'tighter'.

Let's examine Jean's story, paragraph by paragraph, to see what changes took place:

Paragraph 1. It was not necessary to tell the reader Lindsay is a boy; this becomes obvious later in the story. 'Very' is an unnecessary modifier: if you're happy, you're happy. If I had written this story I would have *shown* Lindsay's happiness (for example, he might have clapped his hands for joy, jumped up and down six times yelling 'yippee!' or a broad smile might have lit up his face). In her second sentence Jean (unnecessarily) repeats the fact that Lindsay was happy. In the third sentence Jean doesn't need to tell the reader that Lindsay 'knew that' he was going to be in charge of the assembly; of course he knew it!

Paragraph 2. Why does Jean say it is 'the month of April'? Everyone knows that April is a month – she needs only to write 'April'.

Jean has already said in the first paragraph that Lindsay was 'boss of the assembly'; she now repeats this information ('he was the leader of the assembly') in the second paragraph. The reader only needs to be told once.

Her sentence, 'For this job Lindsay had to do two things' can be eliminated without any problem. She simply has to state what his jobs were. Notice how much simpler is the edited 'He had to decide which child could choose a song for everyone to sing' than the original 'First, when it came time for the children to pick which songs the assembly was going to sing Lindsay had to decide which child would choose the song'. The words 'first' and 'the second thing' (next paragraph) are unnecessary really as there are only two jobs; the word 'and' is sufficient.

The information Jean has included in the second and third paragraphs really belongs in paragraph 1. (A paragraph is a collection of sentences which should be together because each relates to the same idea or topic.) The topic of the first paragraph is that of Lindsay's important job; thus his delegation of jobs should also be in that paragraph.

Paragraph 3. 'Principal' is 'the head teacher' (one word instead of three). In the next paragraph, Jean mentions second class; therefore I feel she doesn't need to tell the reader the story is set in 'the infants' school'. The first sentence in this paragraph contains thirty-four words. The average length of a sentence should be about twenty words (even fewer if it is for young readers). Jean could have used direct speech in this paragraph to break up the look of the page. The word 'responsibility' does not need to be repeated (second sentence).

Paragraph 4. If Miss Newbold is Lindsay's teacher, then the word 'class' does not need to be said. The phrase 'the leader of the assembly' can be written more simply as 'the assembly leader'. 'A child in second class' could have been written as 'a class two child' although I preferred to write, 'someone in second class'. In this paragraph, too, direct speech could have been used. Sometimes people get into the habit of using indirect speech continuously. Dialogue adds sparkle to a story. As in the second paragraph, Jean has told us here that 'this was the month of April'. In infants' school 'number' is used instead of 'arithmetic'.

Editing someone's work is a subjective business; you may or may not agree with changes I have made. However, you must agree Jean's first draft definitely needed some cleaning up.

NEVER BE SATISFIED WITH FIRST DRAFTS, SEARCH,
SEARCH FOR WAYS TO SIMPLIFY AND IMPROVE YOUR WRITING.

HELPFUL BOOKS

Sheridan Baker, *The Practical Stylist*, Thomas Y. Crowell Co., New York, 1973.

Jefferson D. Bates, *Writing with Precision*, Acropolis Books, Washington, D.C., 1980.

Claire Carmichael, *English: The Essentials*, Longman Cheshire, Melbourne, 1986.

F. G. Fowler & H. W. Fowler, *The Oxford Dictionary of Current English,* Oxford University Press, London, 1974.°

William Strunk & E. B. White, *The Elements of Style*, Macmillan, New York, 1979.

Lucile Vaughan Payne, *The Lively Art of Writing*, Follett Publishing Co., Chicago, 1975.

Roget's Thesaurus, Penguin, Harmondsworth, 1984.°

Style Manual for Authors, Editors and Printers, 4th edn, Australian Government Publishing Service, Canberra, 1988. (A style manual shows the generally accepted conventions in writing and publishing.)

Walter D. Wright, *A Basic Course in English*, Methuen, North Ryde, 1986.

°These are what I use. You can use any good dictionary or thesaurus (ask your local bookseller to recommend one).

9 ☆
CO-OPERATIVE
WRITING AND
PUBLISHING
PROJECTS

Co-operative writing and/or publishing ventures are not easy to establish because of problems such as funding, finding a satisfactory workplace and lack of leadership. Sometimes participants in co-operative projects want the honour and glory but don't want to pull their weight. Being part of a team can be plain hard work. It can mean hours of unacknowledged labour, tears of frustration, angry words and hurt feelings. Everyone wants his or her own way. Most want to be in charge. Occasionally, though, participants' long hours of hard work and stress are rewarded. Prizes, media attention or public acclamation can make it all seem worth while. However, it is the intrinsic merits of participating in such a project that are its chief rewards: that spirit of pioneering, the sense of achievement in a job well done and pride in teamwork.

The people who have contributed to this chapter are representative of many others in co-operative ventures; they don't stand around waiting to be told what to do; they pull up their sleeves and get on with the job. They are achievers and are worthy of recognition.

Here are their stories.

CO-OPERATIVE PUBLISHING

Five Islands Press*

Getting a single volume collection of poetry published commercially is probably one of the most difficult ventures facing any writer. An octad of Illawarra (NSW) poets met in late 1987 to address this problem. The upshot of their meeting was the decision to form a co-operative, Five Islands Press, to publish and distribute members' books. Each of the eight writers purchased shares to get the venture off the ground. Then, in order to become legally established, the group agreed on a constitution (with the free help of the Arts Law Society) and registered with the State Department of Co-operative Societies. By doing this, the group then could have access to publishers' subsidies available from the Literary Arts Board of the Australia Council.

Members of the co-operative are very conscious of distribution, believing it to be the most important aspect of small or self-publishing. They have decided to split up the job of distribution with all members being personally responsible for the sale of at least forty copies of their own title; in addition, each member has to sell at least ten copies of every other book published. Other copies will be sold at poetry readings and placed through retail outlets and with small distributors. Advertising will be through established literary magazines. The co-operative is hoping, as well, to build up a sizeable subscription list to sell its eight publications at discount over the initial two-year period when all members will each have had one book published.

Although Five Islands Press is a non-profit making venture its members will each receive a royalty payment (10 per cent) from the sale of their own books. Surplus funds, if any, will be used to publish new titles, including, it is hoped, a group anthology. To cut costs the co-operative employs its own (experienced) members to design and lay out material. It then undertakes its own typesetting on a word processor and laser printer. A 600-book run at a printery costs about $1500.

On the question of control of writing and editing quality, founding member and director Ron Pretty had this to say:

> With this sort of publishing, there is, of course, the problem of self-gratification undercutting quality. We have to make quite sure we have some control over the quality of writing produced by the co-operative. This is doubly guaranteed. First, the members of our

group are not rank amateurs; we have all been fairly
widely published in books, national literary magazines
and anthologies so we know our work is of a certain
standard. When a proposal is made to publish a
manuscript, each member of the co-operative takes a
copy, reads it and makes in-depth written criticisms of
it; published 'outsiders' are also invited to read and
comment on the proposed manuscripts. Authors then
work on these suggestions to improve their work
before it is typeset. Final proofreading of typeset pages
is also undertaken by the author before printing goes
ahead; this is a good guarantee of production quality.

Five Islands Press is determined to make a success of its venture.
Its first three works, published in 1988, were Chris Mansell, *Red
Shift, Blue Shift*; Ron Pretty, *Habit of Balance*; and Robert Hood, *Day
Dreaming on Company Time*.

The postal address of Five Islands Press is in the Appendix.

VOLUNTARY NON-PROFIT PUBLISHING

Women's Redress Press Inc.*

In 1983 a group of women, some of whom were
already employed in the commercial publishing world, met in Sydney
with the common purpose of establishing a feminist press, publishing books by and for women. The initial idea was to form a co-
operative and to package books in conjunction with established
companies, so that costs could be contained but so that the group
would have editorial control over manuscripts. Basic to the Redress
Press philosophy was that all women who contributed labour to
the organisation should be paid for their services. Much enthusiasm
was generated in the early months with over 300 women each
donating $100 to get the enterprise off the ground.

By the end of 1984 four books had been published in conjunction
with Wild and Woolley but financial and organisational difficulties
resulted in a redefining of Redress Press's operations. During an
emergency meeting called to wind up the press, a core of women
decided instead to proceed with publication. They were forced
to compromise some of the group's original principles – such as
payment for labour – but their dedication to the ideal of feminist
publishing by committed feminists saw them proceed under a

radically altered charter. All profits from existing and forthcoming books would be used to finance future projects, all labour would be voluntary. Subsequently, Women's Redress Press Inc. was incorporated under the Association's Incorporation Act as a non-profit-making association.

Rebecca Peters was one of the women at the emergency meeting. Four years later she is proud to report that the Women's Redress Press is currently producing its thirteenth title and is in no danger of folding up. She writes:

> At this stage we feel we've ironed out all production bugbears, but distribution continues to be our biggest problem. When our books are about to be launched onto the marketplace, we mail out flyers to bookshops and to library suppliers, but basically getting the books out involves a lot of foot slogging from place to place by volunteers who all have other life commitments such as families, careers and studies. But once our books are in shops, they sell well and reorders follow. Book sales seem to gain their own momentum. In terms of commercial publication, we don't really compete, but we would expect a normal print run of our books (between 1000–2000 copies) to sell out in twelve months to two years. Because our company is small and not well known we have a lot of trouble attracting reviews. We would dearly love to be able to employ someone in a promotional/marketing capacity but our finances are limited. Besides, we don't have an office!

Despite the press's lack of facilities, there is no lack of enthusiasm among volunteers. When a project is underway, a production group is formed. Drawing on the skills of volunteers, some of whom are professional editors, designers and graphic artists, this group proceeds with such tasks as author and printer liaison. Typesetting is often undertaken on a member's Apple McIntosh word processor; this cuts costs, even taking into account the fact that desktop publishing disallows a full book bounty from the Government (see chapter 12, 'Submitting Your Work', under the heading Entitlements).

People can still join Redress Press by paying $100; this money is seen as a donation, paid into a capital fund for purchase of equipment. Rebecca points out there is no advantage to financial members in terms of priority publication. Most members are not writers, merely women who are committed to the idea of feminist publishing. The press conducts regular monthly meetings with a management committee, comprising seven (or more) members, making decisions about selection of material. Rebecca feels that Redress Press works well as a voluntary organisation because committee members

> don't get bogged down in editorial policy; they don't worry about conforming to some particular theory of feminism. If we like a book and there's enough members prepared to commit themselves to a production group, then we'll publish it, finances permitting.

Selection of manuscripts is based on the management committee's general consensus. To date the press has published twelve books including novels, biographies, poetry collections and an immensely popular short-story anthology. The latter, titled *Room to Move*, published in conjunction with Allen and Unwin, has sold out of its 5000-copy first print-run and is still selling well. Five months after the press's poetry anthology, *Up from Below*, was released, it had covered its costs. Some Redress books have had publishing subsidies from the Literary Arts Board of the Australia Council. Rebecca says the press has found it time-saving to speak to the Board's project officers before applying for subsidies, in order to 'suss out' the likelihood of success.

Redress Press is proud of its accomplishments. Believing it is important for women working in its organisation to come out with increased work skills, the press points out that some women have moved from working in voluntary capacities for the organisation to full-time paid employment in allied fields. The press also believes it gives writers 'a fair go' by not only reading all manuscripts but by offering constructive criticisms of all work submitted. For women writers interested in submitting manuscripts to Redress Press, some basic professional courtesies should be observed. Members prefer to receive enquiry letters before submission of manuscripts; typed (not handwritten) scripts are acceptable; return postage should be included, as well as the writer's address and phone number; if approaches have already been made to other publishers, this should be made clear, and writers should always make sure they keep a copy of the submitted manuscript.

Publications by Women's Redress Press:
Selected Poems (with Wild & Woolley), Pamela Brown

Welou, My Brother (with Wild & Woolley and the Aboriginal Artists' Agency), Faith Bandler
She Moved Mountains (with Wild & Woolley), Colleen Burke
Mother's Day (with Wild & Woolley), Leone Sperling
Occasional Visits (photographs by women), compiled by Cathy Chinnery
Room to Move (with Allen & Unwin), ed. Suzanne Falkiner
Luxury, Kate Llewellyn
Your Hills are Too High, Roslyn Taylor
The Dying, Peg Job
Claudia's India, Irene Coates
Up from Below: Poetry of the '80's, ed. Irene Coates, Barbara Petrie & Nancy J. Corbett
Two Hundred Australian Women, ed. Heather Radi.
The address of Women's Redress Press is in the Appendix.

PRODUCING A COMMUNITY OR SCHOOL NEWSPAPER

Connexions—A Multilingual Community Newspaper

Concerned about bridging the communication gap in their heavily populated migrant neighbourhood of Port Kembla, a group of local citizens (mostly young people) started *Connexions* in 1984. Originally funded by government sources, the *Connexions* staff now use money they have won in competitions (such as the 'Herald Youth Awards') to continue publication of the paper.

An eight-page tabloid, *Connexions* is produced quarterly by approximately ten to twenty people, aged from twelve upwards. It features multilingual and community information, editorial content, sports, a health and legal column, a kids and pet care column, special features, graphics and photography. The multilingual section of the paper, published in languages such as Macedonian, Vietnamese, Italian and Portuguese, is used to convey relevant information to the ethnic community. Translations are undertaken, not by the staff members themselves, but by trained people in community welfare organisations. Sometimes government documents and information are printed in languages other than English.

People are recruited onto the *Connexions* staff by advertising (such as screen-print posters displayed at the local Community Youth Support Scheme workshop) or by personal invitation from the *Connexions* staff. There are a variety of jobs recruits can volunteer for. These include positions of Editor, Photographic Co-ordinator, Administrative Co-ordinator or Sports Editor. Alternatively, they can become a sub-editor, photographer, entertainment reporter, journalist, multi-lingual researcher, graphic artist, advertising representative or layout designer. Perhaps the most difficult, time-consuming newspaper job – distribution – is done by everyone pitching in to help.

In commenting about their involvement in the newspaper, and its value to them personally, participants made the following comments:

> Finding interesting and current stories which are relevant to the local community is sometimes a problem. Formal meetings have also proven to cause a few headaches.
>
> Working on *Connexions* is a good way of developing literary skills and meeting many new people.

Parents and relatives of young people involved in producing *Connexions* said they were very pleased to see their children's work published and read by other people. The *Connexions* project has proved that community newspapers can be a good way of connecting young with old, migrant Australians with people born in Australia.

Emu – A Literary Magazine for Young Australians

If you look at the chapter on markets for young people's writing, you will notice that it is very limited. *Emu* magazine originated as a result of that very limitation.

Editors, Catherine Jaggs and Evelyn Tsitas, take up the story:

> Before *Emu* there was hardly anywhere for young writers to get published. We began the magazine both as an outlet for those young writers and as a desire to have more control over the publishing process.
>
> The first step, after choosing the magazine's name, was the more tedious process of raising money for

printing costs. It wasn't easy to find a printer willing to do a 200 print run, but eventually a Sci Fi buff suggested a small printer who ran off the Star Trek fanzine. We were in business.

As we were only eighteen at the time, we had no money and we didn't want to ask our parents. We were an independent magazine. So we held trash and treasure stalls at Sunday markets, until, six months later, we had a bank balance (about $300 dollars).

Publicity was a problem – how would people know about us, where to submit work and how to subscribe? Jim Hamilton, President of the Victorian Fellowship of Australian Writers, was a godsend, sending our advertisement all over Australia in F.A.W. bulletins.

It took eighteen months to get our first issue out, surrounding ourselves with staple guns, binding tape, typewriters and hard work. When the first issue came back from the printers, it was really like holding a baby.

Six years and ten issues later Catherine and Evelyn report:

Emu is still going strong. It is still the main outlet for young writers on a national level, providing exposure, information and literary criticism for the country's new writers. The Literature Board has been kind enough to give us three publishing subsidies over the years (though we missed out this year) and we are now functioning so well we've been able to engage a subscriptions secretary, Martin Jaggs. We have a helpful loose body of young volunteers called 'Feathered Friends', who, in addition to helping us produce the magazine, attend our occasional soirées. These soirées and the subscriptions (approximately 130) keep us alive.

We are now producing the magazine three times a year. *Emu*'s forty pages contain fiction, non-fiction, reviews, poetry and illustrations submitted by contributors. We have two age categories: 'Just Hatched' is for writers under the age of fifteen, 'Emus' is for those up to the age of thirty. Catherine works as secretary/treasurer, Evelyn is responsible for publicity and distribution; we both select material for publication, then edit, type, do the layout and organise the soirées. We have form letters for everything (to cut

> down on work) but we always provide constructive
> criticism for our writers.
>   Distribution is always a problem – God bless our
> subscribers!

Postscript: Some months after this article was written Evelyn and Catherine were forced, through lack of financial support, to discontinue production of *Emu* magazine. The fact that they continued for so long is a credit to both of them. At the time this book goes into print, there is no literary magazine solely devoted to the publication of young Australians' writing.

Live Wire – An Inter-school Newspaper

In 1984, in response to a call by a Wollongong (NSW) City youth worker, three junior secondary school pupils reported to a meeting to provide the city youth with their own newspaper. It was a disappointing response, but the three were keen to give it a go. With the youth worker's help they produced the first two-page issue, *EKSSWAT* (later renamed *YAPER*, then *Live Wire*) which was distributed to six central Wollongong schools.

Several years later, funded by Wollongong City Council as part of its Youth Work Program, the paper is flourishing. It has a year-round staff average of fifty to sixty, is produced eight times annually and is distributed to sixteen secondary schools in the area. Its twenty pages cover many topics, issues and events of interest to young people. Each issue usually contains feature articles, letters and regular columns (fashion, music, under-18 gigs, school reports, book reviews, music); graphics, including cartoons, drawings, photographs and decorative borders, enhance its appearance. Each article is edited by the editor, sub-editor and youth worker.

Live Wire's present editor, Joanne Burrows, continues:

> The first editorial meeting for each year is always well
> advertised in the participating high schools. Future
> meetings are then advertised in each issue and young
> people are encouraged to become involved in each
> issue though anyone can drop in to help at any time.
> The majority of staff is school students, ranging in age
> from twelve to eighteen years (the average is fifteen)
> but participation is also open to ex-students and
> unemployed people up to the age of twenty-five.
>   In past years there has been a fairly normal structure
> of positions on the paper. Jobs were specialised.

However, this year we have only two, editor and sub-editor. The work for the paper is divided into three main areas: writing, art work (including photography) and layout and design. Participants can become involved in any area and do more than one job if they wish. Articles for each issue are selected on criteria such as content, presentation, appeal to young people, news value. If two articles on the same topic are handed in, then the better of the two is selected.

We've had a few headaches in the past. One was that the social function the newspaper provided (i.e. meeting other young people from different schools) took over from the production. Some people tended to disrupt editorial meetings without realising what they were doing. One reason we restructured work arrangements this year was to put greater emphasis on everyone being involved in all aspects of the paper; that way the responsibility is in the hands of everyone and not just a few.

The other major headache has been lack of funds and equipment. Typesetting and printing costs consume the $6000 budget provided by Council and there is never money to buy equipment. We find it difficult to experiment and improve the paper without additional finances.

On the positive side, our newspaper efforts netted us a merit award in the 1984 Sydney Morning Herald Youth Awards. As well, six former *Live Wire* staff members have obtained employment as either cadet journalists, typesetters or graphic artists due directly to their work and experience with us. Personally, the paper has given me an experience I won't forget. I've been a journalist, layout artist and editor. I meet new people all the time. After working on *Live Wire* for nearly three years, I feel I've benefited greatly.

Six other *Live Wire* staff members also comment on the benefits they have discovered from participating in this co-operative newspaper venture:

I've learnt numerous writing skills and improved my writing technique. My relatives think it's a great experience and my teachers appreciate the improvement in my school work.

Natalie Stirman, 14

As my goal in life is to become a journalist, working on
Live Wire is proving to be an invaluable experience.
The teachers at school, especially the principal, are
pleased with the articles I write about the school, and
my family feels it is a great experience for me.

Gail Barnsley, 16

Live Wire is beneficial in many ways. It helps writing
and literary skills needed for senior years at school
and also helps the individual's social esteem greatly by
participating in various activities related to the paper. I
am interested in journalism as a career and the
experience I gain from *Live Wire* is priceless. As for my
relatives, they all think that *Live Wire* is great for those
involved and they back me up 100 per cent.

Jason Borg, 16

Live Wire is an ideal way of letting other people know
just what is happening around them. As it is a youth
paper, my relatives have probably never heard of it
and never will; however, other students at my school
like it.

Chris Williams, 15

My friends think *Live Wire* is a really great paper. I am
a photographer for the paper. I would like to have a
career in photography and I think my involvement has
helped me. I am also starting to write articles which is
helping me with my essay writing at school.

Amanda Doherty, 17

I'm involved in photography, layout and journalism for
Live Wire. Experience on a newspaper is beneficial,
not only in social aspects but in practical aspects also.
It is an asset for school work, helping in Photography,
Art and English. After work on the paper for eighteen
months, I feel it has helped me a great deal. If I had my
chance I would do it all over again.

Gaye Burrows, 16

Lake High Link – A School Newspaper

Lake Illawarra High School's newspaper began in
1983 as a direct result of funding by the Disadvantaged Schools

Program. Current funding allows two teachers to be released from the classroom to help students prepare the paper. The organisation of the editorial committee consists of two Year 11 student editors who oversee the features, school news, sport, pictorial, entertainment and literary editors (from Years 10 and 11); they, in turn, are responsible for the supervision of assistant reporters drawn from all classes in the school.

The senior editors have a large degree of responsibility: they advise department editors on journalistic techniques; relay issues, stories and events that require coverage to their editors; hold meetings with department editors to check progress of articles and to discuss problems encountered; consult with supervising teachers; write articles and assist with layout. To be appointed to the prestigious position of senior editor, a student must have previous experience in production of the school newspaper, show leadership qualities and be seeking a future career in journalism.

Lake High Link's present editor, Marcela Aguilar, in reply to a questionnaire, made the following comments:

> We produce three editions per year, with each edition averaging twenty-eight pages. The contents are mainly school and community news. All the photographs, drawings and layout are done by the students. One of the past special features was a writing supplement printed in red. This contained poetry, stories, etc. written by students.
>
> This year we have about fifty students working on the *Link*; to recruit reporters we put up a notice for volunteers at the beginning of the school year. All work done by the students is undertaken during their own time. I'd say we have a moderate rate of volunteers. Students from years seven to twelve contribute, but the average age range is fifteen to sixteen years. Sometimes we recruit articles from local primary school students. We find that reporting and interviewing are the favourite tasks with participants.
>
> The biggest headache in producing our newspaper is chasing up articles and meeting deadlines.
>
> When the *Link* won first prize in the 1986 Sydney Morning Herald School Newspaper Competition, the judges said they were impressed by our responsible and independent editorial spirit. They also said our articles were interesting and varied, and reflected a genuine and serious treatment of issues.

> As editor, I get a lot of personal satisfaction in seeing the finished product. Being involved with the paper has taught me to deal with responsibility. It has also improved my English and my capabilities in communication and socialisation. I hope to go into journalism when I leave school; through the newspaper I have come into contact with professional journalists. As well, I've learnt some of the very basic skills needed to become one.

Three other *Lake High Link* participants also comment on their involvement:

> I've got a lot of satisfaction out of it over the past three years. I like the responsibility and the challenge. It is really worthwhile.
>
> Meredith Hooper, 16

> Working on the *Lake High Link* has been a valuable experience. I'm the Features Editor so a lot of work is involved. Organising other people is the hardest task. Writing articles is relatively easy once they have been researched. I hope to go into journalism when I leave school so my experience with this school newspaper is a good stepping stone.
>
> Paula Wilson, 16

> It's a very informative newspaper that includes interesting articles, news bits, literary work and artistic layout that suits every age.
>
> Ms Kelly, Art teacher, newspaper supervisor

COMMUNITY THEATRE – A CO-WRITING VENTURE

Karina Andjelic and Hilary Bell are two young women who have been actively involved in a wide range of activities at the young people's Shopfront Theatre* in Carlton, NSW, for the past few years. During that time they have each individually written plays and musicals, and have been involved in other co-writing ventures. In 1987, aged sixteen and twenty respectively, they combined their talents to write and produce a half-hour community theatre show for elderly nursing home patients, based on patients' own life experiences.

The show, A *Whippersnapper Going Haywire*, is a series of songs, scenes, monologues and poems revolving around the lives of four old people. Karina and Hilary visited the nursing home and talked at length with four interesting old people who volunteered a great deal of information about their lives. The songs in the show retell some of their stories and are arranged so that the four separate lives depicted are intertwined with each other and with world events such as the Depression and World War II.

Writing the show took a month, after which time Karina and Hilary directed it, using Shopfront Theatre actors. It was then presented to an audience of nursing home patients and was, by all accounts, favourably received.

Each young writer comments below on the experience of co-writing this particular show:

Hilary Bell, born in 1966:

Co-writing A *Whippersnapper Going Haywire* was a difficult activity. The main problem as I see it was that Karina and I are both strong-minded and had definite visions of how we would like the play to be – our visions didn't always correlate. We found the best way to overcome this was to divide up the pieces between us and later on to link them up together. Therefore, unless the other violently objected, we each had total control over our own lyrics, monologues, scenes, etc. The most difficult part of the project we discovered was finding a way of connecting all the individual stories into a common scenario.

What I learnt overall from the project was that co-writing is all about compromising, about being open-minded and flexible in regard to each other's ideas. At the same time I found co-writing led to a great deal of rapport being developed. Having someone to bounce ideas off was very exciting and productive. If I were to do it again, I would hope to have the benefit of a dramaturg, or someone who could look at the whole concept objectively and help to iron out stylistic differences. I would also like to have been able to spend more time on the actual writing, and then to have workshopped it with actors.

Other writing achievements: Hilary has written the book and score of a musical, *On the Footpath*, which was given a moving reading at Interplay in 1985. Her musical, *A Pocketful of Hula Dreams*, was performed at Pastels and the Clarendon in Katoomba in 1987, and later revived. In 1987 her musical, *Near and Strange*, was staged at the Shopfront Theatre, while a one-act play, *Conversations with Jesus*, written as part of the National Institute of Dramatic Art's Playwrights' Studio, was professionally produced in 1988. More recently Hilary wrote *Monsters Under the Bed* during her term as writer-in-residence with Newcastle's 2-Til-5 Youth Theatre. Her radio play, *Cruisin*, was broadcast on ABC radio and she is currently writing the libretto for an opera.

Karina Andjelic, born in 1971:

Although I too found *A Whippersnapper Going Haywire* a difficult project to undertake, it proved to have some very good points such as knowing that your co-writer can provide backup with ideas, and vice versa. With co-writing, there is a strange formation which occurs in that it's as if there are not only two writers but another entity as well. This probably comes from having the confidence in knowing that you have someone to fall back on. Co-writing the show resulted in giving me a lot more confidence in my writing; I also lost the panic syndrome I experience when I write alone.

What I saw as the main problem of co-writing, on the other hand, was having to decide who was going to write what and how to combine the separate styles of writing. I found the best way of approaching the project was for both of us together to first come up with a very tight scene-by-scene scenario and then to write different scenes on our own.

If I were given the opportunity of co-writing again, I would welcome it, and I don't think I'd change much at all about the way Hilary and I approached the task.

Other writing achievements: Karina has written several plays, including *Talent* which was workshopped at the 1983 National Young Playwrights' Weekend (NYPW) and was later produced at the Shopfront Theatre. *A Lesson Learnt Too Late* was also workshopped at the 1984 NYPW. Karina's *Lost Generations* was workshopped at Interplay '85 and produced in 1986 at the Shopfront Theatre.

COMMUNITY RADIO

Radio 2CHY/FM – A Student Venture

Up to 90 per cent of the announcers on radio 2CHY/FM 104 are high school students. Transmitting since the 1970s from Coffs Harbour in northern New South Wales, the radio station employs students, in a voluntary capacity, from Orara, Toormina, Coffs Harbour and Woolgoolga High Schools, and John Paul College. A teacher co-ordinator at each of these schools helps the station's administrative manager to screen hopeful Year 8 to 12 students. After six months' training in the studio, learning procedures such as panel operation and voice projection, selected students then spend half a day each month working on air as announcers. To prepare for each session they must select records, undertake trivia research and prepare local announcements. Some students opt for radio journalism, reporting on local news events.

Success in early announcing can result in students presenting their own shows. Once a week for three months they can host programs such as the popular Top Fifties program, the Breakfast Show, Disabled Impact, Classical Music, Christian Music, Country Music or Jazz programs. At one time the station presented a comedy series, and would have liked to have included radio drama content, but unfortunately scripts were not forthcoming from budding writers.

At the moment over 190 students are involved in radio 2CHY/ FM. Some work on air, others are in training, others contribute to the station's newsletter which is regularly distributed to participating schools and some are involved in a students' advisory group which the station's adult Board of Directors refer to frequently.

Involvement in Coffs Harbour's only FM radio station has led participants into media careers. Some are now working professionally on country radio stations, others are in local and city television.

Lee Quinn (15) is an announcer on 2CHY/FM. He also doubles as a production officer and is president of the Student Management Advisory Council. This is what Lee had to say about how he sees 2CHY's role:

> When I first started working here, I was very nervous about announcing, but now I look back and wonder how I could ever have been nervous. I really enjoy the challenge of preparing and presenting a show, whether it is the Top Fifties program or the Breakfast Show. In my last few years at high school, I'm now

thinking of a career in radio or possibly television. My involvement with 2CHY has been a worthwhile investment in my teenage years; it's taught me to be resourceful and responsible as well as punctual and to be well organised. As well, it's helped me to become much more articulate. I recently obtained a part-time job doing promotions' work with a large company as a result of my work with 2CHY.

Note: If you are interested in submitting written material to your local community radio station, contact the Public Broadcasting Association* which has a list of stations throughout Australia.

10 ☆
SO YOU
WANT A CAREER
IN WRITING?

WORK EXPERIENCE

Work experience is generally accepted as being unpaid voluntary labour during the course of which trainees gain valuable information about work practices in their particular fields. Many companies are more than willing to take on work experience trainees of all ages, not just secondary school students, so don't be discouraged if you are an adult who really wants to get started in a new career such as publishing. If you want to gain work experience, write to or make an appointment with the manager of the company you have targeted. Say that you wish to learn about the industry; offer to work for nothing, even if it is only for a short period. Nothing in the world is more appealing to an employer than an eager recruit (especially if he or she is not looking for a pay packet!).

If you are able to get work experience, then be prepared to take some initiative. I have known work experience students in newspaper offices who were not familiar with the proper use of a telephone, let alone a directory. When they wrote something, they handed it in unchecked, full of spelling errors. They sat around waiting to be told what to do. If the boss is busy and you've not been given something to do, find something! Sharpen some pencils, answer an unattended phone, tidy a filing cabinet, watch the photographer developing photos or the compositors laying out the newspaper, listen to how a journalist conducts an interview, make up interview questions of your own, ask if you can go out with the advertising rep. Don't waste the perfectly good opportunity you have to learn as much as you can about your prospective career.

Another thing is to learn as much about the company you are going to work for and *think* about what will be expected of you before you go to work. Once, as the manager/editor of a small provincial newspaper, I interviewed a university graduate who was applying for a journalist position. He was untrained but I desperately needed more staff. When I asked him how he expected he would gather news if he got the job, he had *no* idea. Needless to say, he was not hired.

While you are on the job, be friendly and polite to *all* your co-workers and do not become embroiled in office politics. If someone gossips to you (which they probably will do), try to take evasive action. Do not repeat gossip. Don't make critical comments about the workplace (even if it leaves a lot to be desired), your colleagues (no matter how unpleasant they may be) or your boss. Gossip and criticism are destructive, and they can backfire.

When your work experience period is over, thank your co-workers in person for the time and trouble they have taken with you. A gracious gesture is to send a general thank-you note. If you think you've made a particularly fine impression, you could ask the boss for a work reference. Provide a stamped self-addressed envelope as a matter of courtesy, and remember to thank the person if you are given one.

JOURNALISM

I had no experience in journalism at all when, in my late twenties, I answered an advertisement in a country newspaper calling for 'a part-time social reporter'. Over twenty other people, some with experience, also applied. The editor asked each of us to return in a week's time with several items of a social nature and he would decide, on the strength of the writing abilities shown, who would get the position. The next afternoon I returned with thirty neatly typed (and carefully edited) articles; the editor was so impressed he gave me the job on the spot! What I am saying here is that all the qualifications in the world cannot match a tonne of enthusiasm. If you really want that job, show you are keen. Be prepared to invest your time and energy, even above and beyond the call of duty.

Journalists work in all types of media: newspapers, magazines, journals, radio, television, public relations, even in film scripting and publishing. Depending on their experience and skills, all journalists are graded (D, C, B, A, A2, A1). Training in a cadetship in journalism generally lasts three years. Cadetships are limited in number and there is considerable competition for those offered. However, you can (as I did) bypass the doorway of cadetship if you decide to work on a country or provincial newspaper. Be prepared, though – working conditions are generally much poorer than they are in metropolitan or city offices. Some large newspapers and other publications recruit messengers who are known as copy boys or girls. Although they are not employed in journalistic work, most of them aim at a cadetship once they have become familiar with the workings of the organisation.

Usually the work of a journalist involves specialising in one of the following areas: reporting; sub-editing; feature-article, lead and/or specialist writing; or freelance work, specialising in a particular topic. The ability to write simple lucid English is not the only prerequisite of a journalist. He or she should have a wide general knowledge, an interest in and understanding of public affairs, a well-developed news sense, an analytical mind, a good understanding of people and the ability to distinguish between fact and opinion. If you want a career in journalism, you should also be able to work under pressure. Deadlines are the name of the game in the media industry, and often journalists have to write stories at great speed.

If you are seeking a cadetship, it is a good idea to get some prior work experience with a media company or on the editorial team of your school newspaper, etc. Knowledge of shorthand and typing is required by most newspapers, so you would be advised to at least learn how to type (on a word processor is best). At one newspaper where I worked, a large field of young people seeking cadetships was narrowed down to two applicants of equal merit. The deciding factor proved to be one applicant's typing ability.

If you are interested in freelance journalism, free correspondence courses are offered through the South Australian Open College for Further Education* and Western Australian Technical Extension Service*.

(For other courses in journalism, see below.)

PUBLISHING

You don't have many opportunities to write creatively in the publishing world, but if being surrounded by books and manuscripts is your idea of heaven, you may find publishing a satisfying career.

Someone once said that all editors are frustrated writers; whether or not this is so, it is true that a number of editors have written some excellent books. Many editors come to the job initially by way of proofreading jobs; alternatively many begin their career with a Bachelor of Arts in hand and are given on-the-job training. A Graduate Diploma in Editing and Publishing (one-year course) is offered at the Royal Melbourne Institute of Technology, while part-time courses are sometimes offered by private tutors. In Sydney, a part-time course is offered at Waverley TAFE, while the Department of Continuing Education at the University of New England (NSW) occasionally offers short intensive courses such as Editing Small Publications, as do the Society of Editors* (Vic. and NSW) and Information Age.* Editors need to be able to read analytically, to pay attention to the smallest detail, and to grasp the ideas and structure of a whole manuscript. It helps for an editor to be a good writer also, as awkward sentences in manuscripts accepted for publication sometimes need to be rewritten. People in the editorial department of a publishing house are involved in manuscript appraisal, contracts, administration, public relations work, the search for new publishable material as well as the supervision of the manuscript through the production process – copy editing, proofreading, etc. Editors contribute significantly to the quality of a book produced under their supervision.

Other departments in publishing houses include: rights (involved with authors' contracts and the selling of subsidiary rights – translation, serialisation, etc.); production (responsible for physically turning the manuscript into a book, the staff includes book designers, artists, printers and administrative personnel); promotion and public relations; marketing, sales and distribution; and accounts.

Freelance readers are important adjuncts to publishing houses. Busy editors send promising manuscripts to outside readers who specialise in particular areas of fiction and non-fiction. Often they have worked in publishing. Readers are paid to give written assessments of manuscripts. Some editors also work from home, copy-editing and proofreading when in-house staff are overloaded with other projects.

Publishing houses usually have sales representatives who sell books to the bookshops. Other jobs allied with the industry include distribution and book-selling.

ADVERTISING COPYWRITER

Advertising covers a wide range of activities and may be conducted by an advertising agency or by a firm's own advertising department. Copywriters provide the ideas and the words or script (radio or television) which are the basis of all advertising. They must, therefore, be able to dream up concepts, write well and be interested in people's needs and their reaction to stimuli.

Copywriters often work alongside commercial artists, layout designers, research workers and accounts personnel. If you are interested in copywriting as a career, you need to know the job is high-pressured. You would be constantly working to meet deadlines; sometimes this involves working around the clock until the job is done.

A trainee scheme, organised by the Advertising Federation of Australia* now invites applications from persons aged from twenty-one to thirty years to undertake a nine-month (paid) training course in advertising. This involves working in an advertising agency.

PUBLIC RELATIONS

Public relations work, with its emphasis on the communication of information, is a job where fluency in written (and spoken) English is required. Public relations officers must be familiar with all, and expert in as many as possible, of the various communication media. They may be involved in news presentation, films, speeches, community relations, industrial affairs, staff relations and special events, displays and publications (leaflets, journals and reports). Public and private companies, government departments, professional bodies, political parties and industrial and commercial associations use the services of public relations personnel.

If you are interested in this career, personal requirements for the job include a lively and enquiring mind, a facility for analysing situations, an ability to get on well with people, skills in writing and speaking, imagination, initiative, an ability to work under pressure and an understanding of the news media. People with journalistic experience are often employed in public relations, although on-the-job training is usually conducted by employers to suit their own special requirements. A number of colleges and institutes conduct courses in communications (for example, Bachelor of Arts in Communications) with special emphasis on public relations.

FREELANCE WRITER

The general public believes all writers are fabulously wealthy. This is not so. Several years ago the Literature Board (now the Literary Arts Board) of the Australia Council surveyed full-time writers and revealed that their average income was $6000 per annum (compared to a teacher's salary of $30 000).

Writing for the screen is probably the biggest money-spinner for writers but generally this does not provide a secure income. (The job is finished when the film is made or the television program is taken off the air.) If you write narrative fiction, poetry, drama or non-fiction on a freelance basis, your income is determined by the amount of work you can sell. If you are successful in getting a novel or non-fiction book published, payment (a percentage – anything from 6 to 15 per cent – of the book's retail price) is made biannually. Playwrights are paid about $30 per performance of their play (*if* they can interest a company in producing it); poets fare even more poorly.

The only way a full-time writer can earn a regular income (and even this is not assured) is to write freelance articles for newspapers, magazines and journals. Many writers have part-time jobs to supplement their writing incomes. Part-time jobs I've held include working in a bookshop, conducting writing classes and camps for adults and children, tutoring at university, casual teaching, selling advertising space for newspapers, and journalism. At the moment I am able to be a full-time writer thanks to the generosity of the Literary Arts Board which awarded me a one-year fellowship. Last year the Board received 805 applications for grants and fellowships from serious writers: 108 were awarded.

People who make a living from representing writers are called literary agents. For a percentage of the writer's earnings they assess the writer's work, approach publishers with the manuscript, negotiate contracts and sell subsidiary (for example, film, television, and translation) rights.

COURSES

A number of colleges and institutes throughout Australia offer full- and part-time writing courses. These include: the Australian Film, Television and Radio School,* North Ryde, NSW (training in film, radio and television production)

Canberra College of Advanced Education (Bachelor of Arts in Professional Writing; Associate Diploma in Professional Writing; Graduate Diploma in Media)

Capricornia Institute of Advanced Education, Rockhampton, Qld (communication, journalism and literature)

Chisholm College of Advanced Education, Caulfield, Vic. (book design and production)

Darling Downs Institute of Advanced Education, Darling Heights, Qld (Bachelor of Arts, with journalism major)

Deakin University, Waurn Ponds, Vic. (Bachelor of Arts courses, with prose fiction, poetry, drama, journalism, writing for advertising and public relations strands)

Holmesglen College of Technical and Further Education, Chadstone, Vic. (course in foundations of professional writing)

Mitchell College of Advanced Education, Bathurst, NSW (Bachelor of Arts in Communications)°

New South Wales Institute of Technology, Sydney (Bachelor of Arts in Communications)°

Queensland Institute of Technology, Brisbane (advertising, journalism and public relations)

°Bachelor of Arts (Communication) is a three-year full-time course designed to provide a broad understanding of the social and technological aspects of communication as well as detailed study in specialised areas such as mass communication, professional writing, journalism, public relations, advertising, media planning and production, and radio, film and television production.

Royal Melbourne Institute of Technology (Diploma/Degree – journalism, advertising, copywriting, public relations, editing and publishing)

School of Creative Arts, Wollongong, NSW (Bachelor of Creative Arts, with a major in writing, also a Master of Creative Arts)

South Australian College of Advanced Education, Magill, SA (Associate Diploma of Journalism, Bachelor of Arts in Journalism)

Swinburne Institute of Technology, Hawthorn, Vic. (media studies, publishing and broadcasting)

University of Queensland, St Lucia, Qld (Bachelor of Arts, with a journalism major)

Victoria College, Toorak Campus, Malvern, Vic. (fiction, non-fiction, scriptwriting, poetry)

Western Australian Institute of Technology, Bentley, WA (creative writing, film and television, journalism, theatre arts)

Writing classes are often conducted by regional Technical and Further Education colleges (free) and adult education councils (nominal charge). Private organisations also provide courses by correspondence. These include International/Correspondence Schools*, Stott Correspondence College* and The Writing School*.

FURTHER INFORMATION

Secondary-school careers advisors are trained in directing young people to the appropriate channels for information on careers choice. You may find the following organisations helpful in giving you more information about your chosen writing-oriented career: the Department of Industrial Relations (Vocational Services Branch),* the Public Relations Institute of Australia,* Australian Journalists' Association,* the Advertising Federation of Australia,* Australian Book Publishers' Association,* Australian Society of Authors,* Society of Editors,* and Women in Publishing.*

11 ☆
PUBLISHED
WRITERS SPEAK

INTRODUCTION

'We who write are survivors.'
Tillie Olsen

People are never too young – or too old – to get their writing published. According to the *Guinness Book of Records*, the oldest author in the world was Alice Pollock, whose *Portrait of My Victorian Youth* was published in 1971 when she was 102 years old! The youngest published author is not on record but one of the youngest must surely have been Melbourne boy Michael Daniel who was only eight when he wrote and illustrated his *The Island of the Blind Hippopotamie* (Wentworth Press); sadly Michael had a terminal bone disease and died a few years after this and a second book were published.

Often, against all sorts of odds, writers have struggled for years to find publication. They have defied the demands of motherhood, career or censorship, have overcome illiteracy, lack of education or physical handicaps, have struggled to write in a language foreign to their native tongue; some have written out of desperation to have others hear their plight, others to let the world know of their achievements. In her book *Silences* (Virago) Tillie Olsen writes of the circumstances which have obstructed writers over the cent-uries—circumstances of sex, economic class, colour, the times and climate into which the writer is born.

Elsie Roughsey is an Australian writer who was silenced for many years by her colour, her cultural heritage and her sex. It took fifty-one years before she met the challenge of writing, then another ten years to write the story of her life. Laboriously filling notebooks (in between cooking, cleaning and caring for her five children and her grandchild) she wrote about her girlhood in a mission dormitory, her return to her tribe, the Lardils of Mornington Island, and what she saw as the steady erosion of their tribal way of life by the influence of European culture. Elsie's manuscript found a publisher via a European friend and *Aboriginal Mother Tells of the Old and the New* (McPhee Gribble/Penguin) with its combination of Aboriginal English and tribal language, was finally published in 1984.

Three of Australia's most highly acclaimed writers in the past ten years – Elizabeth Jolley, Olga Masters and A. B. Facey – did not publish until relatively late in life.

A family of seven children and part-time work in journalism gave author Olga Masters little opportunity to develop her interest in writing fiction until she was in her fifties. Almost immediately her work was critically acclaimed: between 1977 and 1981 she won nine prizes for her short stories, with her first collection, *The Home Girls* (University of Queensland Press, 1984), winning second place in the National Book Council Awards.

Elizabeth Jolley had been writing ever since she was a girl but she did not try to submit material until she was in her forties. Although she did have individual stories published earlier, her first book, *Five Acre Virgin* (Freemantle Arts, 1984), was not published until she was fifty-three. Jolley claims the reason she waited for so long to submit material was that her writing was not previously ready for submission.

A. B. Facey never intended to be a published author; in fact he did not learn to read or write until late in life. Facey was a born story-teller; for years he told anecdotes of his life to his children and grandchildren. Later he recorded his reminiscences in longhand in irregular journals. Eventually he took these journals to the Fremantle Arts Centre Press, asking how much it would cost for the press to print a hundred or so copies for distribution to his family and friends. His manuscript was immediately accepted and contracted by an astute editor who spent the next twelve months working on it with the author. In May 1981, at the age of eighty-one and confined to a wheelchair, Albert Facey attended the launch of his autobiography, *A Fortunate Life* (Penguin). Facey died before the end of the year, knowing that his book was a huge popular success, winner of both the NSW Premier's Literature Award and the National Book Council Award. *A Fortunate Life* is now regarded as an Australian classic.

Sometimes people who have never written until mid-life have often been prompted to do so as a result of personal tragedy. From a very early age Anne-Marie Mykyta knew she would be a writer, but it wasn't until her sixteen-year-old daughter Julie died in what became known in the press as the South Australian Truro murders, that she wrote her first book. *It's a Long Way to Truro* (McPhee Gribble, 1981) was followed by a successful stage play, *Border Country*.

Chronic pain resulted in Suzanne Porter writing her first book in her late forties. Diagnosed as having the degenerative disease osteoarthritis, Suzanne turned in desperation to a Pritikin diet. The diet worked and prompted Suzanne to create new recipes within the Pritikin guidelines. The best of the collection were put together in her book, *It's Only Natural* (Greenhouse, 1985), which has been a best-seller.

Ellen Newton (a pen-name) was in her eighties, ill, and had been shut away in a nursing home for seven years when she s.arted writing a diary. Written out of desperation on scraps of wrapping paper and the backs of envelopes, it relieved the need to communicate, even if it was only to herself. One of Ellen's close friends who ran a bookshop heard about the diary, asked to see it, and at once thought it would make a book. She showed it to two publishers who had recently started their own company, and they agreed. *This Bed My Centre* (McPhee Gribble, 1979) was published the same year Ellen Newton discharged herself from the nursing home to live alone in her own flat.

Older writers use life experiences as the basis of their first publication. Joe Thornton was an illiterate labourer for more than forty years; as a result of learning to read and write, he wrote and self-published a phonetic dictionary, *Spelling Wen Yoo Dont No How*, to help others who had similar difficulties to those he had experienced in his earlier years.

When he retired as Chief of Naval Staff, Sir Henry Burrell set about writing his life as a seaman; his *Mermaids Do Exist* (Macmillan, 1986) was published when he was eighty-three years old.

Born in 1935, Barry Cohen spent nearly fifteen years in the rag trade before entering Parliament. In 1969, at the age of fifty-three, he wrote and published his first book, *The Life of the Party* (Penguin, 1987), a collection of yarns that came out of his eighteen years as an Australian politician, followed by a second book, *After the Party* (Penguin, 1988).

Edna Ryan, often referred to as the 'mother' of Australian feminism, was in the workforce for nearly fifty-four years. Her experience as an active member of the Clerks' Union gave her a solid basis when she started researching for a book about a history of women's wages in Australia. At the age of seventy Edna had this first book, *Gentle Invaders* (Thomas Nelson, 1974), published. Ten years later she produced her second, *Two Thirds of a Man* (Hale & Iremonger, 1984); at the age of eighty-three she was preparing notes for a third book on the effects of ageing. This grand woman who fought actively for wage justice for women all her working life, reared three children and still found time for a career in local politics (including Deputy Mayor of Fairfield Municipal Council), left school when she was fifteen years old!

The need to tell one's story, coupled with determination, drive and talent, seem to be the principal requirements for getting published. The list of achievements of people who fought against all kinds of odds to see their words in print could go on. The purpose of this chapter, however, is for writers themselves to tell their own stories. The remainder of the chapter is divided into three sections. The first section features adult writers, some of whom published later in life. In the second section adult authors tell of their successes as young writers. In the third section young people whose works have recently been published relate their stories.

ADULT WRITERS

John Roarty – Novelist

Born in 1921; lives in Ryde, NSW.
Writing achievement: Although he is literally unable to write, John is the author of a book, *Captives of Care* (Hodder & Stoughton, 1981), which was the basis of an award-winning film that has been screened all over the world.

> I am a person with disabilities as a result of cerebal palsy from birth. All my life I've been confined to a wheelchair and have spent more than fifty years in Weemala, part of Royal Ryde Rehabilitation Hospital; when I first came here it was known as the 'Home for the Incurables'. I'm physically unable to write, and because of moderate to severe speech disability, I have some difficulty in making any dictation understood. Nevertheless, in 1980 I spent six months dictating *Captives of Care* whenever and wherever I could find a place quiet enough for recording. In writing the book, I hoped to make people aware of the

patronising, paternalistic and insensitive way people
with disabilities are treated. In my early years at
Weemala, I was treated – as were other disabled
inmates in this institution – as either an invalid, a fool
or a half-wit. Through the pages of my book I set out to
make a good life for people like myself telling the
world of our situation and also in the hope that I could
help in the instruction of paramedical and social
welfare students.

I had no previous major interest in writing before I
wrote my book. However, I had written short articles on
disability which were published in magazines for the
disabled or in Christian publications. Since my book
was published I've had no urgent impetus to write,
probably because dictation is so difficult both for
myself and my scribe. However, I know that I will write
again if conditions necessitate further full emancipation
of people with disabilities. Writing a book is hard
work – harder than I expected.

Advice to new writers: Write of what you know and
believe; write to make others believe.

Ruby Langford – Novelist

Born in 1934; lives in Granville, NSW.
Writing Achievement: At the age of fifty Ruby wrote her first book,
her autobiography *Don't Take Your Love to Town* (Penguin, 1988),
because, in her own words, 'white Australia doesn't have any idea
of how hard it is for us Aboriginals to live and survive between
the two cultures'.

I started to write my story in May 1984 and it took a
year to write the first draft. Usually I wrote at night by
the light of my old electric power machine because
the overhead light was too hard on my eyes. My only
previous claim to writing fame was an essay I wrote for
a competition conducted by *Dawn*, one of the first
Aboriginal magazines in the sixties. The prize then was
one guinea but I believe nowdays you win an all-
expenses paid trip overseas. Such is the story of my
life! When I was in high school – I left after second

form – I was always in trouble because of writing. I'd have to write a composition and I'd get carried away and write about ten or twelve pages. 'Only three or four pages will be fine, Ruby,' the teacher used to say. I was a bookworm then, and I still am. Plus I've always loved writing, it gets all my problems out of my head and onto paper.

The way my book eventually found a publisher happened like this: in 1985 the Australian Broadcasting Commission ran a documentary on the sewing class I belong to. Operating from the Aboriginal Medical Service in Redfern, we had a class of twenty-seven. We were all determined to take a trip to Ayers Rock. We had fetes and sold food stuffs and our craft goods, and, with a grant from the Aboriginal Arts Board, we were on our way. At this time I'd finished the first draft of my book, and my mother, who was travelling with us, told one of the ABC staff, Billy Marshall, 'my daughter's writing a book'. Billy offered to read the book. He liked it but thought it needed a woman reader's viewpoint. He introduced me to a writing teacher, Susan Hampton, who worked with me for two years teaching me the basics of editing and highlighting the story, how to put it into scenes and chapters and the way to write it up in action and dialogue. I knew nothing about who to approach about funding or getting published until I began working with Sue. With her help I was able to get two established writers to read my manuscript and write a report saying it was good enough to be funded. With a grant – from the Aboriginal Arts Board – I was able to work with Sue to finish the book. In 1987 it was accepted for publication by Penguin Books which had earlier published Sue's co-edited book, *The Penguin Book of Australian Women Poets*.

Even if Sue hadn't given me the help she did, I know I would have found a way of getting my book into print because I'm a very determined person. A whole new world has opened up for me with writing, especially now all my children have grown. I will continue writing short stories, mainly about my Aboriginal culture because there just isn't enough written; our history is mainly word of mouth and it's necessary, I feel, to educate people, both white and black.

Advice for new writers: Don't give up, it's a big job but it's also an achievement to write a book. It takes a lot of persistence but it is also very rewarding.

Serge Liberman – Short-story Writer

Born in 1942; lives in North Caulfield, Vic.
Writing achievements: Despite winning several major writing awards, Serge found it difficult and time-consuming to find a publisher for his first collection of short stories. He published the collection himself and is now acknowledged as one of Australia's leading short-story writers.

Books in print:
A Bibliography of Australian Judaica
On Firmer Shores
The Life that I Have Led
A Universe of Clowns

I was born in Russia and lived successively in a displaced persons' camp in Germany and then in Paris before arriving in Australia in 1951 at the age of eight. Although English was an acquired language, I had no difficulty assimilating it. My first intimations of wanting to write did not develop slowly and gradually; rather they came as an acute assault upon me while I was in Fifth Form at high school in 1959. I had been watching the film version of Eugene O'Neill's *Desire Under the Elms* on television and was absolutely struck by its magnificent power and intensity, and, as a consequence, a vista of what could be done with the creative word opened out before me. It was then that the 'bug' for writing hit me, and did so with the suddenness and virulence of any acute contagion. The next morning, I sat down to write my first play which, by day's end, however, saw its consummation and apotheosis in the waste basket.

Inevitably, my work was, at the outset, subject to repeated trial and error and multiple false starts resulting in a large volume of amateur stuff of little intrinsic value, other than serving as practice for what, through continued writing, was to follow. Even now, I tend at times to see my present writing, however proficient and successful and accepted it may be, as practice for still better work in the future.

In time, to write became a need, a compulsion, which, successful in outcome or not, would not be denied. I could as much stop writing as I could give up my day-to-day medical work. Both were necessary – writing and medicine – to satisfy different aspects of my physical/mental/emotional/spiritual being.

My first story, 'great' at the time but sophomorish in the light of hindsight, was published in 1966 in the Melbourne University medical students' journal *Speculum* – I was twenty-four at the time – and my second story in a Tel Aviv writers' workshop journal four years later. Over the ensuing four years I wrote very little. Full-time hospital work and attendant postgraduate study with the intensive demands they made on time and energy, both physical and mental, left little opportunity for my brain cells to take off on those flights of fancy and imagination needed for writing.

A turning point proved to be my move into general practice in the Carlton area. The significance of Carlton lay in the fact that it had at one time been a suburb with a strong Jewish contingent of people that embodied a culture so much my own – European, immigrant, Yiddish-speaking – and whom I intuitively understood. By the time I entered the area, they were a dwindling lot, and I felt the need to put these folk on paper, along with their experiences, their attitudes, concerns, nuances of character and expression, and their high points and bewilderments. They constituted both the raw material for my earlier stories even as I saw in them my audience, although none of them has in any recognisable form appeared in my published work. With continued writing, both my subject matter and my audience have expanded, but I still see my move into general practice as having given my writing both a focus and a direction.

My first published work of any consequence were stories which appeared in small literary journals. By 1979 I had accumulated a considerable body of work which I submitted to a publisher. Within a week, they were back on my desk accompanied by a courteous note reading 'These are not our kind of stories. Good luck elsewhere'. 'Elsewhere' returned them after two weeks, this time with a letter stating 'The market for stories is a bad one and we have no place for stories in our immediate publishing program'. Gritting my teeth – and damn the consequences – I submitted the manuscript for the Alan Marshall Award for creative writing. And in the light of the knock-backs, a funny thing happened: I won the Award with a very nice citation. The publisher sponsoring the Award had first option on the work. Five months later, however, a letter arrived stating that he could make no offer to publish the collection. I accepted the decision with a reasonably level head. Flukes happened and perhaps my prize was a flukish win in a year in which the manuscript was judged the best of an indifferent year.

One fluke could easily be written off. But how explain two? For, a year later, I had another collection of stories entitled *A Universe of Clowns* completed, which I also submitted for the same award and which – this time with a more sober and muted joy – I again carried off. This time, the Award, as well as netting a cash prize, also earned me a most pleasant luncheon with the publisher. But what might have seemed a prelude to an offer of publication which would have been more welcome still proved to be instead an occasion for a recounting of woes about the publishing industry, about fickle markets, poor returns, and so on and so forth.

This time I decided that I was through with waiting. I chose to give my fortunes a little push and become, as it were, master of my own fate rather than rely on others to dictate it. I had some money – not much, but some – in a bank account which I called my 'literary fund', consisting of income gained from prizes, book reviews and published stories, and I decided to 'recycle' it into publishing a book myself. In June 1981 I took the manuscript of *On Firmer Shores*, which contained what I considered the best and most varied stories from my manuscript collection, to the printer. By September, it saw the light of day. Five months later a second printrun was on the way, and it is now in its fourth printing. It has taken much work, true, with mail orders, prepublication offers, telephone calls and foot-slogging between the bookshops, but in a sense that is what any publishing house or its distributor must do to put a work on the market.

Since then, *A Universe of Clowns* has appeared and also *The Life that I Have Led*, which, in manuscript form, won for me my third Alan Marshall Award. A fourth collection recently netted me a commendation in the same competition.

For me writing boils down to one thing only and that is to sit down and write, write, write; write with – or despite – all the attendant elations and agonies of composition; write for a few minutes at a time, or an hour, or two, or three, or for a whole day, but a bit every day for however long surrounding circumstances – work, family and communal obligations and commitments – permit. One cannot build a house without laying the first brick, then the second, then a third, and so on. The house will not build itself nor will a story or a poem or a play or a film script come into being without the physical act of writing and the mental and emotional and, sometimes, spiritual sweat involved in the process. Writing is creating, true, but it is also plain, this-worldly, concerted work.

Advice for new writers: To give advice is to risk being gratuitous. But for what it's worth, I would suggest to would-be writers to avoid saying 'One day I will write', 'When I have time', 'When the children are grown up', 'When I retire', 'When I come back from holidays or overseas'. DO IT NOW! If an idea strikes, write it down, capture it, explore it, harass it, harrow it, torment it, work on it, *now*, while it's at its freshest and most vivid, lest the clarity, radiance and spontaneous crystalline brilliance of the thought pale, wane and become irrecoverably lost.

Mary Baarschers – Freelance Educational Writer

Born in 1930; lives in Hornsby, NSW
I've been writing now for about fifty years, ever since I had short pars accepted for women's papers. Now I'm superannuated, I write as a freelance full-time

professional writer. Although in the past I have written and published several books, my main work now is writing for three Sydney family firm publishers. When one of these publishers needs some work done, I'm approached and then get straight down to work. I might, for example, be asked to condense a classical novel down to ninety minutes' listening time. Mainly, though, I write educational aids dealing with basic reading, spelling and musical subjects. Sometimes I may have an idea or a new approach for a project, in which case I simply phone one of my publishers for a discussion. Rarely do I receive rejections; this is no doubt due to the fact that I am generally writing to publishers' specifications. Often I'm asked to make quite a lot of revisions, but rewriting is part of being a professional writer.

While I do not expect to be paid for contributions to professional journals, local newspapers or for charities, I do expect my publishers to pay me at the stipulated time. Two of my publishers are reliable, though the third is unprofessional; I have difficulty getting money when it is due, despite contracts. Membership of the Australian Society of Authors is imperative for all writers as it is the only body which looks after writers' interests.

Advice to new writers: Study the market and discover what you can do within this scope. Know your subject and be original in your work. The latter is often the difference between rejection and acceptance. You must give the publisher what he or she wants or your work will simply not see the light of day.

Nola Hayes – Scriptwriter

Born in 1924; lives in Castle Hill, NSW
Writing achievements: Nola was a scriptwriter for television and radio for twenty-five years.

Writing in any form – story, poetry, songwriting, radio, stage, TV – means all the world to me. It has not always been for the remuneration; I have written plays, songs and poems for church organisations, merely for the satisfaction of seeing them performed. Writing is the one thing in which I have confidence and of which I have made a success.

I first wrote for television, wanting a change from radio and storywriting. When I tried to break into the field, I used to phone producers asking for an appointment and interview; as a result I was sometimes asked to write scripts or storylines. I attended a few one-day lectures and seminars to get an idea of the medium, and looked through a sample script which showed a typical layout for TV to work on. Once a TV producer said to me, 'I don't care how you set it out; if the story is good, I'll use it.' In television I worked on dramas and comedies as well as a religious series for the Christian Television Association. After a while, however, I found that many series producers had their own 'stable' of writers and I returned to radio where there seemed to be more scope for work, principally with the ABC.

Another problem I had in writing for television was payment – or rather, lack of payment. I had always been paid for my television writing (usually a week after acceptance) but a producer who had previously bought my work and who had commissioned me to write three plays in a series, failed to pay me and to return my scripts. This experience taught me that one ought to be a member of the Australian Writers' Guild.° The Guild is a union that protects its members. It has guidelines for contracts, free advice, its own legal advisers and will negotiate on behalf of members if problems arise. I've been a full member of the Guild for twenty-one years and one of the first things they stress is that writers should never write anything for anyone without signing a contract first, or at least getting the details in writing. Had I been a member back in those early days, the TV producer would never have gotten away without paying me.

Advice for new writers: If your first few attempts at television writing fail, try a course at the Australian Film, Television and Radio School to gain extra polish and presentation.

° See chapter 7, 'Writing Drama', under the heading Useful Contacts.

Sue Edmonds – Songwriter

Born in 1944; lives in Bulli, NSW.
Writing achievements: In 1986 Sue was awarded a grant from the Music Board of the Australia Council to work as musician-in-residence with the South Coast Labour Council in recognition of her work as a community songwriter and musician.

Music cassettes produced: 'Beat Your Breasts' (Ovarian Sisters, Tasmania, 1980); wrote all the music and lyrics for ten of the fourteen songs.
'Red and Rough' (Mixed Bag,* Wollongong, 1987); twenty original songs.

Books in print:
Strike a Light: Contemporary Songs of Australian Working Life, an anthology edited by Gillian Harrison (Hale & Iremonger).
When the Whistle Blows, a songbook.

Songwriting started for me when I was in my mid-thirties when a woman gave me a poem about her life of domestic violence; this was the beginning of my attempts to capture contemporary life in music. What I try to do in my songwriting is to put larger contemporary issues into perspective for myself and other people living ordinary lives. My songs are 'instant news'. I write about current happenings and issues in the world around me – about big busines, about government activity (or lack of it), about trade unions, price rises, increased taxes and so on. Some of my songs are outdated within a week of writing them; for example, I wrote a song about the proposed introduction of the Australia Card the week it was scrapped. I'd describe my songs as being contemporary political folk songs, even as traditional folk songs, though some people wouldn't agree that immediate comment on current issues is 'folk music'. When I worked as musician-in-residence at the Port Kembla Steelworks, a certain Member of Parliament stated publicly I was misusing public funds. He referred to a song I'd written, 'Pushing Shit Uphill', and ignored all the other features of the program, like instrument making and researching of material. Incidentally, I'd written the song in my own time some

two years earlier! When you are a writer you are
vulnerable to such attacks. But I also believe in the old
adage, 'any publicity is good publicity!'

Every songwriter has a different method of writing
material – some write the lyrics, then search for a
melody. For others both lyrics and melody come
together. Fortunately I play several stringed
instruments so when it comes to writing a song, I'm
able to use a banjo or guitar to compose. Generally I
start with an issue – it could be retrenchment or
politicians' payrises – then comes the concept – what I
am wanting to say about this issue. I might spend
several hours strumming on my guitar, repeating
words or phrases, trying to come up with a 'catch line'.
As I experiment with the sounds my instrument makes,
I also play around with words. When, eventually, a
catchy phrase comes to me, I'm able to work around it
to develop a chorus. I've found that if I can compose a
good chorus, one that is strongly rhythmic, then the
verses are more likely to come. It's important to find a
rhythmic melody and to use repetition in music and
lyrics. Repetition of a particular line or chorus makes
people more familiar with the song.

It's possible simply to write song lyrics without
having any musical background, but the difficulty lies
in finding someone to set music to your words. I'd
advise any novice songwriter to learn to play an
instrument. You need to know at least four or five
chords. Let the instrument give you the sounds.
Experiment with key changes and with different
rhythms as you compose. Keep experimenting till it
sounds right.

When you've composed a number of songs, you
may wish to record them. There are two ways of doing
this. You could hire a recording studio (listed in the
Yellow Pages) or you could self-record. The cost of
hiring a studio is expensive, around $20–30 an hour. If
you chose this method of recording, you should know
exactly what you want to do beforehand. Be well
rehearsed; recording is a long, arduous business. A
good idea to save time is to 'rough' record exactly
what you want at home beforehand. As well, have a
good look at the studio before recording day to make
yourself familiar with the set-up. The advantage of

using a studio is that you're guaranteed a good product because you're using first-class equipment and personnel.

If you decide to self-record, you'll need a good quality four-track recorder and someone with technical expertise to run it. You can work from your own lounge room so you can take your time in recording. Try to deaden the sound in the room before you tape. When my Mixed Bag partner Lioba Rist and I recorded 'Red and Rough' we taped all sixteen tracks in her home; we're more than pleased with the product.

We sell tapes at places where we perform, in clubs and pubs and at private functions.

Advice to new songwriters: Become involved in the music scene. Become a performer, go to music festivals, join a folk or jazz club, enter songwriting competitions, subscribe to publications such as *Stringybark and Greenhide Folk Magazine,** take a songwriting class with an adult education organisation, mix with other songwriters and performers. Busking is also a good way of developing your confidence and your ability to project.

Judith Worthy – Romance Writer

Born in 1937; lives in Mitcham, Vic.

Writing achievements: Under her own and pen-names Judith has published over forty romance novels for Mills & Boon, Robert Hale and Silhouette Books. She has also published over a dozen books for young people.

I had been writing short stories for women's magazines, as well as children's stories, for some years while working in a variety of full-time publishing and public relations jobs when I met a man whose wife wrote Mills & Boon novels. He suggested I give it a go so I slogged away every night for several months until I'd written one. It was hard work and as a result I developed a very healthy respect for novelists. Constructing a plot, characters, background and dialogue, at the same time sustaining interest for up to 60 000 words requires considerable will-power, concentration and plain old-fashioned hard grind. For anyone who has a full-time job, it also requires considerable sacrifice of spare time and energy.

My first romance, *Hotel Manana*, written under the pseudonym Catherine Shaw, was set in the Canary Islands. I had been there for a holiday a few months earlier so the background was largely from information and atmosphere gained first hand. Nevertheless, I read a great deal about the islands, their history, geography and so on and also researched into Spanish customs and made some use of my Spanish phrase book. Then, as now, I checked all facts carefully as I believe backgrounds should be as authentic as possible. I prefer to have actually visited the places I write about but some authors manage to write very convincingly from book research only.

I enjoy writing romances. Anyone who ties themselves to a desk and word processor for eight hours a day without enjoying it would have to be crazy! The point is, I like writing for a living. If I didn't, I'd do something else. Writing a romance is not much different to writing anything else. You have to string words together to make a story, believable characters and authentic background, and you have to do it convincingly. The result may not be great literature but we can't all produce great literature; let's face it, there are thousands of so-called 'mainstream' novels which live almost as briefly, are just as forgettable as a Mills & Boon and end up on remainder tables, having made very little income for their authors.

The financial rewards for writing romance vary greatly, depending on who publishes your work, whether it is sold in hardback, paperback, translations and so on. Obviously the returns are fabulous for some authors, but for many others they are merely average and can be quite small. A great deal depends on what kind of romance you write (for example, contemporary, doctor/nurse or historical romance). It is best to start out with the idea of getting published, not making a fortune. It isn't as easy as most people imagine, either to write a romance, or to get it published. Time enough to worry about the money when you've cleared these hurdles. In general terms, however, the returns from romance are better than from many other kinds of writing.

One of the drawbacks of writing romances is publishers' length requirements. For economic reasons, most romances must fit into a given number of pages, so they are either between 50 000 and 60 000 words or 80 000 to 100 000 words (or more) depending on the 'line'. However, many romances are written outside these limits as 'mainstream' novels, but most new authors, unless they are capable of bestsellers, cut their teeth on the wide variety of contemporary romances, medical, historical, Regency, gothic and even science fiction lines. The only thing I dislike about writing romance is that it doesn't leave me enough time to write children's books which is what I most enjoy; however, it is too difficult to make a living writing only for children.

For anyone interested in writing romance fiction, I would advise them to keep up with trends in the market. Read widely in the genre, particularly in the area in which you write. By reading already published books you will learn what is permissible and what isn't. There are a few taboos, but even these vary from publisher to publisher and according to changing public attitudes and reader tastes. To assist writers, some publishers provide tip sheets. Editors are individuals and they influence to a certain extent what is acceptable. Whether there is a stronger trend towards editors requiring revisions because of the demands of the genre today, I don't know, but certainly one of my publishers asks for alterations more often nowadays than when I was first published. Every aspiring author should be prepared to take an editor's advice and revise, even if this is time-consuming. Good editors know their market and can often suggest very worthwhile improvements to a book. Never get annoyed by editorial criticisms or requests for revisions: even best-selling authors sometimes have to do them.

Advice for new writers: The first thing you should do is *read*. Not one or two novels, but dozens. Find a good one (that is, one which you enjoy or whose style you feel comfortable with), analyse why you like it and try to write one as good. Do not copy. Try to be original. Always remember that you are writing a love story;

romance must be the most important element. Don't overdo the background. Absorb yourself in the story and the characters, and be sincere. A cynical approach almost invariably shows. When you've finished the draft, curb your impatience and put it away for a few weeks; then read it through straight after you've read a few by other authors. Ask yourself if your work stands comparison. It's always hard to judge your own book, but if you're honest with yourself you'll have a fair idea if it's any good.

Don't be discouraged if your first effort comes back with an outright rejection. Put it in your bottom drawer and start your third (you should have completed a draft of the second while the first was being considered). Many authors have had to submit up to a dozen manuscripts before *one* was accepted. Practice does make writing publishable. Remember, that bottom drawer can be regarded as a resource for subsequent novels in years to come. No story is ever completely dead; it can always be rewritten with a fresh approach.

David Foard – New Writer

Born in 1948; lives in Oak Flats, NSW.
Writing achievements: David has written four novels, a radio play, twenty short stories and numerous poems. Despite this output, he has not yet been published. He believes in himself and foresees a time when much of his work will be in print.

Writing means everything to me and yet I am a realist. I understand the restrictions placed on my writing by the everyday need to pay the mortgage or eat. Wife and family excepted, writing is the single most important thing in my life. It fulfils a desire to express myself as a storyteller. I write because I have to. It is as much a part of me as sleeping, eating or breathing. I write because I believe in myself. I believe in my stories. I believe in my talent. Every time I complete a sentence, paragraph or full length novel, I achieve success. Have I been published? I am ashamed to say *no*. But it will change.

The compulsion to be published is an inner belief in myself, despite setbacks. Deep down I want to leave behind something of myself. Really, though, the compulsion is to *write*. Only the work in process interests me. I learnt how to write the same way I usually learn everything else. The school of hard knocks is a tough, but honest, taskmaster. I study those who have gone before –study, write, study, write. It is an ongoing process. I never stop. I am still learning.

For me the most frustrating aspect of being a writer is not being near my computer during my days off work. Not sharing my words with professional writers who understand and care. Not seeing my work in print, when other lesser quality work appears in whatever literary magazines or closed shop circles are prepared to print. I keep getting told that the work will sell itself, but it doesn't get a chance. I find now that it is still up to me to sell my words. Looking at other, published writers, it seems to me there has always been someone – a personal contact somewhere – who has helped to make the break. They say there are three secrets to retailing –position, position, position. There are likewise, in my opinion, three secrets to becoming published – personal contact, personal contact, personal contact. *This is frustrating.*

From the business point of view, and having been in business for many years, I can see no responsibility by publishers towards new writers. However, even as a business man I understand that if you don't buy, you can't sell. If publishers refuse to understand this simple fact, they will suffer. Not from the point of view of going out of business (for there will always be an over-supply in the market place) but they will suffer to the extent that the talented writers who *could* make the publishers money (a lot of money) will end up going elsewhere because there would be no loyalty to any firm who refused, as business policy, to nurture the raw writers. Publishers should seek out talent . . . help it . . . nurture it . . . and it will reap greater rewards than if it's left to walk unheralded through the door. I believe, too, it is the responsibility of the published author to put something back into the system; it is as much his or her responsibility to nurture new talent, as anyone's.

Advice for new writers:
Read . . . write . . . read . . . write. When you think you

have done enough . . . read some more . . . write some more. Like any profession, an apprenticeship has to be served. The techniques have to be mastered. It doesn't come overnight. It will take time. If you are good, if you have the talent, it will come out in the end; it is inevitable.

If you give in and 'throw the typewriter off the cliff', then you are just not made from the right stuff and you only get what you deserve. This is not the business for the faint-hearted. Rejection goes with the job. Believe in your work. You will know if you're lying to yourself. Be professional in your attitude. Invest in yourself and your work. Move with the times and get a word processor.

Richard Echin – Wordsmith

Born in 1923; lives in Narellan, NSW.
Writing achievements: Over the years Richard's writing has enriched the lives of family and friends – these are the people with whom he shares his written words.

Writing is simply a part of my life. I started at school and apart from writing compositions on unimaginative topics to satisfy teachers' requirements, I wrote for competitions in the local show. During my high school days I contributed reports and fiction pieces to the school magazine. Nowdays I write for my own pleasure and for that of others. Writing for me is not a hobby in the sense of being something to occupy spare time. When I write it is because it gives me pleasure to do so; or because there has been some stimulus; or because I wish to communicate with someone in a special way. I get the greatest satisfaction from knowing my writing has given pleasure to special people to whom I write lightweight, amusing letters or ditties on particular occasions such as birthdays, anniversaries or graduations. My writing also includes poetry, short stories and song lyrics. During my long teaching career I wrote mini-musicals for primary-school-aged children. Among some pieces written while I was teaching in the upper Murray Valley are two or three which have become (almost) part of local tradition. Two of them were published in *The*

Land newspaper about five or six years ago. As well I have had some poetry published –in newspapers, *Habitat* magazine, a Repatriation magazine and *Rocky Hill Lines*, a Goulburn publication – but I have never received payment. Not a brass razoo.

If I were never published commercially I wouldn't start growing a crop of ulcers because of it. Certainly there would be satisfaction to be derived from being published and knowing that my work was reaching a wider audience, but if my work were never published it wouldn't send me bitter to the grave.

Advice to new writers: When you have written something, share it. Write lots of letters and write as if you are speaking to the other person. If you can talk, then you can write. There is an endless source of things about which to write: start with yourself and the things that affect you; write about things you know about. Writing is like reading—you learn by doing. Use your five senses and you may well find that you develop a writer's special 'sixth sense'. Talk to other people who write. Keep on writing.

Merle Glasson – Poet

Born in 1912; lives in Port Macquarie, NSW.
Writing achievements: Domestic obligations curtailed Merle's writing activities for many years. She wrote, when she could, under pseudonyms (to protect the good name of her family) and succeeded in winning some writing competitions and getting work published occasionally. Her first book of poetry was published when she was seventy. 'My whole life', she says, 'has been a succession of Missing the Bus.'

Books in print:
Gently Jolting Back to Earth (Black Lightning Press)
Landscapes (Black Lightning Press)
Selected Poems (Black Lightning Press)
Woman on the Verandah (Black Lightning Press)

I do not regret being a devoted mother and loving wife. But I should not have spent all those hours making party cakes, sewing for school fetes and placating in-laws. For years it was dinned into me by society that a woman should avoid doing anything that might cause friction between herself and her spouse. My husband was always on tenterhooks that, because I had a university degree, I might not show before his parents and other relatives as a properly devoted housewife. He would have cringed with shame if it became known that he had a wife with 'literary pretensions'. I promised myself that my time would come. It has. Too late. I squandered my best writing years.

During my married years I did manage to have a few poems and humorous articles printed in the *Women's Mirror* and the old *Bulletin*, but all under the carefully maintained cloak of a pen-name. During those years, even if I managed to jot down notes on the 'inspirations' that kept floating by from time to time, I was generally too exhausted from looking after four children and a husband to write. My health was poor (worse than it is at present, and I'm now in my late seventies!). However, I've always had an unshakeable faith in my own worth as a writer, in spite of my failure to produce or to have most of what I managed to produce rejected.

As a child I was encouraged to write by my father who was an English teacher. However, when I found he was sending off some of my poems to children's pages (with his improvements) I stopped showing him my work. Then, in my teens, when I submitted work to women's magazines, my mother – a gentle, sensitive soul – was terrified that her friends and relatives might take my fictitious characters to be portrayals of themselves, so, to please her, I resorted to a number of pen-names, including Agnes Millrose and Sallie Morgen. The greatest support in my wish to become a writer came from Imogen Whyse, founder of the Poetry Society of Australia. She helped with advice and encouragement, and above all, by her enormous love for poetry. Later, I joined a small but very lively group, the Blue Mountains Writers, which was the one other source of real help and encouragement I had. (Even today my oldest and dearest friends still think I should be better employed playing bridge!)

It wasn't really until 1970, after being 'put aside' in what I considered an Arab-type divorce, that I bought an electric typewriter and thought of myself as 'a writer'. When I had what I considered a large enough bundle of poems printed in various journals (including a few prize-winners), I sent a manuscript off to a commercial publisher, full of confidence. It came back without comment. Then a feminist publishing group started, so I sent them two different bundles. Both disappeared, and although I made several attempts to find out what happened to them, I learnt nothing of their fate. One of those manuscripts has been lost forever, unfortunately, as I also lost the carbon copy during house-moving. Meanwhile, one of our Blue Mountains Writers' group, Barbara Petrie, and her poet-husband Dane Thwaites, set up Black Lightning Press, mainly to publish poetry. As I had already attended lectures on self-publishing by two different experts, I realised that the effort of running around doing all my own thing was beyond me, so I was delighted when Barbara and Dane agreed to publish *Landscapes* at my own expense. The total cost was $1566 for 1000 copies.

I had fondly imagined that sales of this book would pay for the cost of the next, and so on, but that was not to be. Even at $4 a copy, this quite nice-looking book had few buyers. Wherever I went – especially on a country tour – I tried to interest booksellers in my book, but with little success. Most said they were tied in with their usual suppliers. I had even less success with my next two books, but I did not really try to sell them. The costs rose for each one, but that was my indulgence. I would rather publish my own book than have an overseas trip or a new car. I am aware that paying to have one's book published is known as vanity publishing, but I am not abashed. For one thing, most of the poems have already been published or won prizes or been highly commended in national competitions, and for another, Barbara and Dane would not publish anything just for the money. It was a great moment in my life when Dane wrote to tell me that he had received a grant from the Literature Board to publish my most recent book, *Selected Poems*. I would not recommend self-publishing unless one has enormous energy and initiative as well as some savings – and then only if the writer has had some success with individual poems or stories.

My 'coming out' as a writer coincided with my readjustment to a new way of life after my Dismissal. I can now say, without looking over my shoulder, that I write. I am a Poet. Nowadays I tend to become tense when friends and neighbours are unable to see that I cannot afford to waste even a half-hour of my new life. In recent years I have written two volumes of autobiography, a few short stories based on first-hand experience, and heaps of verse. There is also in train an odd sort of philosophical work. All my present and future work has one object – to remind people of the beauty and wonder of this universe and of all the living and growing creatures, animal or vegetable, in it, particularly mankind. I feel that just ahead is the fine story, the important poem that will justify my life, the thing that has been waiting for the time when I finally have the freedom, the quiet, a place of my own, and the WILL, all at the one moment, and that all I have managed to achieve so far is nothing. I feel in my bones that I am only now starting. Starting, with only a few years to go!

Advice to new writers: Read, read, read! Old masters, new masters. And write, write, write! Write about what you know, your own feelings, your individual ideas. (I find people who have led long, interesting lives producing silly little stories about mistaken identity, improbable murders, seedy characters they would run from in real life.)

ADULT WRITERS WHO STARTED YOUNG

All the writers in this section were published when they were in their teens or younger; all have gone on to further publication and most are now writing for a living.

Michael Dugan – Freelance Writer and Editor

Born in 1947; lives in Surrey Hills, Vic.
Writing achievements when young: Michael wrote paid articles for

the *Age* newspaper when he was sixteen. Three years later he had his first (non-fiction) book published.

Books in print:
Australian Fact Finders (an educational series of thirty-two titles) (Macmillan)
Aunts, Uncles, Cousins and All (Macmillan)
Billy (Puffin)
Dingo Boy (Kestrel, Puffin)
Dragon's Breath (Gryphon, Puffin)
The Elephant Who Came to Stay (Rigby Educational)
Flocks' Socks and Other Shocks (Penguin)
The Great Overland Riverboat Race (Puffin)
Growing up in the Bush (Kangaroo Press)
Growing Up in the Goldrush (Kangaroo Press)
The Hat Trick (co-editor) (BHP-F.A.W.)
The Hijacked Bath-tub and Other Funny Stories (ed.) (Georgian House)
A House for Wombats (Century Hutchinson)
Of Human Beings and Chestnut Trees (co-editor) (BHP-F.A.W.)
The Maltese Connection (Macmillan)
Melissa's Ghost (J. M. Dent)
Messages in a Bottle (co-editor) (BHP-F.A.W.)
The Moving Skull (Hodder & Stoughton)
Neon Signs to the Mutes (co-editor) (BHP-F.A.W.)
Nonsense Numbers (Thomas Nelson, Ashton Scholastic)
People in Australia (educational series of sixteen titles) (Macmillan)
Race for Treasure (Nelson)
Spelling List (Macmillan)
Teacher's Secret (Puffin)
There Goes the Neighbourhood!: Australia's Migrant Experience (with Josef Szwarc) (Macmillan)
Time and Change (co-editor) (BHP-F.A.W.)

I began contributing to the weekly children's page, 'The Junior Age', in the Melbourne newspaper the *Age* when I was thirteen. My success in publishing here and in winning minor awards in children's writing competitions convinced me I should be a writer when I left school. After my sixteenth birthday I continued writing freelance articles for the children's page as an adult (paid) contributor. The money I earned was considerably more than I could have earned by taking an out-of-school-hours job so I began sending off poems, stories and articles to other papers and magazines as well. Although many were rejected, by the time I left school I had a scrapbook of published items.

When I was seventeen, I set myself the task of writing a book during the summer holidays. Over the next two years this book went from publisher to publisher until a dozen or so rejections made me realise it was unlikely ever to be published. By this time I had written a second novel (for adults) about teenagers and the way they saw life. It too went the rounds with monotonous regularity. Many years later I reread the manuscript and cringed with embarrassment. Then I cut out 30 000 words from it and rewrote it as a novella for teenagers and it went quite well under the title *Weekend* in a paperback series.

After I'd left school and was working in a children's bookshop, my boss, Albert Ullin, told me once I had published a book publishers would give my manuscripts closer attention. He suggested that I look for an established series, find a gap in it, and offer to fill it. This turned out to be very good advice indeed. I noticed that Oxford University Press, in their series 'Life in Australia' did not have a book on transport. I wrote to them offering to supply one. First, though, I had to write several pages of the book to show a sample of my writing, then I had to provide a synopsis for the rest of it. Shortly after my nineteenth birthday I finished the whole book. Some months later I arrived home to find a parcel containing my six author's copies. I stood, transfixed by the sight of my name upon the cover of a book!

Because of my youth the book received a little more attention than such a modest publication deserved. The 'Junior Age' noted its publication and I was interviewed about it by the Melbourne *Herald*. It also led to a commission for another book on the wool industry, but by the time this was published I also had two slim volumes of verse to my credit. My main interest at this time was in writing poetry, so, having achieved my initial goal, I turned back to being a poet. By the time I was twenty-five I had published three small collections of my own verses and edited an anthology of young poets' work. My interest in poetry led, indirectly, to my becoming a children's author when I was commissioned to compile an anthology of Australian nonsense verse. I found that I enjoyed writing for children and that ideas for children's stories and verses came easily.

I hope I continue writing until I die. If I'm not writing something I feel there is an element missing from my life.

Advice for new writers: Plan your story before you begin writing. Make a point-by-point synopsis so that you know how it will begin, develop and end. If the synopsis doesn't work, it is unlikely the story will. However, if the idea still seems good, put it aside and come back to it at a later date. The fresh approach may bring the solution your require.

Sally Farrell Odgers – Freelance Writer

Born in 1957; lives in Latrobe, Tas.

Writing achievements when young: At the age of twelve Sally had a story published in a statewide educational magazine. By the time she was twenty her publishing successes included two novels.

Books in print:
Amy Claire and the Legs (Macmillan)
Angie the Brave (Walter McVitty)
The Bunyip Wakes (Kangaroo Press)
The Cat and the King (Shortland)
Dreadful David (Omnibus Books)
Elizabeth (Rigby Education)
Emma-Jane's Zoo (Omnibus Books)
The Haunting of Ace (Rigby Education)
Henry's Ears (Macmillan)
How to Handle a Vivid Imagination (Rigby Education)
Maria and the Pocket (Macmillan)
Outside (Macmillan)
The Powerful Pickle Problem (Angus & Robertson)
Rosina and Her Calf (Hodder & Stoughton)
Rosina and Kate (Hodder & Stoughton)
Rosina and the Show (Hodder & Stoughton)
Show Us! (Macmillan)
There Were Cats (Rigby Education)

What a Day! (Shortland)
Winter–Spring Garden (Rigby)
The Witch (Macmillan)

As soon as someone taught me to print, I began to write. I must have been about seven or eight at the time. My first story was about a tulip; later I wrote about animals. Publication came when I was twelve years and eight months old. An acquaintance of my mother's used to have stories published in the NSW *School Magazine* and she gave me the address. The story the magazine accepted (and actually paid me for at professional rates) was 'A Plover Called Arnold'. I originally wrote this story for a state-wide competition in which it was placed second in the junior secondary section. The previous year I won $20 in the same competition with a short story, 'Under a Lucky Star'.

I was so excited about winning this competition! When I was presented with the prize money, the local dignitary said something about expecting to borrow my books from the library in later years. I wonder if he ever did? I might add I won the competition the following year with a story called 'Flood!'

The year after 'Arnold' was published in the *School Magazine*, my parents bought me a typewriter. May they ever be blessed – I have never stopped writing since. I guess Mum had become frustrated with taking down my dictated stories; I had to do this because my handwriting was (and still is) excruciating and very slow. By the time I was fifteen my typewriter had produced three more stories which were published in the *School Magazine*. Two of these stories were incorporated into my first book, written when I was sixteen to seventeen and published by Hodder & Stoughton when I was nineteen. *Her Kingdom for a Pony* was followed the next year by *The Room Upstairs*, a ghost story for slow teenage readers.

Why do I continue to write? Not only is writing a life-long habit, but it gives me an extra dimension, an image for myself and an escape when everyday life is depressing. (Also for the money, of course, though if you're interested, I only gross about $135 a week!) I would write whether I was published or not. I find writing fairly easy. The most difficult things are

(a) getting enough time and (b) having two active children under the age of seven. Mostly I write after 9 pm.
when James and Tegan are in bed. The book which I
am best known for is *Dreadful David*; however, I think
my most satisfying personal achievement is my
unpublished *Out of Time*, a sci-fi novel I wrote last
year. My greatest public achievement is the reputation
I have painfully and deliberately gained for being
quick, adaptable and capable. If someone needs
something written to order in a hurry, I can usually
come up with the goods.

Advice to new writers: Be adaptable, be flexible, be
persistent. And heed the old adage: *If you can't stand
the heat, stay out of the kitchen!*

Anne Farrell (Heazlewood) – Fiction and Non-fiction Writer for Adults and Children

Born in 1954; lives in Latrobe, Tas.
Writing achievements when young: A national women's magazine
published one of Anne's stories when she was sixteen. Soon after
she finished her schooling, her first novel was published.

Books in print:
Book Week Bonanza (Macmillan)
The Calf on Shale Hill (Hodder & Stoughton)
Eight Days at Guara (Hodder & Stoughton)
The Magazine Manual (Collins Dove)
A Night to Forget (Bookshelf)
The Organic Gardener's Companion (Reed)
Shadow Summer (Hodder & Stoughton)

Most of my scanty schooling was done by correspondence, and I remember writing 'compositions'
in serial form. As a member of the ABC Children's
Hour Argonauts' Club, I won a book prize for Poem
of the Month, and at least one of the club's annual
literary awards.
    At sixteen I wrote an article about the record flood
that washed over our farm. The *Australian Women's
Weekly* published it and paid me $30. My first
published fiction was also written at sixteen – two

farm/animal stories which appeared the following year in the NSW Department of Education *School Magazine*. I wrote my first full-length book as soon as I finished school. (I couldn't keep up the continuity a novel requires when I had to keep stopping to write other things – and still find this a problem.) It was the expanded version of a children's book begun at fourteen, a farm story about children with ponies and cattle. It took me three months to write in pencil in exercise books, then I typed it. My mother showed it to our cousin, Roy Farrell, who was at that time the Melbourne manager for the Rigby book publishing company. He liked it and took it to Rigby's editor, who wrote:

> . . . it is a very good story for a seventeen-year-old writer . . . it moves along nicely but without any great contrasts or any remarkable high spots of suspense, drama and so on . . . [the writer] will have to resign herself to the fact that first novels are rarely accepted. I am sure that if she continues to write, and if she pays attention to making her work more dramatic and suspenseful, then she will achieve publication at some time in the future.

My cousin took it to a second company which also rejected it, then to a third publisher who commented:

> I strongly recommend Miss Farrell to persevere. She seems to me to be a natural writer; I like her approach and think that in time, and with encouragement and good editing she could do very much better than this . . . she needs to tighten up a bit more on her characters . . . my daughter said that the most interesting character in it was the horse, and I am inclined to agree with her!

On this publisher's advice, my persistent cousin sent the manuscript to Barbara Ker Wilson. She was just about to start Hodder & Stoughton's new children's list in Australia and she liked my book. It was published in hardback in 1973 as *The Gift-wrapped Pony* and I received a 10 per cent royalty. [Ten per cent of the recommended retail price of the book.]

As you can see, I was extraordinarily lucky to have a cousin acting as my (honorary) agent. He knew the

publishing business and had enough faith in the
manuscript to show it around. Even so, this experience
shows that having a relative contact in a publishing
house is not enough to get yourself published by that
house.

Before my first book was published, I had already
written a sequel. Both - of approximately 50 000
words - took about three months to write. I always
tried to improve on areas that were criticised by
reviewers so each book took longer to write. Writing
doesn't get easier, it gets harder!

For me, writing is an extension of reading, and I am
an addicted reader. My first love is fiction and I write
stories for myself rather than to suit a publisher's
concept of the market. I write non-fiction for the
satisfaction of crafting it and for the income it
generates. The most difficult thing in fiction for me is
creating credible and consistent characters. In non-
fiction my main difficulty is keeping sentences short
and uncomplicated. Fortunately I'm better at editing
my own work since spending over four years as editor
of *Organic Growing* magazine. My pipe-dream as a
writer is to have a publisher, complete with market,
who likes the kind of book that I like writing. And I'd
love to be able to develop K. M. Peyton's flair for story-
telling and Antonia Forest's genius for characterisation.
But alas, they don't come with trying.

Advice for new writers: Read widely and learn to read
analytically to notice writers' styles and techniques,
how they achieve their effects. Do a lot of writing,
including things like diaries and letters to friends.
These help develop fluency. Make the most of your
experiences. If you have been utterly terrified or wildly
ecstatic, try to write down exactly how you felt, without
clichés. If your aim is publication, find out the current
essentials and taboos and observe them.

Doug MacLeod - Poet, Dramatist, Editor

Born in 1959; lives in North Carlton, Vic.
Writing achievements when young: At the age of twelve Doug wrote
regularly for a monthly column in the Melbourne *Age* newspaper.

When he was fourteen his first illustrated book of poems was accepted for publication.

Books in print:
The Fed Up Family Album, illus. Jill Brierley (Puffin)
Frank Boulderbuster, illus. Michael Atchison (Kestrel/Puffin)
In the Garden of Badthings, illus. Peter Thomson (Puffin)
Knees, illus. Jack Larkin (Picture Puffin)
The Monster, illus. Peter Thomson (Viking Kestrel)
Sister Madge's Book of Nuns, illus. Craig Smith (Omnibus)
Tales of Tuttle (Puffin)
Ten Monster Islands, illus. Terry Denton (Omnibus)

Plays produced:
My Son the Lawyer Is Drowning

I first began to write for my own enjoyment when I was in grade 2. I wrote nonsense poems as I was utterly obsessed with them – I much preferred writing poetry to stories, probably because I had been brought up on a steady diet of Milne, Banjo Patterson and Edward Lear.

From 1971 to 1973 the *Age* newspaper ran a monthly lift-out for children –an eight-page leaflet called 'Og's Magazine'. The editor published a great deal of what I wrote and it was the encouragement of seeing my name in print that spurred me on to find a publisher for my first book. I was tempted at the time to join the Puffin Club but decided against it because there were so few Australian activities (this was before the Australian branch of the club was fully established). Now I like to think that *Puffinalia*, the magazine of the Australian Puffin Club (which I co-edit), is serving the same purpose in encouraging young talent as the old 'Og's Magazine' did.

I was fourteen when my first book, a collection of nonsense poetry, was accepted for publication, but I was sixteen before the book, *Hippopotabus*, was actually published. It looked a little like a Monty Python product – my main aim was to make people laugh. I took a great deal of trouble over the illustrations, spending many weeks on decorating the book in a style that was perhaps not terribly commercial, but certainly striking. I didn't know much about book design then, so I made some tremendous blunders.

Despite this, it still remains my favourite book.

When I wrote *Hippopotabus*, I knew nobody in publishing. I simply sent off my manuscript to a publisher, the address of which I had gleaned from the title page of another book. This publisher didn't even publish poetry, so it was a silly choice. However, the editor, in his rejection letter, was kind enough to explain that a new publishing company was keen on presenting new work by young Australians so I bundled the manuscript off once again.

Having my first book accepted was the proudest day of my life – it certainly had a profound affect on my future career. The publication gained me quite a lot of publicity. I was sixteen and looked younger, so a lot of radio and TV shows wanted to do an *enfant terrible* story. My art teacher at school was particularly encouraging. And of course my parents were delighted. I didn't mention the book all that much at school . . . anyway, I was too busy there editing the school magazine.

Hippopotabus's print run of 3000 copies sold out and the damage that did to my ego became apparent when I produced another book fairly quickly. I illustrated it in record time and presented it to a friend of the family to have published as soon as possible. It was a nasty little book which lacked everything that had made *Hippopotabus* a success; I'm still embarrassed by it.

I find writing very difficult; it is such a hard slog. The most difficult thing is transferring the ideas to paper – making them seem just as alive in words as they were when I first thought them up. Thinking of ideas has never been a great problem for me, though I suspect there will come a time when I have to go out and search actively for them. I get my ideas from books, daydreams, long and silly conversations, playing Theatresports, being with my family, travelling . . . any number of ways. Attending the Victorian College of Arts (writing stream of the drama school; a three-year course) was very worthwhile for me, if only because it put me in touch with other young people of my own age and outlook. Many of the projects I've worked on since college have involved fellow students. It's wonderful to have that network.

I've continued writing because, I suppose, I used to enjoy myself so much when I started out. I can't pretend to enjoy writing now as much as I did when I was experimenting with all sorts of ideas, and didn't feel compelled to write something which would sell. Every now and then I get the old 'high' feelings if I come up with an idea that I think is good. I loved writing *Sister Madge's Book of Nuns* mainly because it started out as a joke with a publisher. I didn't even use my own name or address on the correspondence which transpired between myself and the editor. So far as the editor was concerned, I really *was* Sister Madge from the Convent of Our Lady of Immense Proportions in Eltham. If I can keep that level of amusement in my future projects, I will be writing until I am a very old man.

Advice for new writers: The usual advice is to *be patient.* Very seldom do I write anything which is good in its first draft. Most of my work is written out many times before it sees print. The permutations are endless. It is also not a good idea to be too precious about your work. Be open to suggestions from other people. Remember they are not insulting you by offering advice and constructive criticism – particularly if you have requested it.

In 1987 Doug MacLeod edited *Kissing the Toad* (Puffin), a collection of short stories and poems by young writers. The book was the result of an International Youth Year Australian Young Writers' project, a competition to find the best writing by young Australians. Here are Doug's comments on the standard of entries received:

For *Kissing the Toad* I was presented with a shortlist of 200 entries which had been culled from an initial 5000. From these I had to select about twenty pieces which could make up the collection. I wanted work that seemed to speak about personal experiences and I also wanted work that had a lighter side. However, very very few of the entries were light-hearted. Clearly, growing up in the eighties is no laughing matter. To be honest, the whole experience of editing the book was a little depressing. I longed for stories which were not grim in outlook. But would these have been true to teenage experience? Apparently not.

Overall I think that not enough drafts were undertaken by many contributors. Stories often had rather hackneyed plotlines and characters that looked as though they were from Sweet Dreams romances. I think these problems can be overcome if contributors read their work out loud and attempt to rewrite sections which don't sound right. Developing the power of constructive self-criticism is the key to being a good writer.

Mavis Thorpe Clark – Children's Author and Non-fiction Writer

Born in 1912(?); lives in Balwyn, Vic.

Writing achievement when young: Mavis wrote her first full-length novel at fourteen.

Books in print:
The Boy from Cumeroogunga (Hodder & Stoughton)
The Min-Min (Hodder & Stoughton)
New Golden Mountain (Hutchinson)
No Mean Destiny (Hyland House)
Soft Shoe (Martin Educational, Horwitz Grahame, Ashton Scholastic)
Solomon's Child (Hutchinson, Puffin)
A Stranger Came to the Mine (Hutchinson, Ashton Scholastic)
Young and Brave (Hodder & Stoughton)

Writing has been my profession, my way of life; it has given me an extremely rewarding life with much travel, interesting friends and interesting experiences. I was probably about eight or nine when I started out. I wrote the occasional fantasy but mostly I preferred to write about the things I knew – the cat, the dog, the picnic in the bush. This necessity to *know* my subject has remained with me. Although my first published book was written when I was eighteen I had already written my first full-length novel four years earlier. This was not published as a book, but was later used as a foundation for a newspaper serial. *Hatherley's First Fifteen* was the title of my first book which was published in Australia and New Zealand by Whitcombe & Tombs, and in England by Harrap. I chose to offer the book to the local publisher because they had an office in my home town, Melbourne.

The book was produced in England and I was not shown even the galley proofs before it was released. However, I was elated when I first saw it, and it set up my future course for me. I consider my books for young people, especially *The Min-Min*, to be my main writing achievement. In my travels in the Outback, I had the very good fortune once (only once!) to actually see a min-min. That sighting became part of the background material for this book. Another extremely satisfying work was my adult biography of Sir Douglas Nicholls, the Aboriginal leader, entitled *Pastor Doug* (also his story for young people, *The Boy from Cumeroogunga*). Another work of mine I feel is very important is *No Mean Destiny*, the story of Jessie Mary Vasey and her founding of the War Widows' Guild of Australia.

I have never found writing difficult, only demanding. The professional writer has to arrange his life in a way that allows him sufficient time to write. This often means the sacrifice of other interests.

Advice for new writers: Most writers serve an apprenticeship, even those who begin at a young age. Writing is like music, it takes much practice to develop a smooth, easy style. It also requires self-discipline. The freelance writer is his own boss. There is no one but himself to tell him to work regular hours, to be consistent and persistent. If he doesn't bring the discipline of a consistent approach to his work, he will probably never get beyond 'hoping' to be a writer.

Simon French – Children's Author

Born in 1957; lives in Wilberforce, NSW.
Writing achievement when young: Simon published his first (highly acclaimed) book at the age of seventeen.

Books in print:
All We Know (Angus & Robertson, Puffin)
Cannily Cannily (Angus & Robertson, Puffin)
Hey Phantom Singlet (Angus & Robertson)

I have always liked writing stories although initially
those were only the ones given by teachers at school.
By the time I was twelve, however, the ideas simply
could not be contained within the framework of school
and I began to write stories with chapters. I vividly
remember two stories I wrote in sixth class. One was
about car racing and featured my friend's older
brother as the lead character. The other was a school
story using kids in my class. At this stage I was already
using my circle of acquaintances as the basis for book
characters.

My first published book, *Hey Phantom Singlet*, took
about two years to write. A lot of it I wrote at school
during class time when I wasn't supposed to be. I used
the kids in my class (and the teachers) as characters,
often recording dialogue and incidents as they
occurred. Sometimes what I wrote was confiscated by
teachers and not returned, with the result I had to
rewrite the missing bits at home. As I typed up each
chapter, I'd take it to school for the kids in my class to
read. They enjoyed reading about themselves and
didn't mind the fictitious elements either, suggesting
other incidents at school for inclusion in the book. As it
turned out, I took notice of too many of these ideas and
Hey Phantom Singlet is a bit too cluttered. I rewrote
the book about six times, hence the two-year
incubation. From time to time I got sick of writing it and
set it aside. At other times there was simply too much
homework to pay the book due attention.

When it was finally finished, I looked up publishing
companies in the yellow pages of the phone book
(where else?) and sent it away. Five publishers
rejected it over a six-month period before Angus &
Robertson in Sydney decided to take it. The company
gave me an advance of $300 (a minor fortune at the
time!) and a contract for 7½ per cent royalties (later
increased to 10 per cent). Having commenced the
book at the age of thirteen and having it finally
published at seventeen, I had a bit of novelty value so
there was some media attention. My family and friends
were rather surprised at my achievement.

I had commenced another book when I was fifteen,
but it still hasn't been published. My second published
novel, *Cannily Cannily*, was released when I was

twenty-three. I've continued writing because I enjoy the highly satisfactory release of emotions, opinions and creativity it allows me. Also, I perceive a need for the kinds of stories I write – stories which portray Australian children in a realistic and believable fashion, echoing their conversations and reflecting their diversity of experience in our contemporary society. Ideas for stories really roll at some times, but at others what seems like a good idea just won't translate onto paper. Rewriting for a final draft can be fairly trying and difficult at times but I also find it challenging and satisfying. Ideas then fall into place and the textures that give depth to a story and its characters really start to happen for me. Material for stories is all around – people I see in public places, conversations overheard, newspaper articles, places visited, kids I grew up with or have worked with, my circle of friends, and, of course, some of my own experiences.

Advice for new writers: It's important to like reading books as much as writing them because reading gives you an understanding of how other writers achieve their style. This does not mean copying methods and ideas from others, but it is fascinating to see how a writer, such as Katherine Paterson, for instance, can portray her characters so vividly and yet with such subtlety. The other aspect which is important is to share what you've written with others at least once during your novel's development. Accept comments and constructive criticism as a challenge and focus on ways to make what you've written appeal to and deliver meaning to others.

Debra Oswald – Scriptwriter

Born in 1959; lives in Marrickville, NSW.
Writing achievements when young: When she was seventeen Debra's stage play, workshopped at the Australian National Playwright's Conference, was produced by a Sydney theatre company and broadcast nationally on radio.

Produced plays:
Dags, a stage play for teenagers and adults; won 1986 AWGIE award

Dancing Daze
Going Under, a stage play
Kindred, short film shown on ABC TV
Two-way Mirror, a stage and radio play
Episodes for ABC drama: *Palace of Dreams, Sweet and Sour*
Five radio plays for ABC
Twelve dramas for ABC TV Education
Several short films

Books in print:
Dags, play (Currency Press)
Me and Barry Terrific, teenage novel (Oxford University Press)

At the age of ten or eleven I first began to write –
stories and 'a novel' –but by twelve I'd decided to
concentrate on writing plays. In sixth grade I co-wrote
a play about the United Nations which my class
produced for parents. Earlier, at the age of eleven, I
won a Young Journalist competition run by the
Australian newspaper for writing a feature article. My
interest in writing for the theatre was, I think, stimulated
by attending plays with my parents at a time when
theatre in Sydney was in an exciting stage of growth,
with the role of playwrights particularly prominent.
Theatre was such an immediate, engaging medium –
it utterly captivated me.

During my teens the subject matter and style of my
writing was an odd combination of original and
unoriginal. Some of my material was very derivative. I
copied the work of writers whom I admired (usually
unconsciously); the rest was original, based on my
own adolescent experiences and feelings. Obviously
the latter was better writing, but 'copying' skilled
writers was probably a useful learning tool. Writing for
me was not greatly difficult. Trouble came in coping
with my savage self-criticism afterwards and trying to
solve problems with reworking material. I showed my
plays to a few school friends and to theatre company
play readers. One of the most encouraging
experiences I had as a teenage writer was when John
Bell at the Nimrod Theatre kindly gave up several
hours one afternoon to talk to me about a play I'd sent
him. I was quite well informed about places to send
plays, being an avid reader of *Theatre Australia*

magazine and a follower of the theatre world generally.
I sent my work everywhere for reading.

Between the ages of fifteen and sixteen, I wrote
Two-way Mirror in various versions. It was a 50-minute
play about adolescent craziness, psychiatric
interference and the intensity of friendship between
teenage girls. When I was seventeen the play was
given a full two-week workshop at the 1977 Australian
National Playwrights' Conference in Canberra. Later it
was broadcast nationally as a radio play on ABC radio
and given a pro-am production at the Downstairs
Theatre at Sydney's Seymour Centre. Being accepted
for the Playwrights' Conference was thrilling, like a
delicious daydream that I'd conjured for myself many
times and which had finally come true. It was a big
boost to be seen as a 'writer' and to be taken seriously
as such.

Pushing on with my writing career, I had a radio play
Our Hopeful Youth broadcast on ABC radio when I
was nineteen and enrolled in the Australian Film and
Television School. At the time the school was
disorganised, frustrating, creatively barren and
demoralising, but in the long run I believe that
attending it was worthwhile. It gave me an income and
an official identity as a writer. While at the school I
watched dozens of movies; this was not only enjoyable
but useful for my later scriptwriting work. Now I hope to
keep writing till the day I drop. I enjoy working in all
media – film, stage, TV, radio and novels. Writing is
never easy. I'm a very disciplined writer because I find
that it is discipline which gets me over the initial terror
of starting every day. The most difficult thing for me is
self-confidence – to stop imagining that my work is
dreadful. After six and a half years of full-time writing I
find this self-doubt has not diminished. I get ideas for
stories from my own and friends' lives and generally
from being a nosy parker. For commissioned work I'm
often given an unfamiliar subject; I find research a
fascinating and productive business.

Advice for new writers: Write. Don't just talk about it or
imagine yourself as a great writer. Write lots of stuff, hit
your limitations, crawl over them and go on to write
better stuff. Write about what you know; choose

characters and subjects you're familiar with and ideas you feel passionately about in your own life. Find a couple of reliable readers whose judgement you trust, who will gently criticise your work on a regular basis. Then send your work to every theatre company and so on you can find. You never know where support will come from. Be humble. See yourself as the young apprentice, devouring every play, film, novel, whatever, to pick up craft skills. Appropriate humility doesn't mean you can't be self-confident as well. It's the smart way to learn how to become a better writer.

Robin Gurr – Poet

Born in 1934; lives in Windsor, NSW.
Writing achievement when young: Robin wrote and illustrated her first book at the age of fourteen but had to wait another six years before it was published.

Books in print:
Harvest of Birds (self-published)
A House of Cards (Edwards & Shaw)
Masques (Outposts Publications, U.K.)
Music in the Grass (Outposts Publications, U.K.)
Song Is a Mirror (Edwards & Shaw)
The Tiger in the Head (Jacaranda Press)

I started writing little stories when I was seven but by the age of ten I was trying to write poems. My mother provided me with moral support in her conviction that my writing – particularly poetry – was worthwhile.

At fourteen I wrote my first (later published) book, *Red Pepper*, the story of a horse and his many adventures. It was largely based on my own experiences and on a horse I had once owned. Although I wrote this book when I was fourteen, it was not published until I was twenty because it hadn't occurred to me when I was younger to look for publication. I wrote it during my school Christmas holidays, just after having sat for the Intermediate Certificate.

Finally it was published by the Australasian Publishing Company in London who included it in their 'York Series' for young readers. The book was accepted on its second submission. The publishers asked for very few editorial changes, perhaps two or three minor ones. I was paid the usual royalties for writing and illustrating it. A minor nuisance was that the illustrations had to be done twice over at the publishers' request, due to a technical oversight on their part.

Red Pepper got some nice mentions in the press with one reviewer even suggesting that it should win the award for Children's Book of the Year. It was certainly encouraging when this book was placed in the school curriculum and quickly became a best-seller. I was a shy girl who preferred not to be noticed at all; I don't think I told many of my friends about the book's publication though privately I felt a certain pride in its achievement.

I soon followed up the first animal book with another similar one which was also published. A number of my poems began to find publication in literary journals and newspapers and I used some of my earlier poems as texts for songs I wrote and performed regularly on an ABC program called 'Young Australia'. Quite a lot of my poems written at this time were published by the Poetry Society of Australia whose president, Imogen Whyse, gave me invaluable encouragement. In my late teens I wrote the text for a song-cycle. The music was written by a young friend who is now an eminent classical composer. These songs are still performed and broadcast overseas as well as in Australia.

I have continued writing for the joy of it but find the better I get, the harder it becomes. On the other hand, the harder it becomes, the better I get. I have achieved many life goals, mainly in various fields of artistic endeavour, but nothing else has ever given me the same senses of fulfilment that writing gives.

Advice to new writers: Believe in yourself. Someone once had to say that to me, and it was the best advice I ever had.

PUBLISHED YOUNG WRITERS

Getting your writing published or your play/film script produced is difficult enough at the best of times. But to be a teenager (or younger) and have work accepted for publication or production is infinitely more difficult.

Nevertheless, a number of young writers – more than many people realise – have been successful. English girl, Daisy Ashford, had her book *The Young Visiters* [sic] published, exactly as it was written (with quite a few spelling and grammatical errors!) when she was nine years old. Over 300 000 copies were sold within a short time of publication and the book has been in and out of print ever since.

Henry MacKenzie Green was one of Australia's youngest published novelists. His book, *Clarence and the Goblins*, was written when he was ten, the same age Australian children's author Christobel Mattingley was when she had her first publishing acceptance, an article in a natural history magazine.

One of Australia's earliest teenage authors went on to become Prime Minister! In 1875, when he was eighteen, Alfred Deakin published a poetic drama, *Quentin Massys*, which is now a collector's item.

More recently Suzanne Holly Jones's novel *Harry's Child* (Jacaranda Press, 1964) was published when she was nineteen; Paul Radley wrote his novel *Jack Rivers and Me* (Allen & Unwin, 1981) at the same age and won a major Australian literary competition with it.

Quite a few young writers have later achieved writing success as adults. One is English author Joan Aiken who wrote poems in her childhood. As a teenager she experimented with short stories (mostly ghost stories) and at seventeen sold her first story, 'The Parrot Pirate Princess', to the BBC. That same year she wrote her first full-length book (for children) and entered it in a literary competition. Unfortunately it was never returned, and, as she had only typed out one copy, the hand-written notes were put away until she was thirty-one when she retyped it and submitted it for publication. It was published in 1960 as *The Kingdom and the Cave*.

The writing career of well-known British author Lorna Wood began very early; she was still in her teens when her first book appeared, a romantic comedy novel for adults called *The Crumb-Snatchers* about a mother and daughter who live on their wits. Popular Canadian children's author, Ruth Nicholls, wrote a fantasy novel, *A Walk Out of the World* (Harcourt Brace, 1969), when she was eighteen, while British novelist Ruth Ainsworth, who published poems in periodicals and won a gold medal for poetry in her teens, has stated that she started writing 'as soon as [I] could use a pencil'. Pamela Brown, whose novel *The Swish of the Curtain* (Nelson, 1941) was published at the age of nineteen, has commented, 'When I started writing I was still a child, and I wrote purely for my own enjoyment. On finding that it amused other children as well I continued to write for their diversion, and have done so ever since.' K. M. Briggs, whose lifetime work included novels, plays, verse and the enormous definitive *Encyclopedia of Fairies* (Pantheon, 1976) began writing as a child, and published *The Legend of Maidenhair* (Stockwell, 1915) when she was only seventeen. Dorothy Clewes, a British author who has published dozens of books for children in her life, began her career with *The Rivals of Maidenhurst*, written when she was seventeen. Many adult writers admit they were compulsive scribblers in their childhood years; it seems the habit persists.

Books about horses have been popular with young writers. The first three books written by K. M. Peyton, the popular British author of the Flambards series, were about ponies and riding. Ms Peyton, who has written since she was nine years old, had seven books published before *Windfall* (Oxford University Press, 1962), which established her reputation. The first of them came on to the market when she was still at school. Two other very successful young English authors were Katherine Hull and Pamela Whitlock. At ages fourteen and fifteen respectively, they wrote a holiday adventure novel featuring ponies and camping called *The Far-distant Oxus* (Collins, 1937, 1960). Illustrated by Pamela, it was such an immediate success when it was published that they wrote another three in the series. Three English sisters, Christine and Diana (twins) and Josephine Pullein-Thompson, successful in their later years as authors, pooled their collective ideas and time to co-write a novel about a horse, *It Began with Picottee* (A & C Black, 1946) when they were still in their teens. Diana's first solo book, *I Wanted A Pony*, was published the same year. Other teenagers who published 'horsey' books while still in their teens were Primrose Cumming (*Doney*), Walter Farley (*The Black Stallion*) and Helen Griffiths (*Horse in the Clouds*).

In 1967 a teenager being interviewed by the 'New York Times Book Review', said, 'teenagers today want to read about teenagers today'. She was S. E. Hinton, whose book, *The Outsiders* (Viking Press, 1967) had just been published. Hinton is not the only teenager who wrote a novel about his or her contemporaries. When he was seventeen John Steptoe, a young black American, wrote and illustrated *Stevie*, a novel using the young people and ghetto neighbourhood of his own life. Here in Australia Kathy Lette and Gabrielle Carey caused a sensation in the late 1970s with *Puberty Blues* (McPhee Gribble/Penguin, 1976), an exposé of teenage life among the drug-taking, sexually promiscuous surfing fraternity. Almost at the same time fifteen-year-old Simon French, bored with school, wrote his acclaimed *Hey Phantom Singlet!* (Angus & Robertson, 1975) during tedious history classes, as we saw earlier. More recently Sonya Harnett published *Trouble All the Way* (Rigby, 1984) and *Sparkle and Nightflower* (Rigby, 1986) because she thought adult writers for the young were patronising and she could do a better job. Sonya was thirteen when she wrote her first book.

Other Australians who had novels published while they were still at school were Anne Farrell (*The Gift-wrapped Pony*), Robin Gurr (*Red Pepper*), Christine Stewart and Julie Yaeger (*Six Horses and a Caravan*), Diana Bell (*The Rebels of Journey's End*), Doug MacLeod (*The Hippopotabus*), Mavis Thorpe Clark (*Hatherley's First Fifteen*), Edward Wakefield (*Ned Willoughby: A Tale of Love and Adventure*), Sarah McLeish (*Rambo the Champion*) and William Kelly (*Vietnam, Australia and Me*). Some of these writers (as well as others) have written of their youthful publishing experiences in this chapter.

Jodilee Eckford – Newspaper Reporter and Book Reviewer

Born in 1978; lives in Basin View, NSW.
Writing achievements: At the age of seven Jodilee was appointed Kids' Editor and junior reporter for a country newspaper. She also reviews children's books for two newspapers.

> My career started when I wrote to the local newspaper, *The Bay & Basin Review*, and told the editor the paper would be a lot better and would be read by more people if it had a page for kids. I did a rough copy of what I thought it should look like and the type of things it should cover. I pointed out that the page should be a total kids' effort and that we should have a say about the things which are important to us. I also thought that we needed somewhere that we could tell of kids' achievements covering weekend clubs and school activities.

The editor was so impressed with my work that he appointed me Kids' Editor and junior reporter. I was seven years old.

I love to read but I found that a lot of books that adults said were great were really just awful. Most of the time books I enjoyed were also books that other kids read and liked. I decided to go straight to the top so I wrote letters to ten Australian publishing houses to tell them what I thought of adults reviewing books for young people. I sent the publishers samples of my work and a collection of reviews I had written on their company's books and included a few of my ideas. Every publishing company I wrote to put me on its mailing list to review kids' books. I think all of the publishers are just great; they have been very helpful and have given me lots of encouragement.

After a short while I realised that I had too many reviews for one paper so I wrote to *The Shoalhaven & Nowra News*, another local newspaper, to ask if they would look at my work. My first review appeared in this paper on my eighth birthday. I am happy to add that they have continued to run my reviews every Saturday in their weekend paper.

I don't get paid for any work I do but I really don't mind. I am allowed to use any equipment at both papers and I get all the typing paper I need. When I am old enough to join the workforce I will have all the work experience behind me that money can't buy. I find that the publicity I get works for me. For example, when I write to any of the business people in the area asking them to donate prizes for my Kids' Page I get the same sort of answer, that is, they say 'I had read your work' or 'I've heard my kids talk about what you're doing', 'I'll be only too happy to donate an item for you' or 'keep up the good work'.

When I grow up I would like to enter the police force or become a teacher. I'm not sure just yet what I'll do but I know that I want to work with kids.

Advice for young writers: If you put in 100 per cent effort, you will get 100 per cent out of it. My Rhee Taekwondo instructor tells me this and I apply it to everything I do. Try it, it works.

Miriam Cullen – Playwright

Born in 1970; lives in North Epping, NSW.
Writing achievement: When she was fifteen, Miriam's play *A Roman Romance* was performed at Sydney's Seymour Centre during the 1985 Interplay Festival.

I wrote *A Roman Romance* over the fortnight of the August holidays when I was fourteen. It was to be a major assignment for the Drama Course I was doing as part of English. The play could be on any subject and of any length. With these broad requirements in mind I started writing. I can remember being very uneasy about writing a comedy. It seemed that many others were writing great emotional dramas of teenage trauma and world issues. However, after encouragement from a friend to whom I had read the first section over the telephone, I kept writing and managed to complete the play by the end of the holidays.

For reasons unknown, I decided to write my play in rhyming verse. Finding the words to rhyme was the most difficult part of writing (ever tried rhyming 'chariot'?). When school resumed I very nervously submitted the script three months before it was due. The teacher returned it the next day, wildly enthusiastic about it, and read it to the class. They were delighted and I was in a state of shock. At our school English classes in each form performed a play and the best from each form was put on during a concert for parents. My play was chosen and no script alterations were deemed necessary. I worked with my lovely teacher on the casting, directing and costuming; the production was praised, and I was still in a state of shock.

The following year the school English co-ordinator gave me an advertisement for Interplay. This was an international festival for young playwrights (aged twelve to twenty-five) which was to eventually involve seventy-two young playwrights from interstate and around the world in a series of performances, forums, workshops and rehearsed readings of plays. I convinced a generous aunty to type up my script and sent it in. I didn't think I had much hope of becoming a delegate as I'd submitted it at the last moment, but I knew that at least I'd get a written comment from these professionals who read the scripts. About a fortnight later the three comments came in the post, together with a letter of acceptance as an Australian delegate!

Participants at Interplay came to Sydney from all over Australia, New Zealand, USA, UK, Canada, West Germany, Mexico, Yugoslavia, Ireland, Japan and American Samoa! The experience of meeting these international young playwrights was incredible; their talents were of a very high standard. Looking back, I can't believe how lucky I was, not just getting in as a delegate, but having my play performed.

For the months leading up to the performance I used to travel for up to two and a half hours every Sunday from my place to the Shopfront Theatre in Carlton where rehearsals were held, under the direction of Kathy Henkel. I greatly enjoyed working with everyone at Shopfront and was quite pleased with the production. I suppose I didn't look at it too critically which is perhaps the case with far too many young writers. The play was performed five times at Interplay, as well as at the Shopfront Theatre.

My school and parents were very happy about my success and I got a page in our school yearbook, an article in the Catholic Schools' paper and another in the local newspaper. (The latter was called the *Northern Times* – my friends went around saying I was on the cover of 'Time' magazine!) Apart from being able to say I had a play performed at the Seymour Centre at the age of fifteen, I suppose it was good to have a backstage glimpse of the creation of a production by a professional theatre group. It was an experience to remember and one I would like to repeat. It made me realise it's possible to achieve anything, and that the theatre world is not hostile to young writers.

Advice to young playwrights: Just write. Have the confidence to realise you can write fairly much as well as the next person. Take the time to put your ideas on paper and know that your ideas are valuable.

Adam Boulter – Film-maker

Born in 1970; lives in Lurnea, NSW.
Major achievements: Winner of four national youth film festivals.
Winner of the Australian Teachers of Media (ATOM) Students' Film
Festival award.

Completed films:
Albie
Funeral for a Friend
Spider Slumber
Whelan

My film-making career began at the age of nine, when,
greatly encouraged by a friend who taught at the
Australian Film and Television School, I filmed a
documentary. It didn't win any awards, but it instilled
in me the will to continue and improve.

I guess my future destination was moulded around
this time as I was acting on stage, as well as learning
how to do stage lighting, sound and stage managing. I
had my own program on a local radio station and later
operated a mobile disco in clubs.

My first film-making success came at the age of
thirteen when I won the National Youth Film Festival
with a short feature film called *Spider Slumber*. When
the results were announced, I couldn't believe my luck;
I'd beaten other entrants five and six years older than
me. Naturally my family was very proud of me; my
teachers were pleased because I'd brought credit to
the school. (Sometimes, though, I feel teachers tend to
take credit for something they haven't really done –
they don't give me a great deal of advice, really. But
mine have encouraged me, so I suppose that's
something.) My first national win was followed by
another in 1985 and then I won again in 1986. I
amassed quite a few prizes, including rental hire of film
equipment to the value of $750, an 8 mm camera,
$150 cash, trophies and marketing and distribution of
my films.

My success in the national youth film awards
brought me media attention with interviews in local
and city newspapers and appearances on national
television shows such as 'The Today Show', 'Willesee

Tonight' and 'The Ray Martin Midday Show'. As a result of making films, I've started making many contacts in the industry. I enjoy the prestige of being treated as an equal by adult film-makers.

I've been very lucky; I've had a great deal of encouragement from my mother and backing and support from friends. Then again, if a local businessman hadn't sponsored me when I first began, I might not have made it this far. Over the years I've had to do a lot of talking to people to sponsor me as making a film is an expensive business. However, I know I have a good package to offer sponsors so I don't feel awkward about approaching them. The NSW Film Corporation, Spectak Productions and Hoyts Cinema all offered to fund *Funeral for a Friend*.

I went into films not knowing anything about the techniques involved in film-making – I've just learned as I've gone along. Making a film is not only an expensive operation but it's also time-consuming. I spend many hours negotiating for money and equipment, organising actors, choosing locations, writing, shooting and editing for each minute of film produced. My most recent production – based on an Elton John song – involved a cast of ten, a crew of twenty, camera cranes, makeup and costume design. A friend, fifteen-year-old Troy Rowley, did the choreography and we all mucked in to build tombstones for the film's graveyard setting. It took about a month to edit the fifteen-minute film.

With regards to the script-writing process, I wrote the first two films I produced; part of the third (*Whelan*) was written by a local writer, Paul Sommers. Sometimes when we go to the shoot scripts change as a result, maybe, of a camera shot requirement or because the sound track doesn't match. You have to be pretty flexible when you're writing a film-script.

At one time I wanted to go to the Australian Film and Television School when I'd finished my HSC but now I'm not so sure. I might just leave school without formal qualifications and see what happens. My ambition in life is to direct feature films. Stephen Spielberg is my hero – his work is pure perfection. I want to emulate his achievements.

Advice to young film-makers: First set yourself a goal. Aim for it. You'll get there. You have no barriers to achievement. Nobody's going to stand in your way. If an offer comes along to gain experience in anything at all, jump at it. Don't be hassled by detractors. Be busy getting to know and understand people. Make contacts in the industry. Get your foot in the door; let those in the right places know who you are, what you're going to achieve and how you're going to do it. Don't get big-headed about media achievement if it comes your way; just think of it as an experience. Everything you do is an experience.

I haven't got where I am without a lot of help from people, but I know that there's something in me that will always help me achieve and it's called *drive*. I'm not scared to use it. And neither should you be.

Michael Winkler – Poet

Born in 1966; lives in Tallangatta, Vic.
Writing achievement: Publication of ten poems written between the ages of twelve and fourteen in a poetry anthology, *Sextet* (edited by Virginia Ferguson).

The first poet I ever read was Bruce Dawe. Here was someone talking a language I understood; I tried to copy his laconic style and imagery techniques. My first poems were all about the bush, verdant forest, babbling brook, etc. Those which I had published in *Sextet* were about the similarities between school and prison, camping on an old gold-town site, the myth of freedom, the loneliness of the non-conformist and so on. The subject matter reflected what I thought was suitable fare for poetry in the Noble Tradition. By the time the book was published, my poetry had entered a New Era – adolescent angst and anguish; the old poems seemed so passé it was embarrassing.

Virginia Ferguson, the anthology's editor, was a rather fabulous character, a primary teacher whose special talents were noted. She formed and led a writers' club for gifted students from primary and secondary classes. She made up 'tasketitions' for us; these were wild and creative ideas and challenges for writing. Never was she critical of material I wrote. Rather, she would say that X was good, with the implication that maybe Y wasn't so terrific. Her enthusiasm was boundless. The teenage novel, *Puberty Blues*, was dedicated to her; it was she who pushed for its publication.

I was ecstatic when Virginia told me she wanted to include my work in her anthology. It encouraged me to write poems with more and more interest and gusto for a few years, until I suddenly stopped writing poems. Why? I don't really know. One of my poems was published in *Kissing the Toad*, edited by Doug MacLeod in 1987, but poetry writing didn't really interest me after I left school.

However, I still write, with the general goal of eventually being a writer, whatever that term means precisely. I tried writing a novel a few years ago (it was abysmal!). At the moment I submit freelance articles to a community newsletter and short stories to other publications. I average maybe twenty to twenty-five rejections to each acceptance. I hope that a few years' maturity might improve me by leaps and bounds. It frustrates me that I can't seem to write better than I do, but I pin hope on the passing of time.

The difficult thing for young people writing seems to be that their work is very rarely of comparable quality to adult writing. Our country is crawling with youth football and other sporting teams. Not so with creative writing outlets for young writers. Those that exist tend not to discriminate between nine-years-olds and sixteen-years-olds. Some merely function for 'under 25s'. It is ludicrous that the writing of ten-year-olds is compared with that of twenty-five-year-olds. The other perennial myth is that you can't write about anything until you have had Experience of Life, and hence something to write about. Jane Austen never went off hitch-hiking; she was never crouching in factories taking copious notes. It is wrong to assume that young people have nothing to write about because they are not widely experienced.

Helen Sargeant – Fanzine Contributor

Born in 1964; lives in Carrum Downs, Vic.
Writing achievements: Publication of over eighty articles and science fiction stories in newspapers, magazines and fanzines. Was a ghostwriter for a full-length novel.

My addiction to science fiction was well and truly kindled at the age of ten when the television premiere of the movie 'Planet of the Apes' was shown. I loved the movie and still do, but I was indignant that the woman astronaut had died before the movie began. I rewrote the script so she lived and saved the day. When I first started writing, if I liked a book I was reading, I'd try to write something like it. I wrote a short-story version of *Wuthering Heights* as well as various episodes of current television series with my friends in the lead roles. I borrowed How to Write books; one of them recommended joining the Fellowship of Australian Writers, which I promptly did.

About the same time the science fiction club at school which I'd helped form started a magazine called *Supernova*. I edited, typed and contributed to all seven issues. About this time I discovered fanzines. Fanzines are amateur magazines, usually produced by a science fiction club to promote the club and display its members' literary and artistic talents. A typical fanzine is *Spock*, the magazine of the Star Trek Club, Austrek. At seventeen I had my first science fiction piece published in *Spock*. Normally *Spock* would have sent me a complimentary contributor's copy, but I had forgotten to include my address on early stories.

My first real professional sale came the same year. At school I had to write an essay with the title 'What is the end?' My immediate reaction was 'if I don't pass my HSC (final exams), it'll be the end of everything'. Thus I wrote about the trials and tribulations facing the HSC student and submitted it, on a teacher's advice, to the *Age* newspaper in Melbourne. The day before my final exam, Mum presented me with a copy of the paper with my article in it. When I saw it there I felt excited, nervous, happy, disbelieving and slightly hysterical; like I could take on the world, and win. Someone was actually paying me (a whole $90) for what I had to say. It was mind-boggling! I was immediately convinced that study wasn't everything – as evidenced by the dismal 50 per cent I scored in my Politics exam the next day.

My scrapbook shows evidence of over fifty articles and stories I've had accepted for publication since my very first piece of writing (a poem) was published – when I was fifteen – in my school magazine *The Voyager*. Some of the fanzines I've contributed to are: *Spock, Beyond Antares, Katra, Metaluna, Big Bang* and *The Mentor*. As a result of my continued publication in fanzines, I was nominated 'Fanwriter of the Year' and invited to run a writer's workshop at a science fiction media convention.

Among my most notable writing achievements are payment (at the age of sixteen) of $25 for a thoroughly researched article on the history of my high school and inclusion in *Starlog*, an American science fiction glossy magazine. An exciting chapter in my writing career came about with the (paid) publication of an article I wrote about Austrek's preparation for the movie *Search for Spock* in the *Australian's* 'Weekend Magazine'. An interesting (and profitable) experience was when I was commissioned by a woman to ghostwrite a short novel for her. She supplied basic characters and chapter outlines and a rewarding bonus of $1000 when I'd finished filling in the rest! As far as I know, the book is now at a publishing house.

In order to improve my writing, I've attended a number of writing courses (including one at Victoria College) and have been taught by professional writers such as Hazel Edwards, Gerald Murnane, Philip Edmonds, Jennie Fraine and David Gerrold. Writing is now such a part of me that if you took it away, there'd be very little left. I write, I suppose, because no one else is writing the things I want to read. Besides, I'm addicted, and as I don't drink or smoke, it's my only vice (apart from chocolate). Ideas come to me easily. I want to write about vampires, robots, pregnant men, the Minotaur; I want to know what would happen to vampires that caught AIDS, what's an alternative to dying? I like to make magic. I like to sit in front of my computer and majik up characters and situations I've never thought of before, all seemingly spilling out from somewhere. Being a wizard, or even playing God, is the addictive part of writing.

Advice for young writers: Write, write, write. Don't let anything stop you, be it peer group pressure, ignorance or commitments. There are always spare moments in the day to write. Write what you feel comfortable with. If you like romance, write that. If you like science fiction, ditto. Don't feel obliged to write 'literature'. Join a writers' group, workshop or correspond with another writer. Compare work with another person. The feedback will help. Don't try this with a non-writing family; they'll praise you, no matter how rotten your work is. Read heaps, try different styles. Be yourself. I'm a mad redhead girl who lives in Melbourne. Not much point me trying to sound like Jane Austen or James Herriot. Send your work out. The most that can happen is that it gets rejected. Rejection slips show that you are at least working.

Sonya Harnett – Novelist

Born in 1968; lives in Box Hill North, Vic.
Writing achievement: Sonya wrote her first book, *Trouble All the Way*, when she was thirteen; it was published two years later.

Books in print:
Sparkle and Nightflower (Rigby)
Trouble All the Way (Rigby)

I wrote my first exercise-book-length story when I was eight. At that time I wrote a lot of highly dramatic stuff – kidnappings, people trapped on cliffs, etc. I'd start with a situation and let it go from there; I still work like that – without a plan – because I never really get *ideas* for stories as such. Generally when I'm writing I listen to music; I find this is good for gunning the imagination.

I started writing my teenage novel, *Trouble All the Way*, as a result of reading a lot of America teenage fiction (for example, books by S. E. Hinton and Paul Zindel) which I thought were trashy. It made me realise that adult writers couldn't write well for teenagers, nor were most teenagers' lives very much like those in the books these authors wrote. Life as a teenager wasn't nearly as exciting: it could be boring and savage and common, so I wrote about an ordinary teenage boy living an ordinary life in an ordinary household. Nothing much happened in it, because being a teenager is often dull.

The book took me about seven months to write, then I spent another year tightening it. When I'd finished it, I didn't know where to send it. I knew nothing about publishers so I finished up looking in the phone book and then wrote to two publishing companies close to home, asking how a manuscript had to be presented. Rigby's sent a more friendly reply so I sent my book to them. I had to make changes their editor suggested. One of the most amusing was when I was asked to cut out some of the stuff about girls. 'Do fifteen-year-olds really think about the opposite sex that much?' I was asked. I nearly laughed myself sick at the question. When the contract was finally signed I felt relief that at long last all the messing around, all the rewriting was over. I asked Rigby's for a $500 advance (it's important to boss the publisher around a little, let them know you're alive!) I got the advance as well as a standard 7.5 per cent royalty.

How did people react to the publication of my book? There's a lot of 'This is Sonya Harnett – she writes books' as a result. It has been an endless conversational piece for my mum. My school teachers as a whole decided to ignore the fact I'd had a book published; they never talked about it, skirting carefully around the subject to the point where other kids began to notice it. Rigby's organised a big author tour for the book and I received a lot of media exposure. Most people seemed more interested in the fact I was young, rather than in the book itself. Of course it was my age which sold it; had I been elderly – thirty or older – I'm sure it would have been rejected.

To this day I don't think of myself as 'a writer'; I write in my spare time, for my own enjoyment. This is probably the reason I've never seen my work as a kind of 'sport' to be pitted against others, to be compared and judged. In the world of your own novel you are a kind of god . . . the world is yours, everyone in it is

yours and you can make everything be as you want it. I
like nothing better than to be writing something I know
is going well; it occupies all my mind and it's a
continuing challenge to make each line better than the
last, to be clever with what you say and to do
something no one else has ever done. The last book
you wrote is always the 'major writing achievement'.
The advantage of writing while you're young is that
your world is always expanding and changing and as
a person you learn more over the years. The piece
you've just completed should be your best because it
should show improvement and greater wisdom than
what you've written in the past.

The best piece of writing I've done is a manuscript I
wrote last year, *Carnival Knowledge*, which is very
black and depressing, but that's how I wanted it. I
hope eventually to get it published. I don't plan a future
in writing. I can't, because maybe I'll never write again.
On the other hand, I may churn out hundreds of books.
You can never say what (if anything) is around the
corner when it comes to writing. At least that's the way
I operate.

I don't think writing is hard to do, particularly if it's
going well and you know what your next line is going
to be. The most difficult thing about it is keeping up the
interest in both yourself (with the story) and in the story
itself (from the point of view of the reader). I have a lot
of half-finished book manuscripts which I just lost
interest in doing, also a lot of material written for my
published books which was never included because it
wasn't good enough. I waste a lot of time writing 'junk'
but it has to be done sometimes, to see if it works or
not. If it doesn't work, throw it out!

Advice for young writers: As a writer you have to
develop a certain arrogant detachment from the rest of
the world. View people and places with an unbiased
attitude and pretend no one can see you – that is the
easiest way. Listen to how people talk and watch the
way they interact for humans are the usual tool of a
book. Make your characters real. And pay a lot of
attention to the world around you. Watch the way
people move, and listen to the world. Never see anything as boring or common. To properly write that a

bird was singing, you must know how it sings; you
should be able to picture it and hear it. Watch the
world, because it's the ground for your work.

Sarah McLeish – Novelist

Born in 1969; lives in Hawthorn, Vic.
Writing achievement: Rambo the Champion, the book Sarah wrote
and illustrated in class when she was thirteen, was published a
year later.

In Grade 6 we had to write a children's book to read
later in that year to the prep students. That first book
was *Rambo the Ram*. Then I wrote *The Adventures of
Milly, Lilly and Tilly*, the story of three stud ewes my
family bought when we started our Hampshire Downs
sheep stud. My third and final book for children was
Rambo the Champion, written when I was thirteen and
later published when I was fourteen. The material for
my book was based on particular events at our farm,
'Baileglas' in Seymour, Victoria. Rambo was a black
ram who was our only truly outstanding sheep! He was
given to me when I was about twelve by my aunt who
managed the farm. The book I wrote about him was a
true story (perhaps a little animated) about his last
show against all his rivals.

The whole book, that is story and illustrations, took
about two weeks to complete. I had to make a few
editorial changes such as the championship ribbons
being red, white and blue, and not blue, white and red.
One of the major editorial problems was when the
illustrations were being photographed for the first time;
all the lines could still be seen where I had erased
mistakes. To fix this, I had to trace every illustration
from the original to ensure that no unwanted white
lines were visible.

Rambo the Champion was originally designed to be
a birthday present for Sue my aunt, and Papa.
Publication had never occurred to me. However both
my grandfathers consulted a family friend who was
actually an author. That was all I really knew about it
until some time later. I had had a particularly horrible
day at school and was all for sitting in front of television

all night and ignoring my homework when Mum came upstairs and said, 'You've got a letter from Hutchinson.' Completely baffled, I said, 'Who are they?' Mum had not connected Hutchinson with the publishers and therefore didn't know either. I remember reading their acceptance letter a few times and then, realising what they were saying, becoming completely ecstatic. And so did Mum!

The book's publication gained me a lot of attention from the press because I was so young. My friends and teachers were surprised and pleased, especially my Grade 6 teacher who originally made us write books for the prep school children two years earlier. My book retailed at $9.95 and I received 10 per cent of that in author/illustrator royalties. Presently I don't have any further writing or publishing ambitions, although I may write some more children's books later, when I've finished school.

Advice for young writers: If a young writer wants to get published, I think he or she should consider writing a children's book because it is easier to write as a child for children. I have often been told to write more books now, even if I get them published later, because as an adult I won't be able to 'hit the same spot'.

Claire Williams – Newspaper Columnist

Born in 1969; lives in Candelo, NSW.
Major writing achievements: For several years, from the age of thirteen, Claire wrote regular newspaper columns. Later she was the founding editor of an inter-school newspaper.

My interest in writing began when I was nine when I converted my bedroom into the 'Book Worm' library. This library had its own 'Book Worm' magazine, complete with short story and poetry competitions, the prizes for which were a year's supply of 'worm' glue (a mixture of tree sap, flour and water). I had no brothers or sisters, and Mum and Dad weren't interested in entering the competitions, so I was the sole entrant . . . and winner of oodles of glue! I read – and wrote – a lot, mostly stories about vampires (which

terrified me), ghosts, poltergeists, witches and spies.
Through my membership of the Puffin Club of Australia
I attended writing workshops and met several authors
and illustrators. I entered some of the Club's writing
competitions, also competitions run by various
Fellowship of Australian Writers groups, local and city
newspapers. Some of these I won and I was placed in
others. What I remember with the greatest pride was
winning a commended certificate in the open section
of the Women and Arts Literary Competition when I
was twelve. I also got a real kick out of giving a public
reading of my poetry during Writers' Week at the
Adelaide Arts Festival – aged eight, I was the youngest
reader on the program.

I was nine when a poem I wrote, 'What a Difference
It Would Be' won a school writing competition and was
published in a local newspaper. It was basically about
conservation, the importance of trees in relation to
ourselves and the threat posed to the environment by
extensive logging operations. The newspaper
interviewed me about the win and published the poem
and my photograph. The attention this gained me from
family, friends and teachers (plus the prize money!)
encouraged me to keep on writing.

I was thirteen when I enquired at a Wollongong
newspaper office about the possibility of writing a
regular column 'Teen Scene' with information for local
teenagers on subjects such as future events, social
activities, comments on world issues and government
legislation concerning youth. To my surprise the editor
agreed; he even offered payment of $10 for each
fortnightly column.

My friends were a great source of ideas for the
column, and were my most honest and supportive
critics. Before each column went to print, they would
read and scrutinise my writing and they replied – as
did other readers – to issues I raised. I remember
sorting through a four-foolscap-page letter criticising
one of my columns which commented on what I felt
was general teacher apathy and ineptness. Actually
my teachers probably wouldn't even have read the
column but for the prompt action of my 'friendly' letter
writer. She set about interviewing all my teachers,
article in hand, questioning them on how efficiently

they used their time! Understandably, teachers regarded me with much suspicion after this little episode.

After a year of writing 'Teen Scene', I found my job as columnist redundant; the newspaper I was writing for employed an additional full-time journalist and all freelance contributions were stopped. Consequently I submitted my published columns to a weekly newspaper in an outer Sydney suburb and was able to persuade the editor there to allow me to write columns for his publication and for five other 'sister' papers. This time I did not receive payment.

Prompted by my publishing successes, I decided I'd like a career in newspaper journalism so I was very pleased when a council youth worker called a meeting to establish an inter-school youth newspaper in my local district. Only three students turned up to the first meeting. I was appointed editor. At the end of twelve months we had a much larger staff and were producing regular issues. I remained either editor or assistant editor for several years before moving to another part of the State. During my stay with the paper I received (as part of the team), a *Sydney Morning Herald* youth award in a state-wide competition to acknowledge young Australian achievers. [The paper Claire refers to is now known as *Livewire*: see chapter 9, 'Co-operative Writing and Publishing Projects'.]

Meanwhile I have undertaken work experience on city, provincial and country newspapers and find I enjoy the challenge of journalism. Eventually I would like to own a large metropolitan newspaper (not necessarily in Australia, probably in England . . . the *Times* perhaps?). If that doesn't eventuate, I'd like to write a sensational Mills & Boon romance, make lots of money and buy a publishing firm! Maybe someone reading this would like to go into partnership with me – they could supply the capital, and I'd handle the rest!

Advice to young writers: Writing is easiest if you enjoy doing it, and if you have something to say that you feel strongly about. The hardest part is knowing how to edit your work. Identifying unnecessary words or badly written sentences is often difficult. It helps to have an objective and constructive critic to pick up faults in your writing. It also helps to bury your short story, poem, etc., and then to reread it at a much later date. That way you can read your work more objectively and critically.

If you are serious about getting published, my advice is to keep writing. Enter competitions, as judges often provide invaluable feedback. Persevere. And realise that you are as capable of reaching your goals as is the next person.

Helen Cerni – Short-story Writer

Born in 1969; lives in Mordialloc, Vic.
Writing achievements: Helen is the winner of a number of national writing competitions for young people.

I first started writing when I was about nine. However, I was fifteen before I won my first writing competition – the Fellowship of Australian Writers' annual play, radio or TV script awards for people aged fifteen to twenty-two years – with a play titled *Ignorance Is Strength*. The play, about a family ignorant of all that is involved in nuclear war, was placed second in the competition and won me a $10 prize.

Since then I've won various prizes ranging from a trophy to $150 for short stories. Mum, who first brought home an application form for me to join the Victorian Fellowship of Australian Writers, has been very encouraging of my literary efforts, as have been my English teachers at school. I find out about writing competitions by reading the F.A.W. bulletin each month. If there were more competitions around for young writers, then I would certainly submit more work. What I found frustrating about those competitions which I did enter was that I only had about a week to send in stories; this is because I have the habit of leaving things to the last minute.

The most difficult aspect of writing I find is coming up with a suitable idea which can be extended to several thousand words for a short story. I've only had two or three rejections since I've been submitting work, but I realise my rejected stories weren't really very good. One of my stories was rejected by a magazine, but later it won a prize in a competition. When it was first rejected I felt depressed, but when it won a prize, I was extra pleased. I've entered several stories in the open section of writing competitions, but it's hard to compete against older, more experienced writers. Writers whose work I particularly admire are Shakespeare, Tolkien and Orwell.

Advice for young writers: Use your own experiences and incorporate these into your stories. I have written two stories based on real experiences which have won prizes. Make dialogue in your stories seem natural; read it out loud and *listen* to it rather than look at it. Finally, get an English teacher or someone familiar with writing to read and correct your stories.

POSTSCRIPT – A CAUTIONARY TALE

Sometimes things can go wrong when you have work published. While I was compiling this book, a young man (who prefers to remain anonymous for reasons which will become clear) wrote to me with a story of his experience of publication. He was fifteen when he submitted an article to a national magazine which subsequently published it. He continues his story:

I was over the moon when I saw that it had been published, but my parents were a little less ecstatic. Unfortunately they could see what I, in an euphoric haze of I've-been-published excitement, could not.

I fronted up to school on Monday still rather tickled, but found myself escorted from the school gate to my locker by an abusive and threatening group of perhaps twenty boys. I decided about then that something was a little wrong. The school corridor seethed with offended and outraged students . . . I had to walk amidst punches and abuse from all sides.

Not having either the panache or the spirit to brazen things out, I sort of existed within a little horrified cocoon of shock. It transpired that a worker in the local grocery shop had made 200 photocopies of the stupid

thing and distributed them to anyone interested. I was
vilified by some bloke on a local television program,
who challenged me to defend myself on the show,
adding that I 'obviously wouldn't have the guts'.

. . . [someone] allegedly made some enquiries
about the legal possibilities of the case. A meeting of
the local Country Women's Association developed into
an argument over the article, with some members
marching out. The 'helpful' school principal told me I'd
'attacked the sacred cow', that he couldn't do anything
but that I 'should watch [my] back'.

. . . Reading the article now, I feel appalled at my
tactlessness. On the other hand, the paranoid reaction
to it did ignore the fact that no malice was intended. I
rang the magazine to tell them about the aggro, and
they said that they'd received quite a few complaints,
but 'don't worry about it'.

As a result I learnt a hard lesson. There are still a
couple of people who won't talk to my parents. I was
paid $10 with $4 taken out for tax, approximately one
cent for every tear shed.

You will probably, at this stage, be wondering what on earth
the young man had done! The fact is he lived in a small country
town and had had the audacity to write a tongue-in-cheek article
about the style of football played by locals! In referring to the rather
patronising response of the magazine staff member when he
complained about how he had been treated, the young man wrote,
'he obviously never lived in a football-obsessed town of 950 people'.

If you are submitting work for publication, remember this
cautionary tale and check first to see if your work is going to
offend anyone. If in doubt, get a second opinion. For further advice
regarding libel, read chapter 4, 'Tools of the Trade', under the
heading Legal Matters.

12 ☆
SUBMITTING YOUR WORK

Manuscript: something submitted in haste and
returned at leisure.

Oliver Herford

The first thing an unpublished author should
remember is that no one asked him to write in the first
place. With this firmly in mind, he has no right to
become discouraged just because other people are
being published.

John Farrar

Editors are no longer father-confessors. Most of them
are acquisition editors who are more concerned with
bringing home the bacon than in trying to re-write the
bacon.

Scott Meredith

KNOWING WHERE
TO SEND YOUR WORK

If you are serious about getting published, then
you must learn to develop marketing skills. In other words, you
must become familiar with what is being published/produced and
by whom. This applies to all forms of writing, whether it is a
children's book, an adult novel, a filmscript, a radio script or an
article for a women's magazine.

Look carefully at the material being produced in the area you are writing for. You will find the requirements of publishers listed in publications such as *The Writers' and Artists' Yearbook*. Subscribe to the *Australian Bookseller and Publisher* and/or *Australian Book Review* (see end of chapter) which have up-to-date information on publishing and writing. Ask publishers to send you their company's catalogue or forthcoming program as well as their guidelines for writers. Supplement these sources of information by attentive reading of reviews in the press and by looking carefully in bookshops and newsagencies at books, magazines and newspapers. Subscribe to literary or specialist magazines if you wish to write for these markets.

The important thing to remember is to research your market.

If you have written a children's picture book text, for example, go to the children's book section of a book shop. Look at the names of the companies publishing those picture books you think are well produced. Alternatively, examine current and back copies of children's book review magazines (*Reading Time* and/or *Magpies* – see end of chapter) and look at who is publishing what.

If you want to write a magazine article, spend hours browsing in newsagents (cheaper than buying a pile of magazines!). Take note of which magazines are publishing the sort of article you intend writing; study the magazine's style, take note of the feature editor's name and the company's postal address. Send a query letter off immediately!

If you have a play manuscript ready for assessment, ask the Writer's Guild* for a list of addresses of theatre companies seeking new plays. Contact the Australian Film Commission* for advice on where to submit a filmscript.

Don't just send your manuscript off 'blind', hoping that you've sent it to the right place. Invest some time in investigating the market place.

HOW TO PRESENT A MANUSCRIPT

One of the greatest moments in your life as a new writer will take place when you finally launch your writing into the wide world. It could be a single poem, a short story, a one-act play or a 35 000 word novel that you are sending off into the unknown. Having sweated blood and turned that inspiration into brilliant prose or poetry through virtue of long hours writing

and editing, you'll probably be in a rush to send it away for a
professional verdict.

JUST WAIT A MINUTE . . .

Before you do submit your manuscript, give it a fighting chance
to make a good impression. Presentation of your work is very
important. You would be surprised how often editors comment
on the sloppy, unprofessional presentation of solicited manuscripts.

Here are some tips on how to present your manuscript to its
best possible advantage:

1 Submit only the best writing you are capable of. Proofread your
   manuscript meticulously for spelling, punctuation, grammar and
   typing errors before you send it. Editors have better things to
   do than fixing up your poor grammar or incorrect spelling.
2 Always include your name and address (you will be surprised
   how many people forget the latter).
3 Always include a stamped self-addressed envelope (s.s.a.e.) for
   return of your manuscript. (This is in case of a rejection. If your
   work is accepted, the organiser/company will sometimes return
   your s.s.a.e., or use it to enclose your letter of acceptance.)
4 Send postage stamps to cover return of your manuscript. If you
   are submitting overseas, ask at your post office for International
   Reply Coupons.
5 Manuscripts must be typed. If you don't have a typewriter, beg
   or borrow one, or have your work professionally typed. A typewriter (or word processor) is a writer's essential tool. Always use
   double-spacing with wide margins (top, bottom and sides) and
   number your pages. Type on only one side of the paper. Most
   publishers prefer A4-size, white paper.
      Include a title-page with
      (a) title of work;
      (b) type of work (one-act play, short story, etc.);
      (c) name and address (and phone number if you have
          one);
      (d) length (if short story or novel).
6 Make sure your manuscript has a fresh appearance. Worn typewriter ribbons are *out*!
7 Be careful how you bind your manuscript. Publishers prefer them
   to be unbound in case they need to photocopy pages at a later
   date. Spiral-bound and wax-bound manuscripts may look impres-
   sive, but they are awkward for photocopying purposes. Put an
   elastic band around the manuscript, or place it in a ring folder.

8 *Always* keep a copy of everything you send away. Manuscripts can and do get lost. Sometimes they are not returned. Carbon paper is the cheapest and easiest way of duplicating.

9 If entering a competition, always obey the conditions stated; for example, if the rules state a poem you submit must be unpublished, it means just that. Young writers especially should be aware *never* to send work which is not their own, original, unaided effort.

WHAT TO DO AFTER SUBMISSION

Be prepared to *wait*. Publishers can take a long time to decide what they wish to publish. It could take eight weeks (or longer) to hear if your submission has been successful. Sometimes editors send manuscripts to freelance readers for a second or third opinion. Editors do not take kindly to being hassled by writers: BE WARNED! (and don't make enemies).

Don't expect to receive a lengthy criticism of your work if it is returned (see below, How to Cope with Rejection). Sometimes, if an editor has liked your work but cannot use it, he or she might suggest an alternative publisher.

Questions New Writers Often Ask

To whom should I address my manuscript?
If submitting to a large publisher, address your manuscript to the Publishing Department; to a small magazine, The Editor; to a theatre or film company, The Script Assessor. Take the time to ring up the company's secretary for the name of the person to whom you are sending your manuscript and address it accordingly. Do not deliver your manuscript personally, and never expect an editor to take time out for a personal interview with you unless the editor has requested it.

Should I enclose a covering letter when I send a manuscript to an editor?
Editors are extremely busy people, so a *short* letter is all that is necessary. You need only say something like this:

> Dear Sir/Madam
> The current debate on intelligence testing in schools which your magazine has recently been highlighting, has prompted me to research and write the enclosed article.
>
> 'Idiots and Genii' is a humorous examination of the extremes to which educational authorities could go in attempting to classify children for the purpose of streaming them into opportunity classes.
>
> I hope you find it suitable for publication in your magazine.
> Yours sincerely
>
> O. Hanry

If you are young, you could state your age. If you have previously been published, it is a good idea to state this (briefly). Some widely published writers enclose a bibliography of their work.

How do I know my work won't get stolen or printed under another name if I do submit it?
Your work is protected by copyright. When you submit a piece of writing, make sure you write the copyright symbol (©) next to your name and the year of submission. Copyright belongs to you till you sign it away. Incidentally, there is no copyright on ideas, only on actual written material.

What is meant by copyright?
Copyright is the legal term designating ownership of created works; that is, if you wrote a story, you own the copyright to that story. No one can claim it as their own or copy it in part or full without your express permission. If they do, you can sue them. Similarly, if you wish to quote another writer's words in your own work, you must seek written permission from them to do so. Sometimes a publisher may ask you to surrender copyright; you are advised not to do this as you have no control over its future publication; besides, you may finish up losing a lot of money if the work becomes a blockbuster.

The Australian Copyright Council* will advise you of your rights, or answer any queries you may have.

Do publishers always contact you after you have submitted work to them?
Reputable publishers will *always* contact writers with rejection or acceptance of their work. Larger companies often send a letter

or card of acknowledgement of receipt of manuscript, but don't expect this as a matter of course; it is merely a courtesy. It is a good idea to keep a record of your manuscript despatches, acceptances and rejections.

What happens if your manuscript is not returned?
Did you include your return postage? Did you remember to include your name and address? If the answers to these questions are 'yes' and you have waited long enough for a reply, write a polite letter of enquiry to the publisher. The longer you can wait for a reply, the better. Publishers hate being bugged by writers for overdue manuscripts. There's an old saying that the longer you wait, the more chance you have of getting work accepted. (Of course the publisher may have lost your manuscript; that's why it's imperative you keep a copy.)

What are publishers actually buying when they buy my work?
This depends. Some publishers buy first world publication rights (that is, the right to be the first in the world to publish your work), first Australian publication rights (the right to be the first to publish your story once in Australia), non-exclusive rights (the right simply to publish your work) or they may wish to purchase your copyright. Always check with the company what rights they are actually buying.

Can you explain what subsidiary rights are?
Subsidiary rights are all rights not sold to a publisher in the initial contract. Thus, if you have only given your publisher the right to publish your novel in volume form, subsidiary rights would include foreign translation rights, the right to sell your work to book clubs, adapt it for film or television, or to serialise it in magazines, and so on.

The Australian Society of Authors* is well equipped to answer questions on contracts. It has a contract service for its members. You could also ask the Arts Law Society* for assistance with contracts.

What is multiple submission?
This is when a writer submits a piece of work to two or more publishers at the same time. There is some disagreement among writers themselves (and editors), about whether writers should make multiple submissions. By submitting work simultaneously, you may cut down on a considerable amount of time waiting to hear from publishers. On the other hand, your work may be accepted by all the companies you submitted to; this can cause embarrassment and hard feelings. If you do decide to make multiple submissions, it is good policy to let each of your editors know at the time of submission.

Do I have to send my entire novel manuscript?
Postage is expensive (especially as you should always send return postage to publishers). Many publishers prefer writers to send a sample chapter or two of their novels, along with a synopsis (that is, a chapter-by-chapter breakdown).

I've written a picture book text, but I don't know an illustrator to do the pictures; what should I do?
Publishers are more than happy to accept picture book texts without illustrations (most prefer it). If you have an illustrator in mind, tell the illustrator *not* to submit finished artwork. It can very easily be lost in the post. Black and white roughs or Polaroids are sufficient. If you are ever sending photographs, always write a caption and the name and address of the photographer on the back of *each* photo.

What chance has a new writer really got? Do editors/publishers give preference to published writers?
Unsolicited manuscripts *do* get read, despite what some people believe. The majority are read in-house. Editors will (naturally) be more interested in the work of a writer who has previously been published. But, rest assured, if your manuscript is good enough it *will* eventually find a market.

What do literary agents do? Should I get an agent?
An agent acts as a foot in the door for a writer. He or she has contacts to sell the writer's work and to solicit assignments. Agents also negotiate the best possible contracts for their clients. For all this they receive a percentage (usually 10 per cent of the writer's income. However, most agents will not represent new writers.

If you are determined to use an agent to sell your work, you will probably first need to build up a good number of publishing credits. Writers' organisations such as the Australian Society of Authors* and the Writers' Guild* will supply names and addresses of agents.

ADVICE FROM EDITORS
AND PLAYSCRIPT ASSESSORS

Note: A wide variety of publishing/production outlets were approached and asked to comment on 'pet gripes' they have concerning submission of unsolicited material from writers. The companies which kindly responded are acknowledged elsewhere in this book.

Comments from Stage Play Assessors

Writers would be encouraged to talk to us and/or find out about our philosophy prior to submitting scripts.

Do make the script easy to read – no smudgy carbons. Where possible, have it typed by someone who knows how to set the page out with good spacing.

The type of company we are (that is, a theatre-in-education company presenting issues-based theatre in a specific community) means that work has to be written specifically for the company; unsolicited scripts very often don't suit our needs.

Please don't send plays in loose page form with no binding to hold script together. We are constantly supplying bulldog clips to prevent the loss of odd pages. Very irritating.

We would sincerely like to attract and encourage new writing talent, but because of our funding situation our resources are limited.

If there were more good scripts written, more unsolicited scripts would be produced. There is *always* a shortage of good scripts. The reading delays are not cruelty or laziness, but an *inevitable* process.

There are no 'rules' . . . A good play is a good play. However, all scripts must be non-sexist, non-racist, etc. And scripts with small casts and minimal sets are more practical in terms of our present funding and resources.

Generally our plays are either commissioned or have had production interstate. It would be rare for an unsolicited script to receive a production.

Clarity of presentation (typed, properly spaced, clear stage directions) is vital. Sadly many plays submitted indicate little familiarity with theatre, particularly contemporary theatre.

Plays should be supported by a biography of the playwright, whether the script is available for workshopping and whether it is a first or final draft.

A brief synopsis of the play saves time.

Comments from Film Producers

Material submitted should preferably be professionally typed and bound.

Writers would be advised not to send material without making contact first as sometimes scripts can be lost or the producer may be particularly busy or even overseas. Therefore the writer will become frustrated, wondering why there has been no acknowledgement, unless initial contact is made.

We do not normally reply to the submission until assessment has been completed and this can take from two to ten weeks.

The only general advice I can give about submitting scripts is that it is foolish, I believe, to send the same piece of material to ten people at once. It's really annoying; nobody is serious about looking at stuff that wants to get involved in an auction situation and, so, my advice to anybody is to pick one person at a time, but not leave material with them for too long.

If a writer is also simultaneously putting out the script to a number of producers, please say so. If a writer sends you and only you a script because he or she considers you may be simpatico or whatever, that deserves preferential treatment: for a start, if you turn it down, the writer then has to go to plan B and start from scratch. This does not mean that circularised scripts are not welcome. They are.

Be aware of the constantly changing trends and markets in the entertainment industry.

It is important that material is as professionally presented as possible.

The ratio of unsolicited material that reaches production is 400 to one. Completed scripts from writers of limited experience are almost a total waste of time as they rarely get read all the way through.

Writing for the cinema is pointless unless the product is such that it can be promoted as an event roughly equivalent to the second coming of Christ.

I would like prepaid return postage if the script is to be returned. Any material sent without an explanatory letter as to what the writer wants from us by way of financial returns, options, etc., will not be considered. We regret we cannot provide a script evaluation service.

Comments from Radio Producers

Write to the Script Editor first and ask how and what material should be submitted.

The material submitted should be original, unpublished writing. Broadcast does not preclude subsequent publication in print.

Comments from Educational Publishers

Many writers who submit manuscripts to us are totally out of touch with what is going on in schools and with what children like.

Some writers set their hearts on a topic and cannot be dissuaded from pursuing it, even when told there is no market demand for it.

Sloppy, even bad, presentation of material is a constant problem.

Anyone who submits a manuscript to several companies at the same time should let publishers know. One author I know made multiple submissions of her textbook to three companies. All three accepted; as a consequence she made two enemies in this limited market.

Comments from Book Publishers

Never submit the one and only copy of your MS. All care will be taken of the MS, but no publisher can guarantee that mishaps will not occur and they will not be responsible for its loss or damage.

Because of the large volume of manuscripts received, our editors are unable to comment or give critical assessments of work.

While manuscripts prepared on traditional typewriters are of course acceptable, the advance of technology has meant that much typesetting can be done from word processing disks should the book be taken for publication. However, this must be at your (that is, the author's) convenience.

It is not necessary for the author to have illustrations prepared as the publisher can arrange for suitable artwork.

People who want to deliver their manuscripts personally are welcome to do so, but it isn't possible at that time for them to discuss their work with an editor.

It will generally take approximately six weeks for the work to be assessed, depending on the volume of manuscripts already awaiting assessment.

Our pet gripe is that authors hardly ever do any research before they phone up or submit manuscripts. I always feel authors should do some homework before approaching publishers as they quite often send scientific manuals, how-to-books or historical works to publishers that do not specialise in these fields. All they have to do is to browse through a bookshop and see what publishers are publishing what books.

Comments from Commercial Magazine Editors

Submit neat clean copy, double-spaced. Grubby copy creates a grubby mood.

Determine the required word length. Do not call and ask: 'How many words fit on a blank page?' If you do, we will not speak to you.

It saves time and effort to telephone or write with ideas, rather than submitting complete works.

Read the magazine articles and attempt to understand the direction, the feel. Think about your article in terms of the magazine. Be smart and check that your idea hasn't been published in an earlier edition.

I find myself losing patience with contributors who don't take the rudimentary precaution of reading (our publication) to see whether there's any point in submitting work. They're easy to spot because they never bother with getting my name right and often send me letters beginning 'Dear Madam or Sir'. People who expect a letterful of advice in reply also obviously have no idea of the extent to which they're trespassing on my far-from-limitless good nature.

The content of the story must be suitable for (our magazine's) readership. Stories are welcome which are written within a framework that lends itself to the magazine.

If your story is accepted, it is subject to any changes or deletions deemed necessary by the editor.

All stories accepted by our magazine become the property of our company.

Articles must be original, accurate and contain nothing libellous. We have excellent full-time writers who contribute to the bulk of our magazine so your article must be of a high standard.

As a weekly magazine we are committed to a production lead of up to six weeks, and forward planning of even longer. This obviously has a bearing on topicality.

We cannot comment on returned manuscripts. We receive a great many every day, and rejection is not necessarily a reflection on a writer's ability. Allow six weeks for acceptance or rejection of a manuscript.

Comments from Literary Magazine Editors

Preference is given to work that speaks with an honest, human voice. We publish work by well-known authors, but one of our main objectives is to encourage new writers.

We don't want hobbyists. Treat your writing as you would any act contributing to the advancement of the world's people. Be critical of your own work and listen to advice, consider it but don't chop and change for every editor's whim. The aim is to write good stories, not stories that win. Those who write only for the marketplace will end up there, peddling the same wares forever.

Don't whinge about rejection slips, we all get them. Try to write better. Always include a stamped envelope and the best story you've got!

GETTING WORK ACCEPTED

Having your first piece of work accepted for publication will doubtless be one of the highlights of your writing career. Enjoy it!

If your acceptance letter comes with a contract, *do not sign it in a hurry*. Contracts are legal documents and can be very tricky, even for experienced writers. Ask a solicitor (for example, from the Arts Law Centre or a writers' organisation such as the Australian Society of Authors – see chapter 4, 'Tools of the Trade', under the heading Legal Matters) to go over each clause for you, and, if necessary, explain the small print. A very helpful book is Colin Golvan and Michael McDonald's *Writers and the Law* (see also end of chapter 4).

Contracts are always negotiable (*before* signature); you do not have to agree with everything written on them. Many authors refuse to sign the 'Option Clause' which makes it compulsory for the author to submit subsequent manuscripts to the publisher who holds their previous book contract; others negotiate about royalties offered, or subsidiary rights, etc. Reputable publishers respect your right to negotiate these points. Never rely on a verbal agreement.

Most newspapers and magazines do not send contracts; the terms they offer are generally spelt out in the acceptance letter. Payment is sometimes on acceptance, sometimes on publication. You should expect a by-line on your article.

A point worth noting: if an editor ever asks you for alterations, or even commissions work from you, never miss the deadline specified. A writer known to be reliable will be given preference to a better writer who can't be trusted to deliver on time.

HOW TO COPE WITH REJECTION

Rejection slips are like colds; everyone gets them,
some people catch them more often than others.
                                        Norman Hidden

The greatest recorded number of publishers'
rejections for a manuscript is 223 for *World
Government Crusade*.
                                Guinness Book of Records

It doesn't matter how good your writing is, sooner
or later (probably sooner), you are going to get a rejection slip.
This can take the form of a slip of paper with the publisher's/
organiser's name and address on it (usually paper-clipped to the
top right-hand side of your manuscript). Rejection might also come
in the shape of a brief but formal, 'We thank you for your contribution
but regret we are unable to use it'. Some publishers have been
known to return manuscripts without any acknowledgment at all,
while others (much nicer!) occasionally state the reason why they
are returning your work ('We feel you have not developed the
characters or plot sufficiently').

There are many reasons why manuscripts are rejected. It could
be that your writing is just not up to standard, the magazine to
which you have submitted it may have enough material for its
next ten issues, you may have sent it to the wrong place, the editor
may have already accepted another poem or short story just as
good as yours on exactly the same topic.

What you have to remember is that there are many more writers
than there are competitions and markets, so there are bound to
be many more rejections than acceptances. Rejections don't just
happen to you. They happen to *all* writers, young, old, amateur,
professional. After receiving 743 rejection slips, the British mystery
writer John Creasey M.B.E. had 564 books published. One of the
twentieth-century's most influential writers, James Joyce, had his
first book *Dubliners* returned twenty-two times. Other books which
were rejected at least once are *Gone With the Wind, Room at the
Top, Catch 22,* and *Watership Down*. Professor Steven Goldberg's
book *The Inevitability of Patriarchy* was rejected sixty-nine times by
fifty-five publishers before it was accepted for publication. History
abounds with stories of rejected books which became classics.

The best way to cope with rejection is to accept that it is going
to happen one time or another and to forget about it. Concentrate
on your current writing project. If you regularly send work out,

you will more likely than not receive the most wonderful of treasures: a letter saying, 'We like your story/poem enough to publish it' or 'Congratulations, you have won a prize in our writing competition'. Don't let rejection be your excuse for giving up. Persevere.

What to Do with Rejected Work

If you believe in the quality of your rejected manuscript, then try it again elsewhere, repeatedly, until you run out of competitions or markets or you decide it really isn't up to standard. If a rejection slip does include the reasons for your work being rejected, then take the hint. Look at your manuscript and develop the plot or characters or whatever it is that the editor says needs fixing.

VANITY PUBLISHING

Sometimes, in a newspaper or magazine, you may have seen an advertisement like this:

MANUSCRIPTS WANTED!
We will publish your book.
FREE appraisal.

For an unpublished writer itching to see his or her name in print, this offer can be very tempting. Unfortunately, these ads are always placed by vanity presses (sometimes called 'subsidy publishers'). These companies invariably praise the novice's manuscript, accept it for publication, then offer a contract which promises royalty payments to the author (usually 40 per cent), *provided* the author is willing to pay the cost of the print run of the book. In other words, *the author takes all the risks*. No conventional publisher would ever ask an author to pay production costs. That is part of the risk the conventional publisher takes, and the reason why it is so difficult to be published through one.

The vanity press doesn't need to sell a single book to make a profit. The author pays the cost of printing, then has to buy the books from the press and *share* the royalties. Most vanity publishers do not spend much time on editing manuscripts nor do they promote their books satisfactorily; the quality of their publications is usually so poor in writing and editing, and the production so shoddy that most experienced reviewers will not waste time looking at them.

Vanity press publication is only for people who want to see their book in print, who don't care how much it costs and who do not care whether or not it sells.

SELF-PUBLISHING

Many famous authors – D. H. Lawrence, Mark Twain, Virginia Woolf, James Joyce, Gertrude Stein, Zane Grey and William Blake, to mention a few – self published at some time in their lives, some because they were unable to get their books accepted by conventional publishers, others because they were dissatisfied with the way their existing publishers treated them and their work.

Any author can self-publish and many do. The greatest benefit of self-publishing is that you, the author, retain complete control over your work. Probably the biggest drawback to self-publishing is the initial cost; you need money to self-publish.

Self-publishing encompasses a wide range of methods. The more ambitious author may wish to publish a full-length, bound novel or family history; others less ambitious may be happy to type poems or stories on A4 pages and photocopy them for distribution to family and friends.

If you wish to self-publish a book for sale to the public you will need to look at the areas of typesetting, design, printing, advertising and distribution. Depending on how much money you have available to publish your book, you can typeset the manuscript yourself on a typewriter or word processor, you can hire a typist to prepare the final manuscript, or you can pay a printer to do the typesetting. If you decide on the latter, it is advisable first to obtain quotes from a number of printers (they are listed in the Yellow Pages of your phone directory). Some printeries do not do the actual typesetting, but may refer you to companies which do. If your book is professionally typeset, you should receive galley or page proofs so you can proofread pages before they are printed.

Discuss with your printer your exact requirements. You will need to decide such matters as size of book, paper quality, number and kind of illustrations, type of cover and binding and the number of books to be published.

Distribution and Marketing

Getting your book to the public is a real problem for the self-publisher. You could attempt to sell copies yourself by word of mouth. You could set up a stall at an open-air market or make the round of bookshops, placing copies on a sale and return basis. Alternatively, you could try to sell by direct mail, through commissioned salespeople or via a distribution company. In promoting your book you could place classified advertisements in select newspapers or magazines. Depending on your resources, you might be able to promote your book through an author interview on television or radio, a media story or author appearances at bookshops and other places where the book is likely to sell well. You might (if you are lucky) be able to persuade people to review your book favourably. Marketing your own book successfully requires a lot of hard work and the ability to 'push' your product.

Entitlements

The government pays a bounty on books which meet certain requirements to help meet the cost of printing; ask your printer about your book's eligibility for bounty. As well, you may be entitled, if your book is sold to libraries, to claim Public Lending Rights (money paid annually to both author and publisher for estimated numbers of copies of books in Australian public lending libraries). You will also need an ISBN (International Standard Book Number) for your title and you will need to deliver free copies to the National Library of Australia and your own State Library to be eligible. Ask about ISBN numbering at the National Library (Canberra, ACT) and when you've fulfilled the requirements make a Public Lending Rights claim as both author and publisher by writing to Public Lending Rights.*

A service is offered to authors and institutions for self-publishing by Boolarong Publications.*

Note: For further information about self-publishing, see Serge Liberman's story in chapter 11, 'Published Writers Speak'.

CO-OPERATIVE PUBLISHING

Sometimes groups of writers such as friends or members of a writing group get together on a co-operative basis to publish a book or a series of books. Each person in the group may put up a sum of money to get their group's work into print. Alternatively, a properly constituted group may be able to obtain funding from a government agency (such as a local council or state or federal arts body) or from a commercial organisation.

The group may decide to publish an anthology of members' work on a one-off or regular basis, or they may decide to publish single volumes of individuals' writings so that eventually the work of each member of the co-operative is published.

The main advantage of this method of publication is that costs (and losses, if any) are shared. Because there are a number of people involved, each writer's manuscript stands a better chance of being workshopped and/or edited than if it had been self-published. Additionally, the large group means that enthusiasm can be generated and this is particularly useful when it comes to promoting, distributing and selling the published work/s.

Books published by co-operatives may be eligible for Book Bounty and Public Lending Rights (see above). As well, contact the Literary Arts Board of the Australia Council for details of publishing subsidies which may be available.

Note: For some examples of successful co-operative publishing ventures, see chapter 9, 'Co-operative Writing and Publishing Projects'.

HELPFUL BOOKS

Robin Bromby, *Writing for Profit in Australia*, Cromarty Press, Narrabeen, NSW, 1987.

Joanna Beaumont, *How to Do Your Own Publishing*, Orlando Press, Rozelle, NSW, 1985.

Bill Hornadge, *How to Publish Your Own Book*, 3rd edn, Review Publications,* Dubbo, NSW, 1986.

Barbara Jefferis, *Australian Book Contracts*, Australian Society of Authors,* Milson's Point, NSW, c.1983.

Writers' and Artists' Yearbook (a directory for writers, artists, playwrights, writers for film, radio and television, photographers and composers; published annually), A & C Black, London.

*Australian Book Review** ($35 p.a.)
*Australian Bookseller & Publisher** ($30 p.a.)
Reading Time (Children's Book Council of Australia)* ($16 p.a.)
*Magpies** ($20 p.a.)

USEFUL CONTACTS

Registers of freelance publishing services, containing names and addresses of professionals offering editorial services, layout experience, publishing consultancy, manuscript evaluations, indexing, etc., are available free of charge from the Society of Editors* in New South Wales, Victoria and Tasmania.

13 ☆
MARKETS AND COMPETITIONS

ADVICE FOR THE AMBITIOUS

Perhaps you feel the time has come in your writing career when you would like to test your talent on the market place.

Listed on the following pages are a number of avenues you might like to pursue. They are accurate at the time of going to press, but circumstances change. Most of the competitions listed here are held annually, but they may be discontinued by the time you get around to entering them. Prize monies, conditions of entry and so on, may change; you would be advised to contact the publishers or organisers at the addresses given below *first*. Ask for a copy of conditions and an entry form. Always include a stamped, self-addressed envelope (s.s.a.e.) for return of material. New writers often neglect to do this. It is a discourtesy not to do so. You may find you do not get a reply if you do not send the s.s.a.e.

Remember, when you are submitting work to markets and competitions always present your work professionally (as outlined in the previous chapter).

SHORT-STORY AND POETRY MARKETS

Literary magazines as well as some commercial magazines, annuals, newspapers and radio stations publish short stories and poetry. Some of the better-known literary magazines which accept poetry and/or short stories for publication are: *Australian Short Stories, Hecate, Helix, Island Magazine, Linq, Luna, Mattoid, Meanjin, Overland, Poetry Australia, Quadrant, Scripsi, Southerly*, and *Westerly*.

Other magazines which have more recently appeared on the market are: *Brave New Word, Fine Line, Fremantle Arts Review, Going Down Swinging, Islands, Northern Perspective, Outrider, Oz-Wide Tales, Peninsula Writing, Phoenix, P76, Scarp, Storytellers*, and many others.

Newspapers which publish poetry and short stories are: *Adelaide Review, Age, Australian, Bendigo Advertiser, Canberra Times, Sydney Morning Herald*, and others.

You can purchase guides which show details of short-story and poetry outlets for established and aspiring writers from:

Arts Council of Australia* (ask for *Poetry and Short Story Guide*)

Australian Writers' Professional Service* (ask for *Writers' and Photographers' Marketing Guide*)

Australian Library Promotion Council* (ask for *Bookmark Diary and Directory*, hardback)

Australian Society of Authors* (ask for *The Australian and New Zealand Writers' Handbook*, hardback)

Australian News Syndicate* (ask for the *Australian Writers' Market*).

Other helpful publications are Robin Cromby's *Writing for Profit in Australia* and the *Writers' and Artists' Yearbook* (see end of chapter 12, 'Submitting Your Work' under heading Helpful Books).

New and existing magazines are often publicised each month in the *Victorian F.A.W. Newsletter*.*

MAGAZINES AND NEWSPAPERS

A visit to any newsagency will quickly reveal the enormous volume of magazines and newspapers to which you can submit material. Generally submission details are outlined on the inside page of these publications. For an up-to-date, detailed list of Australian newspapers, magazines, ethnic publications, newsletters, radio and television stations, obtain *Margaret Gee's Media Guide** (this guide is issued three times a year for a very moderate cost).

Another helpful guide to possible media markets is *Australian Serials in Print*.*

For New Zealand markets obtain the *Media Planner* from the Press Research Bureau.*

Magazine Markets for Young Writers

There are not many magazines – and even fewer newspapers – which publish work by young people. As a result, competition is stiff. Here are some possibilities:

Roles
A quarterly magazine of poetry, prose and plays written by young people under the age of eighteen. Available by subscription from Shopfront Theatre for Young People.*

*Hero**
A glossy bi-monthly fashion and lifestyle magazine aimed at fourteen- to twenty-year-olds. It is available from newsagents. The editors state they are interested in purchasing articles on live events, film reviews and fiction from writers up to the age of twenty-five. Payment. Unpublished work is not returned.

Puffinalia
This quarterly national magazine of the Puffin Club of Australia* (Penguin Books), regularly publishes short stories and poems by writers under the age of sixteen. Occasionally the work of outstanding young writers is featured in a 'Puffineer Profile'. *Puffinalia* is only available by subscription and only members are eligible to have work published or to enter the magazine's numerous competitions. School or family membership is available.

Jetsetter
This magazine, which features competitions, articles on pop stars, art and craft ideas, etc., occasionally publishes verse and short stories by young people. It is available through subscription from Jetsetters of Australia.* Only members' work is published.

*Going Down Swinging**
The editors have stated that they are particularly seeking work from new and young writers.

BHP-F.A.W. Publishing Project
This is an award which takes the form of a special publishing project, an annual book of poetry by young Australians aged fifteen to twenty-two years. Previous titles are *Neon Signs to the Mutes, Of Human Beings and Chestnut Trees,* and *Messages in a Bottle.* Write to the Secretary, Victorian Fellowship of Australian Writers.

Kwopitak*
Fiction magazine (stories and poems) for previously unpublished writing by Aboriginal secondary school students and adults for secondary school and adult readers. One issue p.a. No payment to contributors.

Dolly*
This glossy magazine, popular with young women, has a 'Poet's Corner' where contributors' poetry is published. Payment not specified.

Contagious*
A new magazine for children in the nine to eleven age group, this publication seeks work from writers of all ages. Teenagers and children must indicate their age on all contributions. Work is to be original and unpublished.

Brave New Word*
Strictly speaking, this magazine does not publish work exclusively by young people; however, the editors state they attempt to encourage work by new and unpublished writers. They also offer a literary criticism service (charges unknown).

Geek Speak*
This irregularly published magazine encourages publication of work by young writers as well as old. Its stated aim is 'to encourage liberal and free thought through individualistic and light-hearted expression'. Contributors are not paid.

Kids Zone!*
Originally known as Kids Only!, this colourful monthly magazine for young people publishes poetry, stories and drawings submitted by its subscribers. Payment is $5 per contribution.

Aussie Kids*
Reporters under the age of twelve write most of the stories in this bi-monthly children's magazine.

Jabberwocky*
A children's magazine published monthly which uses poems, stories, reviews and illustrations by young contributors. Available through subscription.

Charlie*
A monthly magazine for young women, published in New Zealand but readily available in Australian newsagencies. Features a page of contributors' poetry. Payment not specified.

Newspaper Market

School or community newsletters
Opportunities exist for you to be published in community newsletters or in school or inter-school newspapers (see chapter 9, 'Co-operative Writing and Publishing Projects').

To find out about community newsletters, approach your local library or council. They generally keep a community groups' register; look up neighbourhood centres as they quite often publish a monthly newsletter of interest to the community they serve. Sometimes, too, the local library publishes a newsletter for its members, so ask about that too. Who knows, your demand for publishing space might just start the ball rolling!

Another possibility is that the local writing group might welcome contributions from members of the general public for its annual anthology. You could find the contact person/phone number in the community register.

If all of these avenues remain closed, you could write to the local council, suggesting that it investigate the establishment of an arts newsletter to allow writers and other artists (for example, theatre enthusiasts, craftspeople and painters) a means of expression, and communication with each other and with the community at large. Don't forget, too, that there might be a community worker attached to council who could be looking around for a keen writer (just like you!) to help establish a regional arts magazine, or a neighbourhood or youth newsletter.

Local newspapers
It may be possible to get your writing published either on a one-off basis or regularly in your local newspaper. Look up the names and addresses of newspapers in your district phone book. Then write a neat letter to the editors, asking if they would be interested in publishing your work. Enclose a sample. You could send a poem or a short story, but you would probably be more successful in getting published if you sent in an article of community interest; it could be a report on the activities of a club you are involved with, a book or film review, or a specialist column (for example, book reviews, gardening, teen scene). More than once a career has been launched because an enthusiastic writer

approached a newspaper editor with an interesting gimmick (see Jodilee Eckford's story in chapter 11, 'Published Writers Speak'; as well as advice on work experience in chapter 10, 'So You Want a Career in Writing?'). Never, repeat never, bowl along to a newspaper office without an appointment, expecting the editor to be wildly enthusiastic about your brilliant writing. Editors are busy people and don't welcome anyone who doesn't have an appointment. Incidentally, don't be too disappointed if your proposal is rejected.

City newspapers

There don't seem to be many opportunities for new writers to get work published in newspapers. However, some city papers, generally in the comic section of Sunday issues, regularly feature poems and prose by juniors. It is simply a matter of looking around your newsagent's display to find out what is available.

BOOK PUBLISHERS

There are more than 1000 book publishers operating in Australia. A comprehensive list of names and addresses of members of the Australian Book Publishers' Association is published annually in both the Association's Directory of Members and *Australian Book Scene* (see below).

If you wish to submit a book manuscript to a publisher, do your market research beforehand. Look in bookshops to see which publishers are publishing which kinds of books.

The list below is not exhaustive, but the following Australian-based publishers publish books in these categories:

Fiction
Angus & Robertson Pty Ltd
William Collins Pty Ltd
J. M. Dent Pty Ltd
John Ferguson Pty Ltd
Fremantle Arts Centre Press
Hale & Iremonger Pty Ltd
Heinemann Publishers Australia Pty Ltd
Horwitz Grahame Books Pty Ltd
Hutchinson Group (Australia) Pty Ltd
Hyland House Publishing Pty Ltd
Macmillan Company of Australia

McPhee Gribble Publishers Pty Ltd
Nelson (Australia) Ltd
Pan Books (Australia) Pty Ltd
Penguin Books Australia Ltd
Rigby Education (Lansdowne-Rigby)
Ryebuck Publications
Transworld (Corgi & Bantam)
University of Queensland Press

Non-fiction
Angus & Robertson Pty Ltd
Bay Books
Century Hutchinson Australia Pty Ltd
Child & Associates Publishing Pty Ltd
William Collins Pty Ltd
Collins Dove
Cromarty Press Pty Ltd
Currawong Press
Darling Downs Institute Press
Five Mile Press
Greenhouse Publications
Hale & Iremonger Pty Ltd
Heinemann Publishers Australia Pty Ltd
Hodder & Stoughton (Aust.) Pty
Horwitz Grahame Books Pty Ltd
Hyland House Publishing Pty Ltd
Jacaranda Wiley Ltd
Lothian Publishing Company Pty Ltd
Macmillan Company of Australia
McPhee Gribble Publishers Pty Ltd
Melbourne University Press
Methuen Australia Pty Ltd
Oxford University Press Australia
Pan Books (Aust.) Pty Ltd
Penguin Books Australia Ltd
Reed Books (A.H. & A.W. Reed Pty Ltd)
Second Back Row Press
Transworld: Corgi/Bantam/Doubleday Australia
University of Queensland Press
Viking (Penguin Books Australia Ltd)

Biography/History
Alternative Publishing Co-operative Ltd
Blubber Head Press

Greenhouse Publications
Hargreen Publishing Co.
Heinemann Publishers Australia Pty Ltd
Hill of Content Publishing Co.
Kangaroo Press
Melbourne University Press
Nelson (Australia) Ltd
Oxford University Press Australia
Pegasus Press
Penguin Books Australia Ltd
Rigby Education (Lansdowne-Rigby)
Transworld: Doubleday
University of Queensland Press

Educational and Academic
Ashton Scholastic
Edward Arnold (Australia)
CBS Publishing Australia
Century Hutchinson Australia Pty Ltd
William Collins Pty Ltd
Era Publications
George Allen & Unwin
Great Western Press Pty Ltd
Hargreen Publishing Co.
Harper & Row (Australasia) Pty Ltd
Heinemann Publishers Australia Pty Ltd
Hodja Educational Resources Co-operative Ltd
Holt-Saunders Pty Ltd
Jacaranda Wiley Ltd
Lansdowne-Rigby
Longman Cheshire Pty Ltd
McGraw-Hill Book Company (Australia) Pty Ltd
Macmillan Company of Australia
Methuen Australia Pty Ltd
Oxford University Press Australia
Pergamon Press (Australia) Pty Ltd
Pitman Publishing Pty Ltd (Longman Cheshire Pty Ltd)
Scribe Publications
Sydney University Press
University of Queensland Press

Children's Books
Angus & Robertson Pty Ltd
William Collins Pty Ltd

Childerset Pty Ltd
J. M. Dent Pty Ltd
Five Mile Press
Franklin Watts
Paul Hamlyn
Harcourt Brace Jovanovich Group
Heinemann Australia Pty Ltd
Hodder & Stoughton (Aust.) Pty
Hutchinson Group (Australia) Pty Ltd
Hyland House Publishing Pty Ltd
Kangaroo Press
Lothian Publishing Company Pty Ltd
Macmillan Company of Australia
Walter McVitty Books
Methuen Australia Pty Ltd
Nelson (Australia) Ltd
Omnibus Books
Oxford University Press Australia
Penguin Books Australia Ltd
Queensland University Press

Plays (including plays for young people)
Alternative Publishing
Currency Press
Heinemann Publishers Australia Pty Ltd
Hodder & Stoughton (Aust.) Pty
Macmillan Company of Australia
Nelson (Australia) Ltd
Playlab Press

Poetry
Black Lightning Press
Boobook Publications
Fremantle Arts Centre Press
Hale & Iremonger Pty Ltd
Pegasus Press
South Head Press
Women's Redress Press

THEATRE COMPANIES

Here is a list of theatre companies in Australia
which will accept unsolicited playscripts. Unfortunately, the majority

of them produce very few such scripts annually; it would seem most either commission plays or produce well-known plays.

New South Wales
Australian Elizabethan Theatre Trust
Belvoir Street Theatre
Browns Lane Theatre Company
Ensemble Theatre
Griffin Theatre Company
Hunter Valley Theatre Company
The New England Theatre Company
New Theatre
Nimrod Theatre Company
Nomads Theatre Company
Northside Theatre Company
The Performance Space
Q Theatre
Riverina Theatre Company
Sidetrack Theatre Ltd.
Sydney Theatre Company
Theatre North Inc.
Theatre South
Toe Truck Theatre

Australian Capital Territory
Canberra Youth Theatre Company
People Next Door
Tau Community Theatre Inc.

Victoria
Anthill Theatre
Arena Theatre Company
The Church Theatre
Four's Company
Melbourne Theatre Company
Mill Theatre Company
Playbox Theatre Company

South Australia
Magpie Theatre
Mainstreet Community Theatre Company
Patch Theatre Centre
Unley Youth Centre

Western Australia
Acting Out
Hole in the Wall Theatre Company Ltd
S.W.Y. Theatre Company
Western Australia Theatre Company

Queensland
La Boite Theatre
New Moon Company
Roadwork
Royal Queensland Theatre Company

Tasmania
Zootango
Salamanca Theatre Company

For further information about theatre (and film) companies, contact the Australian Writers' Guild Ltd.*

FILM COMPANIES

New South Wales
Astra Film Productions
Bruning, Bell & Partners
Anthony Buckley
Damien Parer Productions Pty Ltd
Filmco Ltd
Frontier Films Pty Ltd
Great Scott Productions Pty Ltd
Hanna-Barbera Australia
Independent Productions Pty Ltd
JNP Films Pty Ltd
Hilary Linstead & Assoc.
Limelight Productions Pty Ltd
John McCallum Productions
McElroy & McElroy Pty Ltd
Ross Matthews–Zarwot Pty Ltd
Harry M. Miller Films
Monton & Monton Pty Ltd
Palm Beach Pictures
Pavilion Films Pty Ltd
Port Jackson Film Productions Pty Ltd
Production Pool Ltd

Roadshow, Coote & Carroll Pty Ltd
Samson Productions Pty Ltd
John Sexton Productions Pty Ltd
Smiley Films Pty Ltd

Victoria
Crawford Productions
Film & General Holdings Pty Ltd
Michael Pattinson
Nilson Premiere Pty Ltd
Simpson Le Mesurier Films Pty Ltd
Syme International Productions

South Australia
Forest Home Films

Western Australia
Australian International Films
Barron Films

Tasmania
Tasmanian Film Corporation

ANNUAL WRITING COMPETITIONS

There are many competitions held annually for writers. To list them all here would take pages so I have only included annual competitions for young and/or unpublished writers. If you wish to find out about other competitions, you would be advised to contact the Literary Arts Board of the Australia Council,* your state Ministry of the Arts, or to subscribe to writers' bulletins/ newsletters of the various state branches of the Fellowship of Australian Writers* (F.A.W.) the Australian Society of Authors* or the Writers' Guild*. The Victorian F.A.W. conducts quite a few annual writing competitions.
   Competitions are also listed in:
Writing for Profit in Australia by Robin Cromby (see chapter 12, 'Submitting Your Work' under the heading Helpful Books).
Kulture Vulture: Prize Pickings for Arts Practitioners, by Wendy Rawady, Bicorn Pty Ltd.*
Bookmark, ed. by Michael Dugan & J. S. Hamilton, Australian Library Promotions Council.*

Competitions for Young and/or Unpublished Writers

These competitions would all seem to be annual events. There may well be other writing competitions; thus this list is not exhaustive. One-off competitions are conducted from time to time. Be alert - keep your eye on library noticeboards, newspapers, etc.

Note: Where there are known to be sections for adult writers in the following list of competitions, these are marked with a dagger(†).

Age Short Story Award†
Details: There is a section for previously unpublished writers living in Australia.
Closing date: 30 November.
The Age Short Story Contest
c/- The Literary Editor
250 Spencer Street
Melbourne, Vic. 3000

Anne Elder Poetry Award
Details: Annual award made to the writer of a book of poetry published that year, provided that the book is the first the poet has had published.
Value of award: $700 and $300.

C/- Victorian F.A.W.
1/317 Barkers Road
Kew, Vic. 3101
Tel: (03) 817 5243

Audrey Longbottom Poetry Award
Details: Open to any unpublished poet.
Closing date: 31 July.
Value of award: $20.

B. Cummins
PO Box 15
Berowra, NSW 2081

Australia Day Poetry Competition†
Details: Youth section
Closing date: 1 November.
Value of award: $50.

J. Goodridge
125 William Street
Young, NSW 2594

Australia-Japan Relations Essay Contest
Details: Secondary school students from Years 7 to 12 are eligible
to enter. Essay topics are set each year.
Closing date: late September.
Value of awards: first prize is a return air ticket to Japan. Other
major prizes are typewriters, cassettes, recorders, watches, etc.

Japan Information and Cultural Centre
1st Floor, Aussat House
54–62 Carrington Street
Sydney, NSW 2000
Tel: (02) 29 4349
or
The Consulate-General of Japan in your capital city.

Australian National Association of Young Playwrights Play Contest
Details: See entry form for age requirements.
Closing date: September.
Value of award: not known.

ANAYP Playwrights' Contest
Shopfront Theatre for Young People
88 Carlton Parade
Carlton, NSW 2218
Tel: (02) 588 3948/588 6545

Australian-Vogel Award
Details: Award is given for an unpublished manuscript (fiction,
Australian history or biography) by a writer under the age of
35.
Closing date: 31 May.
Value of award: $10 000.

Australian-Vogel Literary Award
PO Box 764
North Sydney, NSW 2060
Tel: (02) 288 3000

Australian Writers-Authors Group Inc. Literary Awards†
Details: Short-story award (up to 17 years). Entry fee of $2.
Closing date: 30 June.
Value of award: $50.

Competition Co-ordinator
21 Natasha Street
Wynnum West, Qld 4178

Begonia Festival 'Esso' Literary Competition†
Details: Poetry and short-story sections for writers under the age
of 18 years.
Closing date: December.
Value of award: Three prizes, $75, $50, $25 for each section.

> Secretary,
> Begonia Festival Literary Competition
> PO Box 246
> Ballarat, Vic. 3350

Binalong Banjo Paterson Award for Bush Verse†
Details: Youth sections.
Closing date: 13 September.
Value of award: not known.

Dianne Hopkirk
Post Office
Binalong, NSW 2584

Cairns and District Junior Eisteddford (Literature Section)
Details: Prose and poetry sections for 14 to 18 years, 12 and
under 14, 10 and under 12, under 10. Topics set by adjudicators.
Small entry fee.
Closing date: 27 May.
Value of award: Trophies, medallions and award cards.

> Secretary
> Cairns and District Junior Eisteddfod
> PO Box 277
> Manunda,
> Cairns, Qld 4870

Canberra Times Short Story Competition†
Details: Junior section of this award open to writers 18 to 25
years; plus a section for schools in the ACT area.
Closing date: 20 June.
Value of award: $400.

National Short Story of the Year Marketing Department
GPO Box 443
Canberra, ACT 2601

Canning Literary Awards†
　Details: For writers 17 years and under.
　Closing date: October.
　Value of award: varies.

　Secretary
　Canning Literary Committee
　City of Canning
　1317 Albany Highway
　Cannington, WA 6107

City of Mildura Youth Awards
　Details: Open to writers aged between 13 and 18 years. Short-
　story section.
　Closing date: 18 August.
　Value of award: three prizes, $120, $60, $20.

　Sunraysia F.A.W. Literary Competition
　PO Box 1045
　Mildura, Vic. 3500

Dorothea Mackellar Memorial Poetry Competition
　Details: For primary and secondary school children.
　Value of award: $250 plus expenses paid trip to Gunnedah;
　memorial trophies.

　Memorial Trust
　PO Box 63
　Gunnedah, NSW 2308

Eaglehawk Dahlia and Arts Festival Literary Competition†
　Details: Poem of not more than 24 lines, with an Australian theme,
　for unpublished writers up to and including 18 years. Entry fee.
　Closing date: 31 January.
　Value of award: $100 plus medallion.

　Literary Secretary
　Eaglehawk Dahlia and Arts Festival
　PO Box 21
　Eaglehawk, Vic. 3556

F.A.W. Adele Shelton Smith Award for Play, Radio or TV Script
　Details: Open to writers aged 15 to 22 years.
　Closing date: 31 December.
　Value of award: first prize, $120.

F.A.W.
1/317 Barkers Road
Kew, Vic. 3101.
Tel: (03) 817 5243

F.A.W. Fedora Anderson Young Writers' Poetry Award
Details: Open to writers aged 15 to 22 years. Poems must be unpublished.
Closing date: 31 December.
Value of award: three prizes, $100, $30, $20.

F.A.W. address, as above.

Grenfall Literary and Song Competition†
Details: Junior section for writers under the age of 21. Entries in both sections must be on an Australian subject.
Closing date: 24 April.
Value of award: not known.

Festival Secretary
PO Box 77
Grenfall, NSW 2810

International Youth Playwrights' Competition
Details: not known.

International Society of Dramatists
ISD Fulfilment Centre
Box 3470
Ft Pierce, Fl. 33448.
USA

Jessie Litchfield Award
Details: This competition is held to encourage young and un-known writers of fiction. Entries must be of some substance, i.e. about 15 000 words, but groups of short stories are acceptable, as well as collections of poetry and full-length (not one-act) plays.
Closing date: late September.
Value of award: not known.

Bread and Cheese Club
Pen-y-bryn
PO Box 946
Frankston, Vic. 3199

Judah Waten Short Story Writing Competition
Details: Two sections: teenage (13 to 19 years) and junior (below
13 years).
Closing date: 30 September.
Value of award: $100, $50, depending on section entered.

City of Box Hill
PO Box 65
Box Hill, Vic. 3128

Kimberley Art Prize (Literature Section)†
Details: Secondary: short story, poem; Primary: short story, poem.
All entrants must be residents of the Kimberley (Western Australia)
area.
Closing date: approximately 9 May.
Value of award: prizes ranging from $100 to $25.

Officer in Charge
Cultural Centre
PO Box 94
Derby, WA 6728

Kitty Archer Burton Prize for Poetry
Details: Open to secondary schoolgirls 19 years and under.
Competition conducted by the Society of Women Writers
(Australia).
Closing date: 30 June.
Value of award: not stated.

Receiving Officer
Kitty Archer Burton Prize for Poetry
20 Harley Road
North Avalon, NSW 2107

Little Swaggie Award†
Details: Open to young people 14 years and under.
Closing date: 31 May.
Value of award: A bronze statue valued at $100. Publication of
poem in the Bronze Swagman Book of Bush Verse.

Secretary
Winton Tourist Promotion Association
PO Box 44
Winton, Qld 4735

Mattara Children's Poetry Prize†
  Details: Entries must be in English and not have been previously
  published.
  Closing date: Approximately 18 June.
  Value of award: $200.

  Mattara Children's Prize
  Hunter District Water Board
  PO Box 5171B
  Newcastle West, NSW 2302

Melbourne Poetry Day Competition
  Details: Youth and other sections, including a section for senior
  citizens.
  Closing date: 20 July.

  Poetry Day
  PO Box 268
  Mordialloc, Vic. 3195

Moonee Valley Annual Library Week Award.
  Details: Open to young writers only in the Moonee Valley Regional
  Library Service area. Short-story and poetry categories.
  Closing date: 21 August.
  Value of award: not known.

  c/- Moonee Valley Regional Library Service
  Fawkner Branch Librarian
  762 Mount Alexander Road
  Moonee Ponds, Vic. 3039
  Tel: (03) 370 5244

National Book Council/QANTAS Award for New Writers
  Details: This is an encouragement award, open to any book by
  a young writer (under 35 at the date of publication) or to the
  first book of a new writer of any age. An entry fee of $20 is
  applicable.
  Closing date: 15 December.
  Value of award: return airfare to the Frankfurt Book Fair.

  National Book Council
  Level 5/1 City Road
  South Melbourne, Vic. 3205
  Tel: (03) 614 5111

Pursuit Short Story and Poetry Competition
Details: Open to primary and secondary school students. Entries
submitted must be signed by teacher. Also includes sections for
art and photography.
Closing date: 1 May.

Pursuit Short Story and Poetry Competition
Ministry of Education
(Level M1, Rialto)
GPO Box 4367
Melbourne, Vic. 3001
Tel: (03) 628 2211

State of Victoria Short Story Award
Details: An award for writers aged 15 to 22 years. Although it
is sponsored by the Victorian Ministry, it is not restricted to
Victorians. There is also a section for previously unpublished
writers.
Closing date: 31 December.
Value of award: three prizes, $200, $75, $50.

Victorian F.A.W.
1/317 Barkers Road
Kew, Vic. 3101
Ph (03) 817 5243.

Sydney Morning Herald F.A.W. Short Story Award
Details: Short-story competition open to children in NSW schools.
1500 words.
Closing date: 16 September.

c/- Box 3448, GPO
Sydney, NSW 2001.

Sydney Morning Herald Young Writer of the Year Competition
Details: Open to any student attending a secondary school in
NSW or the ACT.
Closing date: 18 May.
Value of award: computer, printer and software package to student
and school attended. Dictionary prizes to regional winners.
How to apply: Tel (02) 235 6620 or 235 6614.

K. & M. Teychenne Short Story Awards
Details: Two sections: 18 years and under (to 1500 words); 12
years and under (to 1000 words).
Closing date: 30 September.
Value of award: trophy in each section.

General Secretary
Latrobe Valley Eisteddfod
PO Box 384
Traralgon, Vic. 3844

Troupe Young Playwrights' Season
Details: Playwrights aged from 8 to 17 years. Best plays are
workshopped and produced. This is a highlight of the Come-
Out Festival (see below) theatre program.

c/- Caclew Youth Performing Arts Centre
PO Box 164
North Adelaide, SA 5006

Warana Festival Awards
Details: Poetry awards for writers under the age of 25.
Closing date: 1 August.
Value of award: not known.

The Organiser,
PO Box 339
Toowong, Qld 4066

FESTIVALS

Most festivals listed here are free of charge, and
often involve writers, illustrators, editors, publishers, book distributors, sellers, publicists, critics and literary agents talking about
aspects of the literary profession.

At national festivals, such as the Adelaide Arts' Festival Writers'
Week or the National Word Festival, invited overseas writers give
free lectures. Recent visitors have included Julian Barnes, Francesca
Duranti, Nissim Ezekiel, Richard Ford, Victoria Glendenning, Kazu
Ishiguro, Gerhard Kopf and Michael Ondaatje. Some overseas writers
are children's novelists who are invited to visit schools while they
are in Australia. In the past we have had writers of the calibre
of Paul Zindel, Joan Aiken, Charles Causley, Jane Gardam, Ted
Hughes and Alan Garner visiting our shores.

To find out about these festivals, keep your eyes on the arts
pages of national newspapers or contact the Premiers' Department
in your state. The Australia Council* should be able to give you
contact names/phone numbers of festival organisers in your state.

Listed below are writers' festivals/seminars held in Australia which
you could attend:

Adelaide Arts Festival Writers' Week. Held in Adelaide every two years in Elder Park, opposite the Festival Centre, in March. For further information write directly to:

> The Writers' Week Co-ordinator
> Festival Centre
> King William Road
> Adelaide, SA 5000

Look for details in national newspapers prior to the event.

Mattara Festival, Newcastle. A week-long community of the arts held annually in October. Readings (including a reading of entrants' work in the Matarra Children's Poetry Prize).

> Venue: Newcastle Region Art Gallery
> Laman Street
> Newcastle, NSW 2300
> Tel: (049) 68 5219 or 26 2333

Melbourne Festival of Arts and Crafts. May.
> Tel: (03) 859 6689

Melbourne Fringe Arts Festival. September.
> Tel: (03) 419 9548

National Playwrights' Conference. Held annually in Canberra in May. The public can watch how a play is workshopped.
> Tel: (02) 516 2205

National Word Festival. Held bi-annually in Canberra at Australian National University in early March. Three days (including weekend). Includes a Young People's Day.
> Tel: (062) 49 7068 for enquiries/brochures

Perth Festival Writers' Week. Held bi-annually in Fremantle in February. Weekend sessions.
> Tel: (09) 335 8244

Salamanca Writers' Festival, Tasmania. First weekend in December, annually. Contact:

> Tasmanian Writers' Union
> GPO Box 783H,
> Hobart, Tas. 7001
> or
> Salamanca Theatre Company
> 77 Salamanca Place
> Hobart, Tas. 7001

The company also conducts a young writers' weekend during the year.

Spoleto Melbourne Writers' Festival. Mid-September. Readings, discussions, book launches. Contact:

> Organiser
> Level 6, 1 City Road
> South Melbourne, Vic. 3205

Sydney Festival Writers' Week. Held annually in January. Weekend sessions.
> Tel: (02) 267 2311

Warana Writers' Festival, Queensland. For details, write to:

> Warana Festival Organiser
> PO Box 339
> Toowong, Qld 4066

Writing and Illustration for Children Seminar. Held annually in Canberra in late September. Weekend only. Write to:

> Children's Book Council of the ACT
> Box 402
> Dickson, ACT 3032

Festivals for Young Writers

As you can see, there are not many national workshops or festivals for young people. However, local groups often conduct festivals, eisteddfods, etc. which involve youth participation. If you hear of one coming up, contact the organisers immediately, and ask if there is to be a writers' section. If one is not planned, it may be because the organisers haven't thought of it; suggest it!

Recently the Australian government, through the Commonwealth Department of Education, published an *Australian Young People's Festival Manual*. The manual explains how to participate in a youth festival, how to organise one and how to create one if you can't be in one! In its 'Dictionary of Ideas', under the Writing heading, it suggests the following:

children's books	poet-trees
illustrated books	local history
creative writing	radio plays
diaries	satirical sketches

festival newspaper	school plays
festival program	script workshops
haiku graffiti	serial
interviews and articles	story mural
journals	T-shirt poems
letters to the editor	youth plays

If you want to get a copy of this excellent publication, contact your local Federal member and ask for one. For further information regarding the establishment of a youth arts festival, contact:

The 1988 and Beyond Contact Office
Commonwealth Department of Education
PO Box 826
Woden, ACT 2606
Tel: (062) 83 7909

Australian Teachers of Media (ATOM) Students' Film Festival
This national students' film festival is held every October in Sydney. Awards are given in the categories of Primary, Junior Secondary, Senior Secondary, Encouragement Award, Best Film at the Festival. School groups or individuals may submit films of twenty minutes' (or less) duration. There are several days when film entries are screened.

NSW Film Corporation, or the Australian Film Commission (addresses below).

Australian Video Festival
There are separate student awards in this video contest in the categories of Documentary, Drama/Narrative, Computer Graphics, Music Video and Corporate Video. There is no limit on the number of entries submitted. A special student screening coincides with the festival. A $5 administration fee per tape is required. Closing date mid-June.

Australian Video Festival
PO Box 316
Paddington, NSW 2021
Tel: (02) 326 1900 or 339 9555

Come-Out Festival
This is a children's festival, held every two years in April in Adelaide. The literature component of the festival, 'Allwrite!', is held during the second week. Features international and local children's authors, young playwrights' season, young writers' workshops, performance poetry, writing for the media, storytelling and much more.

Allwrite! Co-ordinator
c/- Carclew Youth Performing Arts Centre
PO Box 164
North Adelaide, SA 5006
Tel: (08) 267 5111

International Festival of Young Playwrights
Open to writers aged between 14 and 22, this festival is an intense
period of workshops, readings, discussions on the craft of
playwrighting, and a season of public performances. Scripts from
young playwrights from all over the world are submitted. Sydney
has hosted several 'Interplay' festivals at the Seymour Theatre Centre.
Closing date is late January.

Administrator
Seymour Theatre Centre
PO Box 553
Broadway, NSW 2007
Tel: (02) 692 0555

National Youth Film Fesitval
This festival of films by film makers 19 years and under aims to
encourage young film makers and to promote the art of film making.
Deadline for entries is usually late April. Award-winning films are
screened. You need to have an official entry form.

Secretary
Manly Warringah Media Co-Operative Ltd
Narrabeen Community Learning Centre
Pittwater Road
North Narrabeen, NSW 2102
Tel: (02) 913 1474

Tokyo Video Festival
This is a video contest open to amateurs and professionals, groups
(e.g. schools) or individuals. Age is taken into consideration. Thirty-
four awards are made in three categories. The closing date for
submission of video entries is September but applications are due
in April. The awards are large, generally cash and trophies.

Hagemayer (Australia) BV
5-7 Garema Circuit
Kingsgrove, NSW 2208
Tel: (02) 750 3777

WRITING WORKSHOPS

Writing workshops are invaluable for new writers; they enable participants to exchange their writing with others who are sympathetic to the problems they often have, such as lack of confidence in their work. Workshops are regular features of such groups as the Fellowship of Australian Writers, but they are also conducted from time to time by organisations such as universities and other adult education groups. Writing workshops – sometimes residential – are occasionally advertised in city newspapers.

If you feel intimidated about taking your writing along for examination by an established group where you may not know anyone, why not organise a writing workshop of your own? (See chapter 2, 'Writing for a Purpose', under the headings Form a Writers' Club and Form a Writers' Circle.) You could approach a published writer and offer payment to conduct writing workshops on a regular or one-off basis.

The Department of Technical and Further Education often conducts Outreach programs, such as writing workshops, to assist people who are unable to attend central locations; you may be able to get a group going in this way.

Playwrights' Workshops

National Playwrights' Conference
Plays by new (and experienced) playwrights are workshopped annually at this conference held in Canberra.

Administrator
Australian National Playwrights' Conference
PO Box 627
Broadway, NSW 2007
Tel: (02) 516 2205

Playworks: Women Writers' Workshop
Women are encouraged to write for theatre and are helped to improve the quality of their scripts through workshopping by professional actors, directors and dramaturgs (playscript/workshop specialists).

Playworks Administrator
Seymour Theatre Centre
PO Box 553
Broadway, NSW 2007
Tel: (02) 692 0555

Young playwrights' workshops
The following workshops are conducted for the benefit of budding young scriptwriters:

National Young Playwrights' Weekend
Young writers between the ages of 10 and 18 are invited to submit scripts for any drama medium (television, theatre, film, radio, puppets). Playwrights will have the opportunity to work on their craft with professional writers, directors and actors for three days (generally during September). To participate, you need to submit a script.

Shopfront Theatre
88 Carlton Parade
Carlton, NSW 2218
  Tel: (02) 588 3948

Young Playwrights' Workshop
Victoria's St Martin's Youth Arts Centre, an arts centre dedicated to the high quality production of work by young people under the age of 26, seeks play scripts to be workshopped with guidance from professional writers.

Artistic Director
St Martin's Youth Arts Centre
28 St Martin's Lane
South Yarra, Vic. 3141
Tel: (03) 267 2477

Weekly Young Writers' Workshop
The Australian Theatre for Young People conducts a weekly young writers' workshop to encourage students with a particular interest in writing for theatre.

Artistic Director
Australian Theatre for Young People
38 William Henry Street
Ultimo, NSW 2007
Tel: (02) 692 9313

See also entries for Salamanca Theatre Company, *Puffinalia* and the Adelaide Come-Out Festival in this chapter as they have offered workshops for young writers in the past.

Here are some other known venues for young writers' workshops. You will have to contact each of them if you want to get more details, such as when the workshops are held:

Barnstorm Theatre
c/- 10/138 Brougham Street,
Kings Cross, NSW 2402
(conducts playreadings of new Australian plays by young playwrights)
Errol Bray
Tel: (02) 357 2402

La Boite Theatre
57 Hale Street
Brisbane, Qld 4000
Tel: (07) 369 1622

Canberra Youth Theatre
Gorman House
Batman Street
Braddon, ACT 2601
Tel: (062) 485 5057.

Corrugated Iron Youth Theatre
Browns Mart Community Arts Centre
PO Box 2429
Darwin, NT 5794
Tel: (089) 844 3236 or 81 5522

New Moon Theatre
PO Box 1456
Townsville, Qld 4810
Tel: Enquiries (077) 81 4111. Ask for the Drama Department.

The Self Raising Theatre (produces works by young writers)
140a William Street
Bathurst, NSW 2795
Tel: (063) 31 6655

Shopfront Theatre (home of the Australian National Association
    of Young Playwrights)
88 Carlton Parade
Carlton, NSW 2218
Tel: (02) 588 3948

SWY Theatre Company
PO Box 317
45 Attfield Street
Fremantle, WA 6160
Tel: (09) 335 8746

Youthview (Youth Theatre)
PO Box 820
South Perth, WA 6151
Tel: (09) 444 5076

You may be able to obtain information on playwrighting workshops
for young people by subscribing to:

Lowdown Youth Performing Arts Magazine
c/- 11 Jeffcott Street
North Adelaide, SA 5006
Tel: (08) 267 5111

Mitchellsearch Ltd conducts several Enrichment Studies weekends for talented children at Mitchell College of Advanced
Education, Bathurst, each year, including creative writing courses
for children 9 to 13 years. Contact:

The Organiser
Mitchellsearch Ltd
Mitchell CAE,
Bathurst, NSW 2795
Tel: (063) 33 2746

MANUSCRIPT ASSESSMENT SERVICES

A number of businesses offering script analysis
and assessment have sprung up over the past few years. One of
the most accessible is the manuscript assessment service offered
by the Victorian Community Arts Network. Submissions of both
fiction and poetry are read and commented on by a panel of
experienced writers and editors for the small fee of $5 per
submission (up to three stories or five poems). Submissions,
accompanied by a stamped self-addressed envelope and cheque
or money order for $5 (made payable to 'Community Writing
Scheme') may be sent to:

Reading Service
PO Box 403
Carlton South, Vic. 3053

Another recommended script assessment is run by the Australian
National Playwrights' Centre. For a fee of $40 entrants submitting

play scripts receive two written reports. For further information and a script entry form, contact:

Australian National Playwrights' Centre
60 Kellett Street
Kings Cross, NSW 2011
Tel: (02) 357 7888

Listed below are a number of other manuscript assessment services which have advertised fairly widely. Before you send copies of your work to these services, you would be advised to write and ask for the cost of fees. Fees are generally determined by wordage (for example, the fee for a story up to 5000 words could be $125, escalating to $250 for prose in excess of 50 000 words).

Australian Literary Advisers
7 Geerilong Gardens
Canberra, ACT 2601
Tel: (062) 48 8279.

Book Fellows
24 Market Street
Kyneton, Vic. 3444

Richard Butler Script Consultancy
Tel: (03) 718 1146

Detrusa Promotions
44 George Street
Fitzroy, Vic. 3065
Tel: (03) 419 6652

Scriptassess
PO Box 730
Richmond, Vic. 3121

Swan Writers' and Authors' Group
PO Box 394
Gosnells, WA 6110

Viewpoint Manuscript Clinic
35 Post Office Street
Carlingford, NSW 2118
Tel: (02) 871 7630.

Note: See disclaimer, Appendix A.

WRITERS' ORGANISATIONS

If you are a writer, you belong to a community of writers, even though each person works for most of the time in isolation. Many writers welcome the opportunity of meeting with people working in the same field. The *Fellowship of Australian Writers** is an excellent group for a beginner writer to join. This organisation, open to writers aged 16 upwards, issues a monthly bulletin, holds workshops, seminars and lectures, and also administers a number of important writing awards. It has regional branches throughout Australia with offices in all states. Current addresses for each can be obtained by writing to the New South Wales or Victorian branches.

NSW:
Box 3448 GPO
Sydney, NSW 2001

Vic.:
1/317 Barkers Road
Kew, Vic. 3101
Tel: (03) 817 5243

Listed below are writers' and other organisations which offer support, advice and encouragement to all writers.

*Australian Society of Authors**
An organisation for professional writers, it offers an informative bulletin and a number of books and cassettes on writing to non-members.

*Australian Writers' Guild**
Associate membership of this organisation for scriptwriters entitles you to a monthly bulletin as well as access to its script library. The guild conducts regular meetings, workshops and seminars. It can provide you with a comprehensive list of scriptwriting courses available throughout Australia.

*International PEN (Poets, Editors and Novelists)**
This is the only international organisation purely for writers. Writers from abroad are welcomed into new countries and the organisation is active in Amnesty International, pleading the case for imprisoned writers.

*Poets' Union**
This organisation conducts poetry and prose readings as well as

occasional seminars. You can contact the NSW branch for details of that state's activities or for addresses of other state branches.

*Society of Women Writers**
A national organisation, the society aims to encourage women writers attain professional status. The society conducts writing competitions and seminars.

OTHER USEFUL CONTACTS

*Arts Law Centre**
This organisation, which provides practical free legal advice and assistance to arts practitioners also gives advice on other arts-related matters.

*Australian Writers' Professional Service**
This editorial, consultant and critic service conducts correspondence training courses for writers, as well as producing an informative bi-monthly news-sheet called *Writers' World*.

*Australian Broadcasting Corporation**

*Australian Copyright Council**

*Australian Film Commission**

*Australian Journalists' Association**

*National Arts in Australian Schools Project**

*National Book Council**

*Literary Arts Board of the Australia Council**

A FEW DOs AND DON'Ts

- Although this book encourages you to approach writers' organisations and writers themselves, you are cautioned not to be a pest. Being a pest means *expecting* unconditional assistance, especially from professional writers whose livelihoods quite often depend on their getting on with their writing. Don't expect writers to read and comment on your work. Don't write to them and expect a reply without at least including a stamped addressed envelope. Don't expect writers to come to your writers' club and give free lectures.

Writers are best treated in a friendly, non-threatening way; they are usually approachable and happy to give you some time answering questions. But don't expect them to fall in a heap of praise at your feet if they do by any chance agree to read your work.

• If someone is generous enough with their time to read and comment on your writing, the very least you can do is thank them and listen to what they have to say. Many beginner writers are very defensive of their work and refuse to listen to or take heed of constructive criticism; they only want people to say how wonderful their writing is. Very few people can write so well their work cannot stand some criticism.

• Do everything you can to inform yourself of trends in literature. Read, read, read – as much good quality literature as you can. If you want to write scripts, go to the theatre as often as you can. If you want to make films, watch them critically. Extend yourself as much as you can, in every way that you can. Try to enrich your life experience by becoming an active participant as well as an active observer. Make things happen, then absorb them into your very being.

> And it does no harm to repeat, as often as you can, 'Without me the literary industry would not exist: the publishers, the agents, the sub-agents, the sub-sub-agents, the accountants, the libel lawyers, the departments of literature, the professors, the theses, the books of criticism, the reviewers, the book pages – all this vast and proliferating edifice is because of this small, patronized, put-down and underpaid person.'
>
> Doris Lessing

HELPFUL BOOKS

Australian Book Scene (magazine), published annually, D. W. Thorpe.*
Books for writers, authors, poets and publishers are available through
The Book Connection.* Write to them for a free price list.

☆
APPENDIX
USEFUL ADDRESSES

Note: For addresses of annual writing competitions and festivals, writers' workshops and manuscript assessment services, see chapter 13.

Advertising Federation of Australia
PO Box 166
North Sydney, NSW 2060
Tel: (02) 957 3077
(*Chapter 10*)

Arts Council of Australia
PO Box 181
Civic Square, ACT 2608
Tel: (062) 48 9813
(and in each capital city)
(*Chapter 13*)

Arts Law Centre
11 Randle Street
Surrey Hills, NSW 2010
Tel: (02) 211 4033
or (008) 22 1457 (toll-free)
(*Chapters 4, 12, 13*)

Aussie Kids
PO Box 70
Bankstown, NSW 2200
Tel: (02) 708 4811
(*Chapter 13*)

Australia Council
PO Box 302
North Sydney, NSW 2060
Tel: (02) 923 3333
(*Chapters 12, 13*)

Australian Book Publishers' Association
161 Clarence Street
Sydney, NSW 2000
Tel: (02) 29 5422
(*Chapter 10*)

Australian Book Review
Level 5
1 City Road
South Melbourne, Vic. 3205
Tel: (03) 347 1800
(*Chapter 12*)

Australian Bookseller & Publisher
(*see* D. W. Thorpe)

Australian Broadcasting Corporation
GPO Box 9994
Sydney, NSW 2001
Tel: (02) 339 0211
(*Chapters 7, 13*)

Australian Copyright Council
22 Alfred Street
Milsons Point, NSW 2061
Tel: (02) 92 1151
(*Chapters 4, 13*)
(*see also* Copyright Agency Ltd)

Australian Film Commission
8 West Street
North Sydney, NSW 2060
Tel: (02) 922 6855
(*Chapters 12, 13*)

**Australian Film, Television & Radio
School**
PO Box 126
North Ryde, NSW 2113
Tel: (02) 887 1666
(*Chapters 7, 10*)

Australian Journalists' Association
428 George Street
Sydney, NSW 2500
Tel: (02) 221 5366
(*Chapters 10, 13*)

**Australian Library Promotion
Council**
313 Swanston Street
Melbourne, Vic. 3000
Tel: (03) 650 2864 or 650 2691
(*Chapter 13*)

**Australian National Association
of Young Playwrights**
(*see* Shopfront Theatre for Young
People) (*Chapter 7*)

Australian News Syndicate
PO Box 80
Bondi Junction, NSW 2022
Tel: (02) 389 6499
(*Chapter 13*)

Australian Serials in Print
D. W. Thorpe
20–24 Stokes Street
Port Melbourne, Vic. 3207
Tel: (03) 645 1511
(*Chapter 13*)

Australian Society of Authors
PO Box 450
Milsons Point, NSW 2061
Tel: (02) 92 7235
(*Chapters 4, 10, 12, 13*)

Australian Society of Indexers
GPO Box 1251L
Melbourne, Vic. 3001

Australian Writers' Guild Ltd
60 Kellett Street
Kings Cross, NSW 2011
Tel: (02) 357 7888
(*Chapters 7, 13*)

Australian Writers' Professional Service
PO Box 28
Melbourne, Vic. 3001
(*Chapter 13*)

Bicorn Pty Ltd
8 White Way
Bulleen, Vic. 3000
(*Chapter 13*)

The Book Connection
1 Sterling Street
Dubbo, NSW 2830
(*Chapter 13*)

Boolarong Publications
12 Brookes Street
Bowen Hills, Qld 4006
Tel: (07) 854 1920
(*Chapter 12*)

Brave New Word
382 Richardson Street
Middle Park, Vic. 3206
(*Chapter 13*)

Charlie Magazine
PO Box 37–461
Parnell
Auckland
New Zealand
Tel: Auckland 39 7973
(*Chapter 13*)

Children's Book Council of Australia
PO Box 1055
North Sydney, NSW 2060
(*Chapter 12*)

Collected Works Bookshop (and
Catalogue),
1st Floor, Flinders Way Arcade
238 Flinders Lane
Melbourne, Vic. 3000
(*Chapter 5*)

Contagious
The Publishing House
PO Box 611
Unley, SA 5061
Tel: (08) 271 1024
(*Chapter 13*)

Copyright Agency Ltd
42 Alfred South Street
Milsons Point, NSW 2061
Tel: (02) 959 4727
(*Chapter 4*)

Department of Industrial Relations
(Vocational Services Branch)
(in your capital city)
(*Chapter 10*)

Dolly **Magazine**
140 Joynton Avenue
Waterloo, NSW 2017
Tel: (02) 662 8888

Experimental Art Foundation Bookshop
(Dark Horsey Distribution)
PO Box 21
North Adelaide, SA 5006
(*Chapter 5*)

**Fellowship of Australian Writers
(F.A.W.)**
NSW:
PO Box 3448
Sydney, NSW 2025
Vic.:
1/317 Barkers Road
Kew, Vic. 3101
Tel: (03) 817 5243
(*Chapter 13*)

(Details of other F.A.W. addresses are not
listed here as they frequently change.
Current addresses can be obtained
from the two state branches above)

Five Islands Press
PO Box 1946
Wollongong, NSW 2500
(*Chapter 9*)

Friendly Street Poets
PO Box 79
Unley, SA 5061
(*Chapter 6*)

Geek Speak
348 Abercrombie Street
Chippendale, NSW 2008
(*Chapter 13*)

Going Down Swinging
PO Box 64
Coburg, Vic. 3058
(*Chapter 13*)

Hero
2–4 Bellevue Street
Surry Hills, NSW 2010
Tel: (02) 212 5344
(*Chapter 13*)

Information Age
PO Box 433
Paddington, NSW 2021

International Correspondence Schools
398 Pacific Highway
Lane Cove, NSW 2066
Tel: (02) 427 2700
(*Chapter 10*)

International PEN
(Poets, Editors & Novelists)
PO Box 153
Woollahra, NSW 2025
Tel: (02) 498 4083
(*Chapter 13*)

Jabberwocky
PO Box 10230
Auckland 4
New Zealand
Tel: Auckland 6 0689
(*Chapter 13*)

Jetsetters of Australia
PO Box 132
Hampton, Vic. 3188
Tel: (03) 598 2191
(*Chapter 13*)

Kids Zone!
PO Box 554
Leichhardt, NSW 2040
Tel: (02) 660 0918
(*Chapter 13*)

Kwopitak
Aboriginal Education Resources Unit
151 Royal Street
East Perth, WA 6000
Tel: (09) 420 4534
(*Chapter 13*)

Literary Arts Board (now **Literature Board**)
(*see* Australia Council)

Magpies
c/o The Singing Tree
10 Armagh Street
Victoria Park, WA 6100
Tel: (09) 361 8288
(*Chapter 12*)

Margaret Gee's Media Guide
Information Australia – Margaret Gee
Media Group
384 Flinders Lane
Melbourne, Vic. 3000
Tel: (03) 62 5995

Mixed Bag
PO Box 107
Woonona, NSW 2517
(*Chapter 11*)

National Arts in Australian Schools Project
(*see* Australia Council)

National Book Council
Suite 3
21 Drummond Place
Carlton, Vic. 3053
Tel: (03) 663 8655
(*Chapter 13*)

Poets' Union (Sydney Branch)
Box 250
Wentworth Building
University of Sydney
Sydney, NSW 2006
Tel: (02) 808 3459 or (02) 660 3271
(*Chapters 5, 6*)

Press Research Bureau
Molesworth House
101 Molesworth Street
Wellington
New Zealand
(*Chapter 13*)

Puffin Club of Australia
Penguin Books Australia Ltd
PO Box 257
Ringwood, Vic. 3135
Tel: (03) 871 2400
(*Chapter 13*)

Public Broadcasting Association
645 Harris Street
Ultimo, NSW 2007
Tel: (02) 211 3288
(*Chapter 9*)

Public Lending Rights
PO Box 812
North Sydney, NSW 2060
Tel: (02) 923 3379
(*Chapter 12*)

Public Relations Institute of Australia
PO Box 166
North Sydney, NSW 2001
Tel: (02) 953 6661
(*Chapter 10*)

Reading Time
(*see* Children's Book Council of Australia)
(*Chapter 12*)

Review Publications Pty Ltd
1 Sterling Street
Dubbo, NSW 2830
Tel: (063) 82 3283
(*Chapter 12*)

Shopfront Theatre for Young People
88 Carlton Parade
Carlton, NSW 2218
Tel: (02) 588 3948/588 6545
(*Chapter 13*)

Society of Editors
Vic.:
PO Box 176
Carlton South, Vic. 3053
Tel: c/- (03) 329 5199
NSW:
PO Box 567
Neutral Bay Junction, NSW 2089
Tel: c/- (02) 406 9222
Tas.:
PO Box 32
Sandy Bay, Tas. 7005
Tel: c/- (002) 20 6261
(*Chapter 10*)

Society of Women Writers
GPO Box 2621
Sydney, NSW 2006
Tel: (02) 98 6117
(*Chapter 13*)

South Australian Open College for Further Education
208 Currie Street
Adelaide, SA 5000
(*Chapter 10*)

Stott Correspondence College
383 George Street
Sydney, NSW 2000
Tel: (02) 29 2445 (offices in other cities)
(*Chapter 10*)

Stringybark and Greenhide Folk Magazine
Box 424
Newcastle, NSW 2300
(*Chapter 11*)

Tasmanian Writers' Union
c/- PO Box 207
Sandy Bay, Tas. 7005
(*Chapter 6*)

D. W. Thorpe
20–24 Stokes Street
Port Melbourne, Vic. 3207
Tel: (03) 645 1511
(*Chapter 5*)

Victorian F.A.W. Newsletter
1/317 Barkers Road
Kew, Vic. 3101
Tel: (03) 817 5243
(*Chapter 13*)

Western Australian Technical Extension Service
Prospect Place
Perth, WA 6000
(*Chapter 10*)

Women in Publishing
PO Box 41
Artarmon, NSW 2064;
and
c/- Heinemann Publishers Australia Pty Ltd
PO Box 133
Richmond, Vic. 3121
(*Chapter 10*)

Women's Redress Press Inc.
PO Box 655
Broadway, NSW 2007
(*Chapter 9*)

The Writing School
PO Box 653
Mona Vale, NSW 2103
Tel: (02) 913 1255
(*Chapter 10*)

All opportunities, markets, services and
so on listed for writers in this book are
published in good faith. The author does
not give any personal recommendations.
The choice of services is the sole
responsibility of the individual reader.

Any organisation which has changed
its address and/or phone number since
publication of this book, or which would
like to be included in future issues of *The
New Writer's Survival Guide*, please contact
the author, care of Penguin Books.

SOURCES

Epigraphs used in this book come from a wide range of sources. However, a number were quoted from the following books:

Allen Andrews (ed.), *Quotations for Speakers and Writers*, Sun Books, Melbourne, 1969.

James Charlton (ed.), *The Writer's Quotation Book: A Literary Companion*, Robert Hale, London, 1985.

R. D. Walshe (ed.), *Speaking of Writing*, Reed Education, Frenchs Forest, NSW, 1975 (now out of print).

Stephen White, *The Written Word and Associated Digressions Concerned with the Writer as Craftsman*, Harper & Row, New York, 1984.

Writers at Work: The Paris Review Interviews, Series 1-5, various editors, Penguin, Harmondsworth, 1972-78.

☆

ACKNOWLEDGEMENTS

Grateful acknowledgement is made to the following writers who contributed material for use in this book: Marcela Aguilar, Mary Baarschers, Adam Boulter, Joanne Burns, Colleen Burke, Helen Cerni, Mavis Thorpe Clark, Bill Condon, Anna Couani, Miriam Cullen, Alma De Groen, Michael Dugan, Lois Dunkerley, Richard Echin, Jodilee Eckford, Sue Edmonds, Sally Farrell Odgers, David Foard, Simon French, Hayes Gordon, Robin Gurr, Sonya Harnett, Nola Hayes, Anne Heazlewood, Catherine Jaggs, Paul Jennings, Ruby Langford, Serge Liberman, Alison Lyssa, Jean McIntyre, Allan Mackay, Sarah McLeish, Doug MacLeod, Debra Oswald, Dorothy Porter, Ron Pretty, John Roarty, Helen Sergeant, Tom Shapcott, Ivan Southall, Evelyn Tsitas, Lee Quinn, Claire Williams, David Williamson, Michael Winkler, Judith Worthy.

Every effort has been made to trace contributors to obtain formal permission but in several cases this has not been possible.

The author would also like to thank the following people who helped to make the project a success: Pat Adam, Betty Bennell, Rosemary Blatherwick, Marie Brajak, Barbara Burton, Jean Cowie, Michael Denholm, Sue Hampton, Malcolm Jamieson, Ruth Jones, Merrilyn Julian, Judy Keneally, Kathy Lette, Sue Lovell, Peg McColl, Anne Pettigrew, Christopher Pollnitz, Janet Raunjak, Juliet Richers, Jan Williams, Kate Williams, Susan Wilson, Denise Yates.

Thanks are due also to the following companies and organisations which contributed material to the book: *Adelaide Review*, Australian Nouveau Theatre Ltd (Anthill), Australian *Playboy*, Australian Writers' Guild, Bruning, Bell & Partners Pty Ltd, Anthony Buckley, *Connexions* community newspaper, Crawford Productions Pty Ltd, *Dolly* Magazine, *Emu* Literary Magazine, Fairfax Magazines Pty Ltd, Five Islands Press, 5UV Writers' Radio, Fremantle Arts Centre Press, Freewheels Theatre-in-Education Company, Harry M. Miller Films, Heinemann Publishers Australia Pty Ltd, *Lake High Link* school magazine, La Mama, *Live Wire* inter-school newspaper, Longman Cheshire Pty Ltd, Magpie Theatre, Melbourne Theatre Company, John McCallum Productions, McGraw-Hill Book Company (Australia) Pty Ltd, Monton & Monton Pty Ltd, New Theatre, Pan Books (Australia) Pty Ltd, Pascoe Publishing Pty Ltd, Penguin Books Australia Ltd, Playhouse Theatre

Company Perth, Q Theatre Group Pty Ltd, Radio New Zealand, Radio 2CHY/
FM Coffs Harbour, Salamanca Theatre Company, Syme International Productions,
Theatre Works (Eastern Suburbs Community Theatre Company), The Stage
Company, William Collins Pty Ltd, Women's Redress Press Inc., also the staff
of Collins Bookshop, Wollongong, and staff at the Australia Council's library.

Special thanks to Michael Dugan for his advice and assistance over many
years, to Pat Farrar for getting me started, and to my cheerful editor, Beryl Hill,
for seeing the book to its conclusion.

The author acknowledges with gratitude the generous support and encouragement given to her in her writing career by the Literary Arts Board of the Australia
Council.